Business Explained
THE BUSINESS ENVIRONMENT

MALCOLM SURRIDGE
Senior Lecturer and Assistant Director of External Affairs, Great Yarmouth College; Senior Examiner AEB A Level Business Studies

TONY BUSHELL
Principal Lecturer in Business and Management Studies, City College, Norwich

PHILIP GUNN
Head of the School of Management, Great Yarmouth College; Assistant Chief Examiner AEB A Level Business Studies

Collins Educational
An imprint of HarperCollinsPublishers

Dedication
To Rosemary, Diana and Sheila, with love

© Collins Educational 1993

This book is copyright under the Berne Convention.
No reproduction without permission. All rights reserved.

Malcolm Surridge, Tony Bushell and Philip Gunn assert the moral right to be identified as the authors of this work.

Published by
Collins Educational Ltd
An imprint of HarperCollins Publishers
77-85 Fulham Palace Road
Hammersmith
London W6 8JB

First published in 1993
Reprinted 1994

British Library Cataloguing in Publication Data is available on request from the British Library

ISBN 0-00-3274802

Typeset by Dorchester Typesetting Group Ltd
Cover designed by Ridgeway Associates
Printed by Scotprint Ltd, Musselburgh

THE BUSINESS ENVIRONMENT

Also in the HarperCollins Business Explained Series

People, Marketing and Business
Malcolm Surridge, Tony Bushell and Philip Gunn

Finance, Information and Business
Malcolm Surridge, Tony Bushell and Philip Gunn

Contents

Study Skills vii
    Effective Study vii
    Writing Answers viii
    Using the Business Explained Series viii

1 Introduction to Business 1
    What is Business? 1
    Classifying Businesses 2
    The Size of Businesses 3
    The Dynamic Nature of Business 3
    Business Within Society 3
    Business as an Integrated System 5
    Business Plans 6
    The Types of Business Organization 8
    The Business Environment 10

2 The Economy and Business 16
    The Role of the Economy 16
    Measuring Economic Activity 17
    A Model of the Economy 20
    The Government and the Economy 23
    The Economic Issues: Inflation 24
    Employment 27
    Economic Growth 31
    Privatization 32
    The Balance of Payments 34

3 Business and Economic Policy 37
    Fiscal Policy 37
    Monetary Policy 43
    Other Policies to Control the Economy 48
    Prices and Incomes Policy 50
    Supply Side Policies 50
    The Influence of Business Upon the Economy 51

4 The Competitive and Technical Environment 55
    New Ideas 56
    Developing Ideas 62
    Protection of Ideas 64
    The Competitive Structure of the Industry 67
    Technology and Competition 71
    Markets and Price 73
    The Relationship Between Price and Quantity Demanded 74
    Supply of Goods and Services 76
    Supply and Demand Together 77
    The Effect of Price Changes 79

5 Business, Government and the Law 86
    The Legal Structure 86
    Sources of Law 87
    Competition Policy 91
    Contract Law 92
    Other Legislation 94
    The Impact of Legislation 95
    The State's Role in Business 96
    Recent Government Policy 97

6 Business and Society 101
    The Demographic Time Bomb 101
    The Length of the Working Week 105
    Business and Social Responsibility 107
    Business and the Environment 109
    Business and Ethics 118

7 Business and Trading Abroad 124
    The UK's Changing Trading Pattern 124
    Methods of Trading Abroad 125
    Marketing Overseas 131
    Means of International Payment 132
    Exchange Rates 132
    The European Community's Exchange Rate Mechanism 134
    Trade and the Balance of Payments 136
    Barriers to Trade 137
    International Economic Organizations 138

8 Business and Europe 141
    The European Community 141
    The Institutions of the EC 142
    European Monetary Union (EMU) 145
    The Creation of the Single European Market 146
    Developments in Eastern Europe 154

Suggested Answers to Essays 159

Dictionary 165

Index 175

ACKNOWLEDGEMENTS

A number of people have been of great assistance in the production of this book. We are most grateful to Murray Lauder for reading and commenting upon the whole manuscript. His ideas were invaluable and improved the manuscript in many ways. We are very grateful to Martin Liu of HarperCollins for his thorough and professional work in helping to prepare this book for publication. We also wish to thank David Chell, Clare Gunn and Kevin Gunn for reading and offering comments upon specialist parts of the manuscript. In spite of their help we are, of course, entirely responsible for any errors or omissions which may remain.

We wish to record our thanks to Barbara Francis for her suggestions as to sources for the various materials necessary to write this book. We are indebted to the many businesses, big and small, who offered materials for publication in the book. Without their co-operation the end result would have been much poorer.

Finally, we wish to acknowledge the following examination boards for permission to reproduce questions from past examination papers: Associated Examination Board, Northern Examination and Assessment Board, and Cambridge Local Examinations Syndicate. Any answers or hints of answers are the sole responsibility of the authors and have not been provided by the Boards.

Every effort has been made to contact all copyright holders, but if any have been inadvertently overlooked the publisher would be pleased to hear from them and to make the necessary arrangement at the first opportunity.

Study Skills

> ▷ ▷ **QUESTIONS FOR PREVIEW** ▷ ▷
>
> 1 How can I organize myself to study effectively?
>
> 2 How can I become more aware of business that exists around me?
>
> 3 What do examiners expect in answers to business studies questions?
>
> 4 What other sources of information about business studies exist?
>
> 5 How is the Business Explained series organized and how can it help me to study the subject?

Effective Study

MANY OF you who are about to start an A level, BTEC or similar course in business studies will have had relatively little experience of taking more advanced courses where much is expected of the student outside the classroom. It is broadly true to say that the higher the level at which you study the more work the student is expected to undertake outside the classroom or lecture theatre. Do not be daunted! By organizing yourself and your time you can develop the skills and techniques which are essential for success at this level.

Probably the first thing you need to sort out is somewhere to study. You will need a desk or table to work on and possibly some shelves for your books. It should also be somewhere you can work without disturbance – well away from distractions!

You need to organize your week so as to allocate regular times for study. It makes sense to use the same times each week so that you and your family and friends become used to the arrangement. This might seem unnecessarily formal to you but it is essential that you work steadily throughout your course. You cannot expect to do well by leaving everything to the last minute. Indeed, the growing emphasis on coursework will make such an approach impossible.

The actual studying you undertake may take a number of forms. Business studies is a unique subject in that it is going on around you all the time. Pick up a newspaper or magazine and it will inevitably contain a number of advertisements. Similarly, your favourite TV programmes may be interrupted by advertisements. As your knowledge of the subject increases, you will discover that you can learn much about the firm and its competitors from the way and place it advertises. Equally, as you walk down your local high street you will find a lot of evidence of business taking place. Delivery vans and lorries will be regularly seen and many famous retailers such as Marks & Spencer and W H Smith will have branches. Business studies will help you to understand why they have chosen such a location and why some businesses succeed and others fail.

You can learn a lot about business from talking to relatives or friends who are at work. You may care to ask some of the following questions:

- What do you like most and least about your job?
- What does your business (organization) do?
- Where and how does it advertise?
- Do you work mainly with machinery or with people?
- How large is your business? How do you measure the size of it?

- Are there trade unions where you work?
- Has the business changed a lot over the last few years?
- Do you use computers a lot in your work? If so, in which department – production, design, administration?
- With which other businesses do you do business?

Examples of business studies in action are all around you: make the best use of the examples and evidence offered to support your classroom study. You will gain marks in examinations and coursework by being able to quote relevant, real-life examples.

Writing Answers

Your teacher or lecturer will set you essays, case studies and possibly coursework throughout the course. It is important that you do as well as possible when completing this work, particularly where the marks you score contribute to your final, overall grade.

When tackling essays or other coursework you should resist the temptation to leave everything until the last moment. A successful piece of written work requires careful preparation. You will need to research your answer by using class or lecture notes and texts such as this one. You may also follow up references given in the books you read. Finally, but importantly, you may use quality newspapers and periodicals, such as *The Economist*, to give relevant up-to-date examples in support of your answers. Again, examples from the real world around you should prove valuable. With this material to hand, you should carefully plan your answer before you commence writing.

A level in particular requires more than a simple regurgitation of facts. Marks for factual content alone probably represent less than 30 per cent of the total available. It is what you do with your knowledge that will determine how good a mark you score.

Examiners are looking for evidence of *analysis* in your answers. This means that you must be able to apply your factual knowledge to unfamiliar situations presented to you by the examiners. For example, you may be given a case study describing a large firm which is experiencing communications problems. You might be asked to explain why this firm experiences problems and to recommend some solutions. You may use your notes on barriers to communication as a guide but you will also need to *apply* them to the firm in question, thus analysing that firm's particular problems.

Most questions will also require some *evaluation*. This involves judgement or assessment. So, continuing with our example from the previous paragraph, it may be necessary to identify (justifying your choice) the major barrier to communication or perhaps the most likely cure.

Analysis and evaluation are important components of answers to most types of question and not just case studies. Your teacher or lecturer will be able to help you develop the necessary technique to write well balanced answers.

When the piece of work is returned to you it is important that you read carefully your teacher's or lecturer's comments in order to eliminate weaknesses and improve future performance.

Using the Business Explained Series

This series of books comprises three titles:
- *Finance, Information and Business*
- *The Business Environment*
- *People, Marketing and Business*

It is designed to make business studies both understandable and enjoyable. By adopting the language and approach that we have, we aim to provide a rigorous treatment of the subject whilst not confusing you, the reader.

The series has been written for a typical student who is following an A level, BTEC, GNVQ or similar course in business studies. In particular, consideration has been given to students who will be working alone. Much of your studying will take place outside the classroom and these books are intended to act as a support to the teaching that you receive.

The three books in the series can be read in any order. We have deliberately avoided writing the books in any sequence. Not only can you begin with any book, but with any chapter. If you encounter business terms with which you are unfamilar then simply look them up in the Dictionary at the end of each book.

We recommend two ways in which you may use this book apart from as a class text.

Method A

Reading about business studies in this book and others, as we saw earlier, is an important part of your studies. It will help you to strengthen your knowledge of the subject and its techniques. You may wish to read a topic area prior to your teacher covering it in class. Indeed you may be asked to do so! Alternatively, it could be that you choose to read such an area after you have been taught it.

At the end of the chapters we have included an Exam Preparation section. This will allow you to practise the skills you are attempting to acquire and to assess how well you understand the subject matter. Because many examination boards are now using case studies most chapters contain at least one to allow you to familiarize yourself with this style of question.

We have also included regular Key Points which act as a summary of the principal elements covered in the preceding section. When you reach the end of each chapter you should reread the points for preview and confirm that you now understand them.

Method B

Throughout your course, your teacher or lecturer will set you essays, case studies or similar questions. You will be able to use this book in several ways to help with such assignments. It will, of course, provide you with much of the information needed to answer questions set on A level, BTEC, GNVQ and similar courses. In addition, you may also make use of the references offered at the end of each book.

Finally, you would be well advised to look at some of the past examination questions and the suggested solutions at the back of the books. This should give you valuable guidance on what your teacher (or the examiner) is looking for when setting questions.

As the examination approaches your studying should become more intensive with the main emphasis on the revision of material covered earlier. In the meantime the best of luck with the course!

CHAPTER 1

Introduction to Business

> ▷ ▷ **QUESTIONS FOR PREVIEW** ▷ ▷
>
> 1. What do we mean by the term 'business'?
> 2. In what sense are businesses dynamic and how do they interact with society?
> 3. Why can businesses be described as integrated systems and how should they plan their activities?
> 4. What forms of business exist in the UK?

What is Business?

A DICTIONARY and Thesaurus give many meanings of the noun 'business':

- A trade or profession – for example, 'What business are you in?'
- The purchase and sale of goods and services – for example, 'Smith and I do business together'
- A commercial or industrial establishment – for example, 'This business employs 400 people'
- Volume of commercial activity – for example, 'Business is good at the moment'
- Commercial policy – for example, 'Overcharging customers is bad business'

Other meanings exist, but they are not relevant here. So you can see the problem that needs to be cleared up before we start a study of business. What do we mean when we use the term 'business' in this book?

It is essential that our study examines all the internal and external pressures that affect the many organizations from which we earn or receive money, and all the organizations with which we spend our money either voluntarily or by compulsion. Therefore, in general we mean 'commercial or industrial establishments' like ICI, Marks & Spencer, Abbey National Building Society or Commercial Union Insurance.

But we cannot exclude local government which places planning and development restrictions on businesses, or national government which passes laws that affect every business, and collects taxes on profits and VAT on purchases. Trade unions influence the pay and conditions that employers provide, and pressure groups can cause firms to alter the way they make or package their products. Similarly, we must consider the impact of international organizations such as the European Community and the International Monetary Fund. This book, together with the two others in this series, will consider all the forms of business which exist, what comprises these businesses and the external influences to which they are subject.

So when we think about 'business' in this book, we mean commercial and industrial establishments and everything that affects them.

Business studies is not a single, tidy subject with its own body of knowledge and its own language. Rather, it is a blend of many specialist subjects. Economics is the basis of business studies and provides a firm foundation upon which to build. Money (as represented by finance and accounting) is the language of business, and needs to be controlled and kept secure. People make business, and their behaviour must be understood and influenced when possible. Laws control business and protect society from its worst excesses. Communication is the lifeblood of business and pervades every aspect of it. Mathematics and statistics are the key to understanding, describing and solving many of the problems faced by businesses. We do not need to study each of these in as much depth as a specialist might – we need a working knowledge of each, and to understand the interaction of each of them with the others. The good student of business studies understands the components which comprise business studies and the way in which the elements fit together to provide an integrated approach to the subject.

For example, a company thinking about developing a new product or service ought to consider if there will be sufficient demand for it, and whether the level of demand would be affected by price (*economics*). Can the company afford to produce it and make a profit at the price customers would be willing to pay (*finance*)? Has it got people with the right skills and expertise to design and make the good (*people*)? Is the product covered by any special legal regulations as the upholstery or toy industries are (*law*)? Ought the company do some marketing research to find out what people think before they spend too much money (*mathematics* and *statistics*)? In everything mentioned here, the company will be giving and gathering information and ideas all the time (*communication*).

If any one of these activities turns up a problem, it will affect all the others. For example, if the law says that only flame resistant foam may be used in the product, it may put up the costs, the price may have to be raised to cover it, that may mean fewer customers and less income, which may mean the company cannot afford to employ expert staff, so it may have to drop the whole idea.

ACTIVITY 1.1

Your cousin is about to set up in business as a window cleaner. In conversation with him, you mention the elements which make up business and remark that he will be affected by them all once he starts trading. He is surprised and asks for examples which relate to his business.

Using the six headings outlined earlier, give examples of how he will call upon skills or knowledge from these subject areas in running his business.

Classifying Businesses

Another difficulty facing you is the very wide range of activities that can be described as business. If you look at the *Yellow Pages* trade directory, there are over 2 700 trade classifications, starting with 'Abattoir equipment' and ending with 'Zoos'. We need a much more general structure to allow access to the subject.

The most common and accepted classifications take three stages in the production of goods and services:

- Primary activities
- Secondary activities
- Tertiary activities

Primary Activities

Most commodities or goods that we buy start their life as raw materials in the ground, the seas or the fields.

All the activities concerned with extracting ores, oil or other basic materials; growing grain, fruit and vegetables; breeding animals for meat and fishing are called primary activities, and this part of the production chain is called the primary sector. The industries that make up this sector include mining and quarrying, agriculture, forestry and fishing.

Secondary Activities

Converting these raw materials into useful products, either by manufacturing or processing, is called secondary activity. For example, converting iron ore into steel, and then using the steel for manufacturing cars; or purifying water and pumping it to homes for drinking; or milling wheat to make flour, and then baking it for bread – all these are secondary activities, and together these industries constitute the secondary sector.

Tertiary Activities

Distributing these goods to make it convenient for the consumer to buy them – transportation, wholesaling, retailing, direct mail – are tertiary activities. So, too, are all the supporting services to industry: banking, insurance, travel, street lighting, refuse collection and any other supporting activities (such as holidays, health services, education and training). All these make up the tertiary sector.

SUB-DIVISIONS

There are many sub-divisions to these general categories. Farming can be sub-divided into arable (crops) and dairy (cattle), and these can be sub-divided again into types of crop and types of cattle. We could carry on sub-dividing until we are back to the 2 700 classifications found in the *Yellow Pages*. But the three main sectors we have described above are enough for our purposes.

ACTIVITY 1.2

Look in your daily or local newspaper and turn to the pages where jobs are advertised. Select ten advertisements and categorize the firms that placed them according to whether they are in the primary, secondary or tertiary sectors. Why do you think that firms from certain sectors of the economy placed most of the advertisements – particularly if you looked in a national newspaper?

The Size of Businesses

Another difficulty we have to deal with is the variation in the size of different businesses and the scale of their operations. For example, the Ford Motor Company is a business that manufactures cars on a very large scale in many countries of the world. Rolls Royce manufactures a small number of exclusive cars in the UK for a particular type of customer. Dennis Beeston & Co service and repair cars for a small number of customers in Bradwell, near Great Yarmouth. The one thing they have in common is that they are businesses to do with motor cars – but there is little else.

There are many ways to measure the size of businesses. Probably the most commonly used is the value of turnover or sales, although the number of employees is also used on occasions. Can you think of any alternatives?

Look back now at your answers to Activity 1.2. Do you think that there is any relationship between the size (and probable wealth) of firms and where they advertise for employees? Might this have biased your mini-survey?

The Dynamic Nature of Business

Another aspect of business that we must take into account is the fact that it is dynamic. It is always changing in response to changes within it, and in response to changes outside it. It has an energy of its own that affects its environment, just as its environment has energy that affects the business. In other words, businesses and the environment in which they operate affect one another.

A writer on psychology, Kurt Lewin, described this idea as 'a field of forces' that create a balance between opposing forces. Imagine a balloon that has been inflated. It is the shape and size that it is because the pressure (forces) inside is exactly equal to the forces outside. If you increase the forces outside without an equal response from inside, the balloon will get smaller. The opposite is also true. If you increase the forces inside the balloon without an equal response from outside, the balloon will get bigger. This idea is very useful in helping us to understand what might happen to a business, or to businesses in general, as the environment in which they exist changes. We can call this the 'concept of balancing forces'.

The energy inside a business comes from the people who manage and work in it. When a team of people are working together in harmony, committed to the same aims and objectives and all pulling in the same direction, it is likely that it will be creating forces which will affect its environment. For example, if it develops a new and revolutionary product that the consumers want, and none of its competitors have responded to this new 'force', almost certainly it will get larger and the competitor will get smaller as a result. Similarly, if the company invests in new technology, and as a result reduces its costs, it can either lower its prices to gain a bigger share of the market (thus taking business away from its competitors) or it can make more profit to finance further growth.

We will study the various internal forces that make businesses dynamic. Whether a company grows or contracts depends upon its ability to respond to the changes in internal and external forces.

Business Within Society

People in society demand goods and services for a number of reasons. For example, we need food

---

KEY POINTS 1.1

- 'Business' in this book means commercial and industrial establishments and everything that affects them
- The study of business calls upon knowledge from many disciplines
- Businesses can be classified by describing where they come in the production chain: primary, secondary or tertiary
- The size of a business can vary enormously even between firms in the same industry
- There are a number of ways in which the size of a business can be measured

and drink in order to survive. It is very difficult nowadays for an individual or family in the UK to provide for themselves all that they want in the way of basic needs. So they depend upon businesses to supply their needs. Also, we need good health care to keep us fit and free from disease. Not many of us are expert enough to do this for ourselves. We also need recreation and leisure pursuits to help us relax and enjoy friendship.

ACTIVITY 1.3

Make a list of all the goods and services you have used today. Now tick those services which you think you could provide yourself. Why do you choose not to produce for yourself the goods and services which you have not ticked?

Another reason is because we have very high expectations. As a very affluent society, we do not see our needs in terms of survival, but in terms of our standard of living. And this standard is set not in relation to necessities, but in relation to how much other people have. Today's luxuries become tomorrow's necessities. Televisions and cars are good examples of this. How many people do you know who do not have a television? Politicians and the media make comparisons between what we have and what others have so that our expectations are never allowed to rest.

In response to this demand, appropriate means of supply develop. These may be businesses which produce goods in response to the demand in order to make a profit, or the government of the day providing the health care required. It is almost certain that if a demand exists, a means of supply will respond. So business is shaped by the demands of society.

However, you can probably quote many examples of business shaping society. For example, do you think that 'Coke is it!' whatever 'it' is? Yet, worldwide, more people buy this soft drink than any other. The power of advertising can and does create expectations that influence our society. The temptation to improve our looks or to become more attractive to the opposite sex, as promised in many advertisements, is too great for many of us, and we buy the product whether or not the promise is realistic. Advanced economies become more advanced. Developing economies try to grow by serving and competing with them. Some will provide raw materials while others, like the textile industries in Korea and Taiwan, use cheap local labour to produce low-price goods. Some of them get into debt to such a degree that they use their new wealth to pay the interest rather than improving the standards of living in their own country. Poland and Mexico actually got to the stage where they could not even pay the loan interest. Western businesses are shaping the societies of the developing nations as well as their own.

Our standard of living is greatly influenced by job opportunities. The more successful business is, the more jobs there will be (if we assume that technology does not take over!). This in turn influences the amount of money that is spent on goods and services. Failure of business can have the opposite effect. When British Steel closed down a major factory at Corby, it had a disastrous effect on the local community because the firm had been the major employer and purchaser in the town.

During the 1980s, many incentives were offered to businesses to start up, grow and become more efficient. The spirit of enterprise was encouraged by the Conservative government under Margaret Thatcher. The philosophy of the free market economy has given businesses a much greater influence in the shaping of society than previously: and, almost inevitably, they shape society to demand more of their goods and services.

As demand grows, more raw materials are used and more waste is generated. Lewin's concept of

KEY POINTS 1.2

- Businesses shape and respond to their environments
- The internal and external environments of business interact with one another
- Our society demands a wide range of goods and services, few of which we can produce for ourselves
- Our changing demands and rising expectations have implications for businesses

balancing forces warns us that as one force alters, it affects the other variables in the environment.

Should businesses be allowed to behave in such a way as to risk these undesirable consequences? Is it ethical or not to pursue profit at all costs? It is possible to control some aspects of business behaviour by law, but it is not possible to cover all eventualities. Should some moral responsibility, therefore, be borne by owners and managers? There is no ethical code for managers as there is for, say, doctors and other professions, so how can they be controlled?

Business as an Integrated System

- Which comes first, the chicken or the egg?
- Which comes first, the product or the customer?

CASE STUDY

(The Negative Version)

John returned home from work looking more frustrated and fed up than usual. He hardly said a word to his wife and family, sat down and drank his cup of tea without looking up. Going through his mind were things that had happened at work that day: things like the decision by his boss to change production from 500-gramme packets to 400-gramme packets without consulting him. He could have told the boss that the 500-gramme packets were an urgent run for their best customer, but he had not been asked. It seemed to John that the only way to run the job properly was to run it himself – but how could he with a boss who does not consult.

His wife Jenny sat down beside him and asked him what was wrong. John explained his frustration as he had done many times before, only this time Jenny sensed that it was about time he did something about it.

'Why don't you set up on your own?' Jenny asked. 'You will never be happy working for somebody else. Take the bull by the horns before it's too late. You've got skills and experience and lots of energy. I'll support you.'

'It's not as easy as that,' replied John. 'What could I do? Where would I get enough money? Who would buy from me?' At the same time John found the idea of being his own boss very attractive. Perhaps it would be worth making a few enquiries, he thought.

(The Positive Version!)

John came home from work very excited. He could not wait for the children to go to bed so that he could discuss his decision with his wife, Jenny. At last they sat down with a cup of tea, and John said, 'Jenny, I'm going to set up in business with two of the lads from work. We know we've got the skills and experience, it's just a matter of deciding exactly what we're going to make and sell. How do you feel about joining us and running the marketing side of the business? You'd be brilliant.'

Jenny smiled. She had often thought about running their own business. It seemed a very attractive proposition, but too many people started their own business only to fail within a very short time.

'On one condition,' she said, 'and that is that we do everything properly: don't rush in and don't take unnecessary risks.'

'That's right,' agreed John, 'we'll take it one step at a time and plan carefully before we take any action.'

The conversation went on into the night, and the main outcome was that they would take the best advice they could find at each step along the way.

QUESTIONS

1. Why do you think that John and Jenny are more likely to succeed with their business in the second case than in the first? You should give as many reasons as you can.

2. If John and Jenny asked for your advice about their intended business in the first case study, what would you advise them to do?

A business can be run by one person. That person can do everything: the production of the good or service, the accounting, the selling, the delivering and any after-sales service. This person will be very busy, too busy to become an expert at any of the tasks in the business. She or he will be talking to a customer one minute, paying a supplier the next, making the product the next minute, answering the phone, trying to find time for a cup of tea and so on. All these jobs are essential to the success of the business, no one being more or less important than another.

In a medium-sized company, there will be enough selling activity to justify the full use of one or more person's time. It will become a specialist department where real expertise can be developed. Similarly, several people may make the product in such a way that it is more efficient and less costly. A specially trained accountant may take care of all financial matters and ensure that the company keeps spending in line with income. Perhaps a special section is set up to employ the right sort of person for each job, train them, make sure that the workplace is safe and that the company looks after its staff well. Each of these functions is important to the success of the business.

As with the one-person business, all these activities are going on all the time, non-stop, day-in and day-out. But in the case of the medium-sized business, no one person knows everything that is going on at any one time. There is a need for planning and co-ordination to keep everything pulling in the same direction.

A good example of this need for planning and co-ordination may be seen in your school or college. The National Curriculum requires that certain subjects are taught to all students and that some of those are taught across the curriculum (Information Technology, for example). Teachers and lecturers will attend training days and staff meetings in order to plan how this will be achieved and to ensure that everyone is doing what is required of them.

An example from industry might include every department in a company. If the people doing the selling learn that there is going to be an increase in demand for the company's product, they need to tell production to make more. Production need to buy more raw materials in time to have the goods ready when the customer wants them. If production needs more workers to make the goods, the personnel section will need to find, employ and train enough people. The accountant must ensure that the company has enough money available to pay for the additional raw materials and wages. And someone must make certain that all these interdependent activities happen at the right time to avoid holding anyone else up – particularly the customer.

You can see how complicated business can be in a medium-sized company. Just think how much more complicated it can be in a very large company, with several factories and many different products. Or a multinational company like Ford or Unilever. Or a large government department, or a worldwide charity.

All the various activities that are continuously going on affect each other. We can apply Lewin's concept of balancing forces to these internal activities – as one alters, so it affects others, and they must respond or the business will go out of balance.

A business is like a stewpot. There are a lot of ingredients and each one affects the flavour of the dish. If one is missing, or there is too much of another, the flavour will be different, and perhaps not very nice.

In our study of business, we have to understand how each of the functions operate, how they contribute to the well-being of the whole business, how each one influences and affects the others, and how to keep them all in balance. We must also see the business in its environment. How it affects the environment and is affected by it is very important.

Business Plans

Before starting any business it is essential that plans are drawn up. Small businesses have a very high mortality rate: only 20 per cent survive the first five years. A major reason for this is that the new owners of businesses do not fully understand all the aspects of running a business, or the environment in which their business is to operate, or both!

It is important to research the market to make sure that buyers exist for the good or service that is to be sold and to get some idea of the prices that should be charged. Hopeful entrepreneurs should then calculate carefully the costs of supplying the good or service in order to find out whether a profit can be made.

The process of planning a business is important. It helps to draw attention to aspects of the business which might be unsuccessful or difficult and to skills which the entrepreneur may not possess.

A good business plan will help an entrepreneur to obtain finance. Bank managers are likely to be more impressed by a carefully prepared plan than by a simple expression of a business idea – no matter how great its potential.

A good business plan will contain some or all of the following:

> *Figure 1.1 – A Business Plan Checklist*
>
> **Objectives:**
> What are your personal objectives?
> What are your business objectives?
> Are they specific?
> Have you thought of the consequences?
>
> **The business:**
> History if already established.
> Accounts for previous years's trading.
> Present financial position.
>
> **Management:**
> Experience of proprietors/managers.
> Responsibilities of managers.
> Is the team complete or is further recruitment necessary?
>
> **Market:**
> How large is it?
> Is market research possible/available?
> What is the competition?
> What advantages do competitors have?
> What advantages does your product/service have?
> What are the distribution channels?
> What advertising or marketing will you need?
>
> **Products:**
> Do they meet customers's needs?
> Have they been tested, including production methods?
> How have costs been calculated?
>
> **Pricing:**
> How have prices been arrived at?
> Are they competitive?
>
> **Suppliers:**
> Are adequate supplies available?
> Is quality known to be acceptable?
> What credit is available?
>
> **Physical resources:**
> What premises are available?
> Are they adequate?
> What is the cost?
> What machinery/vehicles are required?
>
> *Source:* Barclays Bank plc

- A full account of the entrepreneur's business experience and qualifications
- A clear statement as to what product or service is to be sold and the intended target market. How is it different from other goods or services that are already being sold on the market?
- An assessment of the costs that the business will incur in starting production and continuing over the first year or so. These should be broken down into monthly payments so that periods of financial difficulty can be identified and planned for
- The amount of capital that the owner of the business has contributed; the amount that she or he has borrowed (or wants to borrow) from others, and the rates of interest that the business is already committed to pay
- Details of the place in which the product is to be produced and sold (this might be a factory, office or shop). Does the business own part or all of it, or is it rented?
- The aims and objectives of the business. What are the intentions of the entrepreneur with regard to her or his business? Does she or he hope for rapid growth or slower growth, concentrating on a particular segment of the market. In other words, what is the overall aim of the business? What objectives will be pursued in order to achieve this overall aim?

> # KEY POINTS 1.3
>
> - **It is unlikely that one person can carry out all the activities necessary to operate a business**
> - **Planning and co-ordination are essential for business success**
> - **The many components of business all interact and contribute to the operation of that business**
> - **Business plans highlight areas of weakness and can help avoid problems before they occur**

The Types of Business Organization

Companies

Read the Case Study below. In it, Sue thought she faced a choice between forming her clothes shop business as a sole trader or taking a partner. She could, however, have formed a private limited company to run her clothes shop. Her business could then have been called 'Thomas's Clothes Ltd'. All private limited companies have the term 'Ltd' (or 'Limited') after their name. It is likely that you know of such a business that trades

---

CASE STUDY

Sole Traders and Partnerships

Sue Thomas has just been made redundant from her job as a manageress in a local factory. She has plenty of ideas on how to spend her redundancy payment of £5 000. After much thought she has decided to open a clothes shop for women and children in her home town.

Her cousin Paula Marsh is a manager at a local bank and unsurprisingly Sue has turned to her for advice. They spent a long while together discussing plans for Sue's business and Paula was able to give her some good advice. Paula and Sue chatted about finding a suitable empty shop and how much rent Sue could afford to pay; they also discussed Sue's likely sales. Paula argued that some research was essential to find out whether Sue would have sufficient customers to make her business profitable.

'Are you going to form a company, Sue', asked Paula, 'or will you find someone to join you in a partnership?' Sue was unsure what these terms meant and asked Paula to explain.

'When you walk down the High Street in Wimberly [a nearby town],' began Paula, 'you must notice the names above the shops and other businesses that are there. In the side roads there are little businesses like Jones's Newsagents who deliver your papers each morning. We call this type of business a sole trader or sole proprietor. It is owned and managed by just one person; although, if large enough, there may be other employees. It's very easy and cheap to set up and consequently is a very popular type of business.'

'Sounds just right for me,' exclaimed Sue, 'I'll start my business as a sole trader.'

'Hold on, Sue! There are other possibilities. When you bought your new house you saw it advertised in West, Marsh and Curwen, the estate agents in Morris Street. They are an example of a partnership which exists when at least two people decide to join together to run a business. They usually all put in money and share any profits that are made.'

'Yes,' said Sue slowly, 'I can see that taking a partner would have advantages.'

Task One

Talk to someone (possibly a friend or relative) who runs her or his own business as a sole trader. Ask why she or he decided to set up this type of business. You should also ask whether she or he can think of any disadvantages of running this type of business. Finally, putting yourself in the role of Paula, write a memo to Sue setting out what you have found out.

Two weeks after their first meeting, Paula and Sue went together for lunch in a local pub.

'Thanks for your memo, Paula. I can see that it would make sense to form a partnership because of the difficulties of running a business on your own. I am worried about taking a partner, though. I would have to find someone I could trust and who agreed with my business ideas. What if we argued? I would also have to share my profits with that person.'

Paula was reassuring. 'There are advantages, you know, Sue. It would be much easier for you to have a holiday and your partner could help you with routine jobs like paying bills and ordering clothes from suppliers. It would also help to have someone to discuss your ideas with and, importantly, your partner should have money to invest into the shop. This should make it bigger and allow you to advertise to attract more customers to the shop. It's not all bad!'

Task Two

Using your local *Yellow Pages* or some other local directory, find at least a dozen examples of partnerships. They are recognizable because they will be made up of several names and will not have 'Ltd' or 'plc' after the business's name. What sort of businesses are run as partnerships? Why do you think such businesses choose to operate as partnerships?

somewhere near you.

Private limited companies offer a number of advantages. Many people can put their money into this type of business, enabling the company to grow and buy more expensive equipment and property to help it trade. People who put their money in companies are called investors or, more commonly, shareholders. They buy a 'share' of the company and, as well as receiving a share certificate, are entitled to some of the company's profits. This extra money allows the business to trade on a larger scale and may also let it employ experts (such as engineers and lawyers) which should help the business develop further.

Possibly the main advantage of forming a company to run your business relates to the term 'Ltd' that follows the name of the business. This tells people who might want to invest their money in the company (in the hope of making a profit), that if the company were to fail, then all that they could lose, at worst, is the value of their investment. This is very reassuring to potential investors because if their liability is not limited in this way then their personal possessions (home, car, etc) could be sold to meet the business's debts if it were to fail. Businesses which are structured in this way so as to protect the people who invest in them are said to have 'limited liability'.

With a few exceptions, it is only companies that can enjoy the benefit of limited liability. If Sue established her clothes shop as a private limited company (as suggested earlier) then the law would treat the business as separate from her personal affairs. This means that any customer who was unhappy with the clothes they bought from the shop would have to take legal action against the company, not against Sue. As outlined earlier, since the business is legally separate, the owners (or shareholders) are not responsible for its debts.

Surprisingly, it is not expensive to establish a private limited company and it would be possible for Sue to set up her business using this legal structure. Apart from limited liability, it would offer the major advantage that she could invite other people to put money into the business. By allowing people to buy a share in the shop, Sue would have more capital. However, in return for their funds these shareholders would have the right to say how the business should be managed.

In looking at the establishment of a business, we have met a number of new, and important, business terms. Before moving on you should make sure that you fully understand the meaning of the business language we have introduced in this section. Indeed, it is crucial that you learn to use the business terms that you encounter as you progress through the subject.

Public Limited Companies

Increasingly companies are making headlines in the newspapers. The winning of a major overseas order, the prosecution of directors for fraud, or the collapse of a famous firm because of financial problems are all newsworthy items. Most of the companies who appear in the media in these ways are public limited companies. They are identified by the letters 'plc' ('public limited company') after the name. You should be able to think of some famous businesses which trade as public limited companies.

Although public limited companies have similarities to the private limited companies we discussed earlier, there are also some important distinctions, including the following:

CASE STUDY

W H Smith and Boots to join forces in DIY

Boots and W H Smith are to pool their Payless and Do It All businesses into a joint venture. With sales of more than £500 million, the new company will trade from 230 stores under the Do It All banner and concentrate on home improvement.

Payless and Do It All each have 4 or 5 per cent of the DIY market. The new combination will rank alongside or slightly ahead of Texas, owned by the Ladbroke group but behind the largest firm B & Q which has a 13 per cent market share.

Source: adapted from the *Independent*, 6 June 1990

QUESTIONS

1 List the advantages enjoyed by W H Smith and Boots as a result of their joint venture.

2 Can you think of any group(s) of people associated with the new venture who might suffer as a consequence of the merger?

- Public limited companies are entitled to sell their shares on the Stock Exchange. This is a large market in which people can buy and sell shares. Public limited companies can raise extra funds relatively easily since they have an enormous number of potential buyers of their shares
- Public limited companies tend to be much larger
- Public limited companies tend to be owned and managed by different groups of people. Boards of directors run public limited companies. They comprise professional managers who are paid salaries and probably do not own shares in the company. Public limited companies are owned by shareholders who have little say in the running of the company. In private limited companies it is quite common for the owners (the shareholders) to manage the business

The Public Sector

Some goods and services are provided for which people do not have to pay directly. Many people do not pay for their education: the services of schools and colleges are free to the users. When you visit your doctor you do not have to pay directly for the consultation. Similarly, you do not have to pay tolls to travel on the UK's roads. The reason why these goods and services are apparently 'free' is that the government or local authority provides them by using money taken from taxes. These goods are said to be provided by the public sector.

The public sector of the economy is that range of goods and services which are provided by the government, local authorities or nationalized industries (such as the National Health Service).

As well as providing 'free' goods and services the public sector is also responsible for providing some goods and services for which consumers have to pay. Examples of this later group include:

- Coal produced by British Coal
- Rail travel provided by British Rail
- Swimming pools and libraries operated by your local authority or county council

Public sector businesses have fallen from favour in recent years and many have been sold to shareholders, thus becoming public limited companies, as part of the government's privatization programme.

The Business Environment – About This Book

The other books in this series will consider the internal operation of businesses. In this book we shall consider the environment in which businesses operate. This is not to suggest that all the influences on business come from external factors: far from it! Many important influences on businesses come from within the organization. For example, the appointment of a new manager who reorganizes the firm is a typical internal influence and such influences are within the control of the firm. The recent decision by the Rover Group to adopt new working practices (the so-called 'Japanese' practices) shows how managers can exert enormous influence upon a business.

However, it could be argued that the increasing level of competition from other car producers had forced the reforms upon the Rover Group. This highlights the integrated nature of internal and external factors. There are, however, a number of particular external factors which can significantly affect the behaviour and performance of businesses, which we shall look at in detail in this book.

Business in its Environment

The business environment is the central theme developed throughout this book, but it is neces-

---

KEY POINTS 1.4

- **Many small businesses are owned by a single person and they are termed sole traders**
- **Businesses can raise more money if partnerships are created**
- **Companies are owned by shareholders. Shareholders's liability is limited to the amount of money they have invested in their shares**
- **Public limited companies are far larger than private limited companies**
- **Some businesses are operated by, or on behalf of, the state. These businesses are said to be the public sector**

sary for us to outline its meaning at this stage.

We could define the business environment as the external conditions in which businesses exist and operate. At this early stage you should already have a few examples of external factors which comprise this environment. You could make up your own list, perhaps starting with competitors and their behaviour.

Businesses are subject to constant change. New governments are elected, laws change, new products are introduced – all these changes alter the environment in which businesses operate and exist. To survive, businesses have to respond. If they do not, they are unlikely to survive.

Changes in the business environment have two impacts upon firms:

- Some changes constrain business activity, making it more difficult for firms to operate. An example of this might be legislation to protect employees which limits the ways in which firms can treat their workers
- Other changes enhance the activities of businesses. The government offers support to exporters in a number of ways. For example, it supported the UK stand at Expo '92 in Seville (Spain) by contributing over £10 million with the aim of promoting UK exports. This eases the task of business in this area

Businesses can, to some degree, influence their own environment and this is an important factor in their survival. We shall consider later in the book exactly what form these actions may take.

The Legal Environment

The UK government and recently the European Commission have passed many laws which affect the way in which businesses work. These impact upon a number of areas of the business activity.

This series covers in detail the following three areas which are major elements of the legal environment:

- *The competitive structure of markets.* A number of laws have been passed since 1948 to try to promote free and fair competition between businesses. The aim is to avoid businesses having too much power and being able to exploit consumers by charging high prices and/or providing products of poor quality
- *Consumer protection.* Firms must conform to laws designed to protect the consumer. Acts such as the Trade and Descriptions Act and the Sale of Goods Act are intended to look after the interests of consumers by making businesses liable for their goods and services
- *Employee protection.* This involves a large range of legislation relating to employment. It includes such key Acts as the Health and Safety at Work Act 1974 and the Sex Discrimination Acts 1975 and 1986 which can constrain and enhance business activity

The Economic Environment

The economy comprises millions of people and thousands of firms as well as the government and local authorities, all taking decisions about prices and wages, what to buy, sell, produce, export, import and many other matters. All these organizations and the decisions that they take play a prominent part in shaping the business environment in which firms exist and operate.

The economy is complicated and difficult to control and predict, but it is certainly important to all businesses. You should be aware that there are times when businesses and individuals have plenty of funds to spend and other times when they have to cut back on their spending. This can have enormous implications for business as a whole.

When the economy is enjoying a boom, firms experience high sales and general prosperity. At such times, unemployment is low and many firms will be investing funds to enable them to produce more. They do this because consumers have plenty of money to spend and firms expect high sales. It naturally follows that the state of the economy is a major factor in the success of firms.

However, during periods when people have less to spend and many firms face hard times as their sales fall. Thus, the economic environment alters as the economy moves into a recession. At this time, total spending declines as income falls and unemployment rises. Consumers will purchase cheaper items and cut expenditure on luxury items such as televisions and cars.

Changes in the state of the economy affect all types of business, though the extent to which they are affected varies. In the recession of the early 1990s the high street banks suffered badly. Profits declined and, in some cases, losses were incurred. This was because fewer people borrowed money from banks, thus denying them the opportunity to earn interest on loans, and a rising proportion of those who did borrow defaulted on repayment. These so-called `bad debts' cut profit margins substantially. Various forecasters reckoned that the National Westminster Bank's losses in the case of Robert Maxwell's collapsing business empire amounted to over £100 million.

No individual firm has the ability to control this aspect of its environment. Rather, it is the outcome of the actions of all the groups who make up society as well as being influenced by the actions of foreigners with whom the nation has dealings.

ECONOMIC SYSTEMS

There are a number of ways in which a government can organize its economy and the type of system chosen is critical in shaping the environment in which businesses operate.

An economic system is quite simply the way in which a country uses its available resources (land, workers, natural resources, machinery, etc) to satisfy the demands of its inhabitants for goods and services. The more goods and services that can be produced from these limited resources, the higher the standard of living enjoyed by the country's citizens.

There are three main economic systems:

a Planned economies

Planned economies are sometimes called 'command economies' because the state commands the use of resources (such as labour and factories) that are used to produce goods and services. The actual system employed varies from state to state, but command or planned economies have a number of common features.

Firstly, the state decides precisely what the nation is to produce. It usually plans five years ahead. It is the intention of the planners that there should be enough goods and services for all.

Secondly, industries are asked to comply with these plans and each industry and factory is set a production target to meet. If each factory and farm meets its target, then the state will meet its targets as set out in the five-year plans. You could think of the factory and farm targets to be objectives which, if met, allow the nation's overall aim to be reached.

A planned economy is simple to understand but not simple to operate. It does, however, have a number of advantages:

- Everyone in society receives enough goods and services to enjoy a basic standard of living
- Nations do not waste resources duplicating production
- The state can use its control of the economy to divert resources to wherever it wants. As a result, it can ensure that everyone receives a good education, proper health care or that transport is available

Several disadvantages also exist. It is these disadvantages that have led to many nations abandoning planned economies over recent years:

- There is no incentive for individuals to work hard in planned economies
- Any profits that are made are paid to the government
- Citizens cannot start their own businesses and so new ideas rarely come forward
- As a result, industries in planned economies can be very inefficient

A major problem faced by command or planned economies is that of deciding what to produce. Command economies tend to be slow when responding to changes in people's tastes and fashions. Planners are likely to underproduce some items as they cannot predict changes in demand. Equally, some products, which consumers regard as obsolete and unattractive, may be overproduced. Planners are afraid to produce goods and services unless they are sure substantial amounts will be purchased. This leads to delays and queues for some products.

b Market economies

The best examples of this type of economy are to be found in small South-East Asian states like Hong Kong and Singapore, though even they are not pure examples of market economies. Even they contain some businesses owned and run by the state.

In a true market economy the government plays no role in the management of the economy. Workers are paid wages by employers according to how skilled they are and how many firms wish to employ them. They spend their wages on the products and services they need. Consumers are willing to spend more on products and services which are favoured. Firms producing these goods will make more profits and this will persuade more firms to produce these particular goods rather than less favoured ones.

Thus, we can see that in a market economy it is consumers who decide what is to be produced. Consumers will be willing to pay high prices for products they particularly desire. Firms, which are privately owned, see the opportunity of increased profits and produce the new fashionable and favoured products.

Such a system is, at first view, very attractive. The economy adjusts automatically to meet changing demands. No planners have to be employed, which allows more resources to be available for production. Firms tend to be highly competitive in such an environment. New advanced products and low prices are good ways to increase sales and profits. Since all firms are privately owned they try to make the largest profits possible.

Not surprisingly there are also problems. Some goods would be underpurchased if the government did not provide free or subsidized supplies. Examples of this type of good and service are health and education. There are other goods and services, such as defence and policing, that are impossible to supply individually in response to consumer spending. Once defence or a police force is supplied to a country then everyone in that country benefits.

A cornerstone of the market system is that

production alters swiftly to meet changing demands. These swift changes can, however, have serious consequences. Imagine a firm which switches from labour-intensive production to one where new technology is employed in the factory. The resulting unemployment could lead to social as well as economic problems.

In a market economy there might be minimal control on working conditions and safety standards concerning products and services. It is necessary to have large-scale government intervention to pass laws to protect consumers and workers.

Some firms produce goods and then advertise heavily to gain sufficient sales. Besides wasting resources on advertising, firms may also duplicate one another's services. Rival firms providing rail services, for example, could mean that two or more systems of rail are laid.

Finally, firms have to have confidence in future sales if they are to produce new goods and services. At certain times they tend to lack confidence and cut back on production and the development of new ideas. This decision, when taken by many firms, can lead to a recession. A recession means less spending, fewer jobs and a decline in the prosperity of the nation.

c Mixed economies

Command and market economies both have significant faults. Partly because of this, an intermediate system has developed, known as mixed economies.

A mixed economy contains elements of both market and planned economies. Some resources are controlled by the government whilst others are used in response to the demands of consumers. Technically, all the economies of the world are mixed: it is just the balance between market and planned elements that alters. So, for example, Hong Kong has some state-controlled industry, while Cuba has some privately owned and controlled firms.

The aim of mixed economies is to avoid the disadvantages of both systems while enjoying the benefits that they both offer. So, in a mixed economy the state will intervene to supply essential items, like health, education and defence, while private firms produce cars, furniture, electrical items and similar, less essential products.

The UK is a mixed economy: some services are provided by the state (for example, health care and defence) whilst a range of privately owned businesses offer other goods and services. The Conservative government under Margaret Thatcher switched many businesses from being state-owned and controlled to being privately owned as part of its privatization programme. This has taken the UK economy further away from the planned or command system. We shall consider fully the debate surrounding this in Chapter Two.

The Competitive Environment

Any business may be influenced by the actions of other firms in the same industry – its competitors. Even supposed monopolies such as British Rail face competition from other forms of transport. Competitors may set standards of quality, reliability and after-sales service which have to be matched if the business is to be successful. A major reason why the British motor vehicle industry lost out to rivals such as Renault and Volkswagen in the 1970s and 1980s was that customers considered its cars inferior to those of foreign producers. In turn, the successful European car producers are now under threat from other producers, particularly the Japanese.

The Technical Environment

Technology has had a huge impact on business and is predicted to continue to do so at an increasing rate in areas such as biotechnology and microelectronics. Changes in technology can render whole product ranges obsolete and can rapidly alter methods of production with extensive commercial and social effects.

Twenty years ago, most British newspapers were produced in Fleet Street in a traditional, labour-intensive fashion. Developments in information technology meant that the owners of newspapers realized that they could replace expensive employees with computers. Trade unions, fearing heavy job losses, fought the changes bitterly, most notably at the News International plant at Wapping. However, the new technology arrived and many newspaper printers and compositors lost their jobs. (You may be able to think of other jobs that were created directly or indirectly by this new way of producing newspapers.) Technology has changed the industry and this has been further reflected in recent years by a number of new newspapers (for example, the *Independent*) which are produced using the new technology.

The Social Environment

Business is affected by changes in society and has to respond accordingly. We shall see in Chapter Six that business also helps to shape society which in turn affects business.

Over recent years there has been a move towards the consumption of healthier foods. Many people have become vegetarians. Others have taken the decision to become fitter through exercise. A large group – the so-called Green Movement – has become increasingly aware of the damage we are doing to the planet and has demanded environmentally safe products. Business has had to react to these and other changes in its social environment by producing the right products and services to meet the new demands.

In addition, business has had to adjust its manufacturing processes to ensure that the public do not believe it to be a polluter of the environment.

Pressure Groups

A pressure group is any group of people who group together to promote a particular view or interest. Trade unions have flourished since the 1850s and are pressure groups. Recently, we have seen the creation of a number of pressure groups concerned with protecting the environment. Friends of the Earth and Greenpeace are two notable examples of this type of pressure group.

Pressure groups exist to attempt to influence the actions of governments by making both voters and politicians aware of their opinions. For example, Greenpeace has campaigned to persuade the government to pass laws to prevent the dumping of sewage sludge, chemicals and other toxic items into the seas around the British Isles.

Pressure groups can rely upon campaigning or, in more extreme circumstances, resort to direct action. Such direct action can take a number of forms:

- People can block access to building sites to prevent construction work going ahead
- Protesters can boycott the products of the companies concerned in an effort to change their minds by reducing sales
- Trade unions have blockaded factories or organized sit-ins to affect decisions concerning the workplace
- More violent actions can also occur – properties have been bombed and senior managers of some companies murdered as extreme protesters have attempted to get their way

Businesses also try to influence the behaviour of the government. They form pressure groups to attempt to make their action more effective. For example, the Confederation of British Industry (CBI) was established in 1965 and regularly lobbies the government. Its objective is to get the government to introduce policies which will help businesses to prosper.

In recent years the number of pressure groups has increased. There are several reasons for this development. Modern methods of communication has made people more aware of issues such as pollution and animal welfare. Reductions in the working week has given the public time to devote to such issues and rising real incomes has allowed them to afford such activities.

In later chapters we shall consider the themes we have identified above in much more detail. However, it is important to understand that the themes which comprise the business environment do not work singly or in isolation. They work together and interact with one another. We should keep this in mind as we now consider each factor in detail.

EXAM PREPARATION

SHORT QUESTIONS

1. Which of the following are businesses: a firm of solicitors, a car manufacturer, a bank, a university, a holiday company, a doctor's practice?

2. Find examples of two well-known firms in each of these categories of business: primary, secondary and tertiary.

3. Give one example of a way in which changes in society alter business activity.

4. List four subject areas which are a part of business studies.

5. Give two benefits that a business may derive from drawing up a business plan.

6. What is meant by the term 'limited liability'?

7. State two differences between a public limited company and a private limited company.

8. Give three examples of businesses which operate within the public sector.

9. Give two reasons why most newly established businesses are set up as sole traders.

ESSAYS

1. Why do businesses of different sizes exist? Are there any relationships between the size of the business and the industry in which it trades?

2. Outline the external factors which shape the business environment. Which of these factors do you think will be the most influential over the next five years?

CHAPTER 2

The Economy and Business

▷ ▷ QUESTIONS FOR PREVIEW ▷ ▷

1. What is meant by the economic environment and how do we know when changes are taking place in this environment?
2. What general influences affect the level of activity in the economy?
3. What are the implications for businesses of inflation?
4. How do unemployment and economic growth affect businesses and how should businesses respond to these factors?
5. What is privatization and what does it mean for businesses?
6. How does government policy towards international trade and the balance of payments affect the business environment?

The Role of the Economy

IT IS difficult nowadays not to have some knowledge of the state of the economy. If you read a good newspaper or watch the news on television you are bound to come across an item of an economic nature. It might be one about unemployment, inflation or perhaps the balance of payments. Here we are concerned with the impact of such economic factors upon businesses large and small. Other external influences such as the legal system and the actions of competitors are discussed elsewhere in this book.

We shall see as this chapter develops that all business organizations are affected to some degree by economic forces, such as the rate of inflation and the amount of skilled labour available. We can define the economic environment as being

> those factors relating to the state of the economy which contribute to the framework in which businesses make decisions.

Whatever the size or nature of the business, its activities are subject to economic forces. Clearly, firms will benefit if the economy becomes more prosperous and we enjoy an economic boom; wages rise and customers have more money to spend. Equally, they will suffer if, for example, prices and interest rates rise and British products become internationally uncompetitive.

The Case Study opposite shows how the economic environment has a number of effects on small firms (and large ones, too!). They suffer from high interest rates which makes it expensive to borrow and result in falling sales. We should not consider any part of the economic environment in isolation.

In this chapter we shall take an overview of the operation of the economy and the implications of this for businesses.

The Economy – A Complex Entity

The economy is an immensely complex entity. It comprises millions of buyers (or consumers) and hundreds of thousands of businesses all making decisions to spend, hire labour, use certain machinery, produce more (or less), lend (or borrow) money, provide services and so on. This scenario is then further complicated by the action of the government which intervenes in the working of the economy for both economic and political reasons. Foreign trade and thus the activities of overseas producers, governments and consumers add another dimension as does the behaviour of trade unions and pressure groups. Finally, any

The Economy and Business

> ## CASE STUDY
> ### Small Firms Face Squeeze
>
> The Confederation of British Industry (CBI) will present a deeply pessimistic report on small companies this Tuesday. There is evidence that small companies are suffering as much from increasingly restrictive lending policies by the banks as from high interest rates.
>
> Small businesses are complaining that banks are preventing them from expanding, and sometimes even surviving, by turning off the lending tap. The clearing banks, which have announced poor results over the last few days, are struggling to stem a mounting tide of bad debts among their UK business customers.
>
> 'For the first time in years, small firms are as gloomy as big ones,' says Tom O'Connor, chairman of the CBI's smaller firms council.
>
> Last week's CBI quarterly industrial survey, covering all sizes of companies, showed that only 19 per cent had experienced an increase in orders in the previous four months, while 38 per cent had suffered a drop.
>
> *Source:* adapted from the *Independent on Sunday*, 5 August 1990
>
> **QUESTIONS**
>
> 1. Research the following terms from the cutting above: restrictive lending policies, clearing banks, Confederation of British Industry and bad debts.
>
> 2. What links do you think exist between the banks suffering 'bad debts' and the small firms' falling orders and difficulties in borrowing money?

attempt to analyse the economy and its operation is further complicated by the involvement of people. This human element means that the economy does not always behave in a predictable manner: people do not consistently make rational decisions. People do not always take the highest wage or purchase the best product. We shall later consider the interaction of these groups that create the complex entity that is the economy.

Why is the Economy so Important?

The managers of all enterprises, whether public or private, large or small, manufacturing or service-oriented, have to be aware of what is happening in the economy and of the likely consequences for their businesses. Let us take an example. Before a major retail chain, such as Marks & Spencer, sites a store in a town or city, its management will have to be convinced, amongst other things, that the local people will have sufficient income now and in the future to make the new store profitable. The inhabitants' income level depends on the prosperity of the local and national economy.

Some firms are more susceptible to the difficulties resulting from economic change than others. If the economy experiences a downturn with rising unemployment and falling consumer expenditure, then large businesses are generally better equipped to ride out this rough period because they are likely to have greater financial reserves to cover losses. In addition, their greater assets make them more able to raise loan capital than a smaller organization.

Some firms sell products (such as food) or provide services (such as public transport) which are not subject to lessening demand in periods when incomes stagnate or fall, but which do not enjoy rising demand during times when incomes are buoyant.

The UK is a major trading nation and many of its firms sell a high proportion of their goods and services abroad. Factors such as the exchange rate of the pound (discussed fully in Chapter Seven) are therefore very important to them. Other businesses may sell in exceptionally competitive international markets and inflation in the UK, for whatever reason, may cause them acute difficulties as overseas rivals undercut their prices.

The economy affects the sales levels that businesses can expect to reach, the rate of taxation they have to pay, the cost of their labour and raw materials and so on. Its importance cannot be understated.

Measuring Economic Activity

There are a large number of statistics produced regularly on the operation of the world's major

CASE STUDY
City Says Fresh Rate Cut Unlikely

Speculation that Norman Lamont, Chancellor of the Exchequer, will take advantage of sterling's strength to make another quick cut in interest rates was disparaged yesterday by City analysts.

Mr Lamont is unlikely to risk taking British base rates from their current 10 per cent below the German rate of 9.75 per cent, analysts believe.

Source: *Independent*, 12 May 1992

QUESTION

1 Write down two reasons why UK businesses may be discouraged upon reading the above newspaper report?

---

economies. The UK's economy is no exception in this respect. You will probably have noticed that often the headlines in newspapers or important items on television news programmes relate to economic data and the implications for individuals and businesses. A prime example of this occurs when interest rates are increased: the media responds by highlighting the adverse effects on businesses with debts and householders with mortgages.

Data is provided on a wide range of aspects of the economy's operation. Statistics are available to show:

- The level of unemployment
- The level of inflation
- The UK's trade balance with the rest of the world
- Production volumes in key industries and the economy as a whole
- The level of wages
- Raw material prices

and so forth.

The main statistics illustrating the economy's behaviour relate to the level of activity in the economy. That is, they tell us whether the economy is working at full capacity using all, or nearly all, available resources of labour, machinery and other factors of production or whether these resources are being under-utilized. The unemployment figures for the economy give an indicator of the level of activity. As the economy moves towards a recession and a lower level of prosperity it is likely that unemployment figures will rise. An alternative measure of the level of activity is national income statistics which show the value of a nation's output during a year. Economists use the term Gross National Product to describe this data. Changes in the level or trends of such key data have great significance for businesses, as we shall see later.

There are numerous sources of data on the economy of which we can make use. The government publishes much through the Treasury, Department of Trade and Industry, the Bank of England and the Department of Employment. The Central Statistical Office, which was established during the Second World War, publishes about half of the government's economic data. Much of this is contained in its annual publication, *The Annual Abstract of Statistics*. It also publishes the equally valuable *Social Trends* annually. Additionally, private organizations, such as the banks, building societies and universities, publish figures on various aspects of the economy's performance.

Economic statistics are presented in many forms, the most common being graphs and tables. Although these statistics can be valuable in assisting managers, they should be treated with some caution when predicting the future trend of the economy and thus helping the business to take effective decisions.

We can list a number of pitfalls in relation to the use and interpretation of statistics:

a Revised data

Certain data, for example that relating to Britain's trade performance, is often revised after it is first published. The revisions may be sufficient to upset a trend which a business believed to be taking place. In recent times substantial revisions of data relating to the UK's trade with the rest of the world have made the government's role in planning the economy more difficult.

b Seasonality

Certain statistics change regularly at certain times of the year. For example, unemployment figures usually fall during the spring as seasonal work in agriculture and the leisure industry becomes available. Does such an improvement precede an economic boom?

The Economy and Business

CASE STUDY

How the UK Stands at a Glance

Public sector borrowing (£bn excludes asset sales & privatization proceeds, '84/'85 to '92/'93, Source: Hansard)

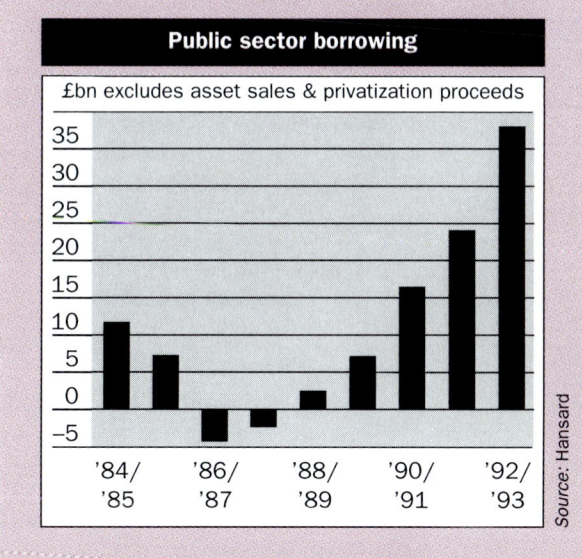

Average earnings (annual increase in average earnings %, '79 to '91, Source: CSO)

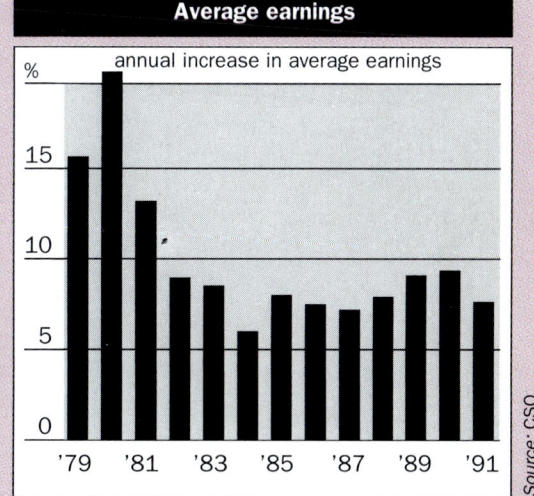

The data relates to the UK economy over recent years.

QUESTIONS

1. What do you think that the rise in public borrowing (borrowing by the government or its agencies) tells us about the yields from taxes during this period?

2. Why might the government receive less in taxes? You should be able to think of at least two reasons.

c Reliability of sources

Much data displayed is collected for other purposes and therefore may contain a fair degree of inaccuracy. Many income figures are based on tax returns to the Inland Revenue and include estimates as to the extent of the black economy. The black economy is that part of the economic activity of a country which is carried out in secret to avoid paying tax, or because the activity is illegal – for example, smuggling or running a brothel. Data on the activities of the private sector is notoriously inaccurate owing to incomplete returns of survey forms by firms.

d Government influence

The government and opposition parties frequently disagree over the accuracy of economic statistics. The opposition parties will inevitably argue that data such as the rate of inflation and the level of unemployment has been handled in such

KEY POINTS 2.1

- The economy is made up of millions of people and hundreds of thousands of businesses
- The behaviour of the economy is critical for firms
- Measuring and predicting its behaviour is difficult, partly because economic statistics are unreliable and easily misinterpreted

a way as to present the government in a favourable light. Obviously this charge will be vigorously denied by the government.

We can conclude that at any time it is difficult to measure accurately the true level of activity in an economy. Without this information, forecasting the future of the economy and taking business decisions becomes difficult and risky.

A Model of the Economy

Economists spend a lot of time trying to develop models of the working of the economy. The London Business School, like many universities and also the Treasury, has a model of the economy which it has entered into a computer. The reason for this is that much of its work is concerned with forecasting future economic trends so as to aid decision-making by business and government. The London Business School's model can be fed with economic information, such as changes in tax rates, and it will then predict how the economy will behave. Such predictions are an invaluable aid to business decision-making because, for example, businesses can find out whether people's incomes are likely to rise or not.

In order to develop a simple model of the economy we need to assume that there are two main sectors in the economy: households and firms. Households supply firms with the factors of production that firms need to carry on their concerns. Thus, households provide labour services, both skilled and unskilled, in return for the payment of wages. They may also supply land for which they are paid rent. Finally, households might supply the finance which is essential to the business. If the finance is in the form of a loan they receive interest payments, but if they have purchased shares in the business they may be entitled to a share of the profits. Most households provide some factor services to a public or private business. Anyone at work is providing labour, and if you or someone in your family has bought shares in the privatization programme (in, for example, British Gas, British Telecom or the water authorities) then they have supplied share capital. We receive payments for these factor services.

The other part of our simple model portrays firms supplying households with all the goods and services that they require. In return for these the households pay the firms. These two sets of actions create the model of the circular flow of money which is shown in Figure 2.1.

You will have noticed that there are two flows. One which is monetary and one comprising goods and services. A flow of factor services from households to firms for which there is an opposite

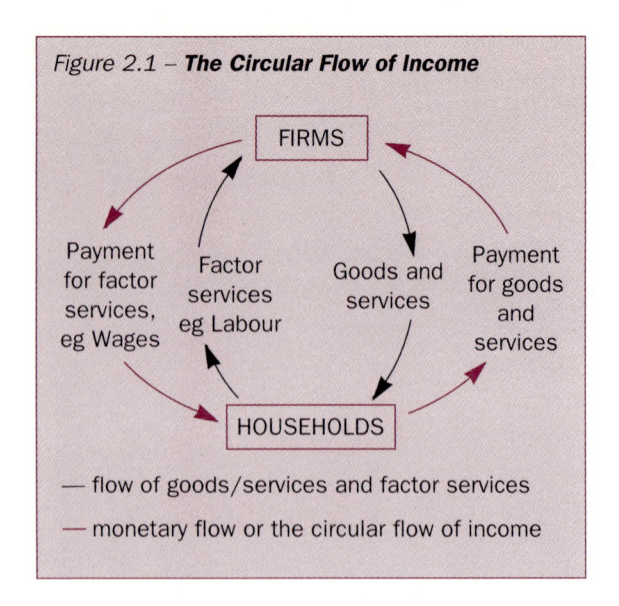

*Figure 2.1 – **The Circular Flow of Income***

— flow of goods/services and factor services
— monetary flow or the circular flow of income

stream of factor payments and a flow of goods and services which households pay firms. It is this monetary flow in which we are most interested.

If we assume that all the goods and services which are produced are in fact sold and that households spend all their income, then we have arrived at what economists call a neutral equilibrium. The level of income which is spent and received by the two groups will not alter since as one group receives it, they spend it with the other. Economists refer to the size of this monetary circular flow as the level of national income.

The fact that the economy is in a neutral equilibrium means simply that the level of national income, and hence the level of economic activity, are stable and unchanging. (An equilibrium is a point of balance in which there is no inherent tendency to change). If the economy was in equilibrium it does not mean that everyone who wants a job has one or that the UK is importing exactly the same value of goods and services as it is exporting.

Altering the Level of Economic Activity

It is almost inevitable that the level of economic activity (or level of national income) will not be in a neutral equilibrium. In a free economy such as the UK's there is a tendency for funds to be withdrawn from the economy, thus reducing the size of the circular flow, as well as there being additions from outside it. The government may also deliberately set about altering the size of the circular flow and hence the level of economic activity.

There are various ways in which the level of activity in the economy can be altered and we shall first consider factors which increase that level.

Injections

An injection is simply an addition to the circular flow of income which does not arise from the spending of households. It was unrealistic to assume earlier that there would be no such additions. These additions or injections will, of course, increase the size of the circular flow and thus the level of activity in the economy. There are three recognized ways in which funds can flow into an economy. They can be generated through:

- Investment
- Government spending
- Export sales

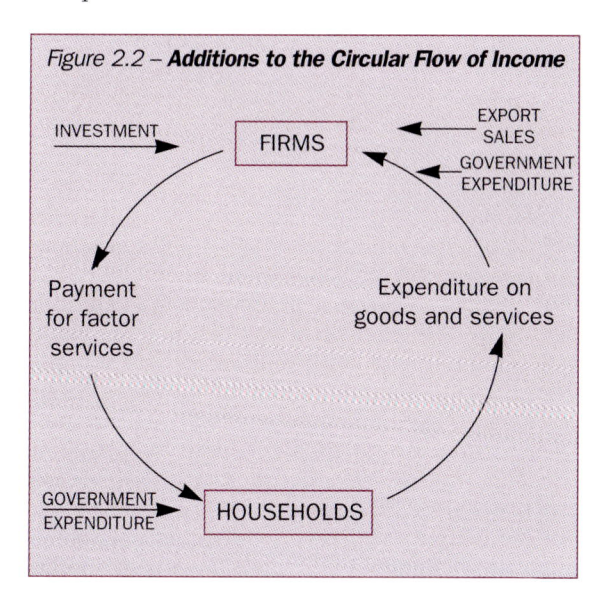

*Figure 2.2 – **Additions to the Circular Flow of Income***

INVESTMENT

Investment is expenditure on productive capital goods. That is, goods which can be used to produce other goods and services. Thus, investment is usually held to be expenditure on factories, machinery and other physical assets. It is important to realize that economists use the word investment in a different context to the layman. An economist referring to investment does not mean the purchase of paper financial assets such as stocks or shares. Clearly, if the ownership of a company's shares is transferred from one UK citizen to another there is no overall impact on the economy.

Investment can be categorized into net investment and gross investment. Net investment is investment which actually increases the nation's stock of capital goods. It is such investment that enables the economy to grow. However, some investment is necessary to replace capital stock that is worn out or obsolete. This loss of value of assets is called depreciation. When this replacement investment is added to the net investment the total achieved is termed gross investment.

You should note that investment increases the circular flow since it comprises extra spending that has not originated in the circular flow. The main influences on the amount of investment that takes place are:

- The rate of interest since firms often have to borrow to undertake the investment
- The firm's expectation about the future behaviour of the economy. If they believe the economy will boom and that the level of economic activity will increase, then they are more likely to enjoy increased sales. They may well decide to invest in new machinery or in a new factory

On the other hand, if the level of investment declines then there will be less injections than previously into the economy and the rate of growth of economic activity (or national income) will fall. Economic statistics show us that over the last few decades the level of gross investment in the UK economy has fluctuated. This will have been one of the factors affecting the level of national income and the environment in which businesses operate.

GOVERNMENT EXPENDITURE

Government expenditure takes many forms and, particularly over the last 50 years or so, has been a very substantial total. This heading covers spending by both central government and local authorities. Government spending results in an injection of funds into the circular flow.

Let us take as an example a decision by the Department of Transport to build a new motorway. This will lead to a variety of spending which would not have taken place otherwise. The authorities will have to employ surveyors, lawyers, accountants and construction workers and will have to purchase large quantities of construction materials. All of the spending generated in this way will be an addition or an injection to the circular flow.

Government spending can, of course, take many other forms. Major financial items are the provision of health and social security benefits. The latter tends to put money directly into the hands of people who need it badly and who are, therefore, likely to spend all or most of it in the near future. If it so wishes the government can use its own expenditure to rapidly affect the level of injections and thus the circular flow. Pursuing such policies, however, can have undesirable side-effects, as we shall see later in the next chapter.

EXPORTS

Exports are an injection because they result in income entering the UK's circular flow as a result of the spending decisions of foreign households, firms and governments. Notice that this spending by foreign households is a loss (or a withdrawal from) their domestic circular flows.

Britain is a major trading nation and, as such, can be described as an open economy. It exports approximately one-third of all the goods and services it produces. The amount the UK imports varies but over time will be roughly the same proportion. The UK's trade is recorded in the balance of payments figures which are published monthly and then collected into annual accounts. If you look at the UK's trade figures you will see that rarely, if ever, does the value of exports equal the value of imports.

Figure 2.3

Fall in exports adds to gloom over economy

A SHARP drop in visible exports [physical goods as opposed to services like banking] in September reinforced City fears that exports have started to falter and will not provide the boost to recovery that had been widely forecast.

The underlying picture was that the improvement seen earlier in the year has come to an end, and that the situation is already worsening.

Visible exports fell 4.5 per cent in September to £8.65 billion, reflecting a broad-based decline, including lower sales of cars abroad.

The slowdown in economic activity in continental Europe, especially Germany, is expected to depress demand in key markets, giving British exports little scope for making up lost ground in the months ahead.

Source: adapted from the *Times*, 23 October 1991, Colin Narborough.
© Times Newspapers Limited 1989.91

The balance of payments accounts are split into two broad sections: the current account, which records imports and exports of goods and services; and the capital account, which records international monetary flows in and out of the UK, such as foreign loans and investment in the UK. We shall consider the balance of payments more fully in Chapter Seven.

Exports have always been important to the UK economy and are indisputably an engine of economic growth. They provide domestic employment not only in the exporting industry but also in the industries which supply components and raw materials to that industry. Exports bolster the circular flow and promote employment in a range of industries. They also stimulate innovation and competition and generate a satisfying standard of living. Most of the world's most prosperous economies are successful exporters, notably Japan and Germany. Few isolated economies have been economically successful.

Withdrawals

Withdrawals (or leakages) are that part of the circular flow which are not passed on as spending with UK firms. This is income which individuals, firms or governments take out of the circular flow with the likely result that the level of economic activity in the economy declines. The three forms that withdrawals can take are:

- Savings
- Imports
- Taxation

SAVINGS

Both businesses and individual citizens can take the decision not to spend all of the income that they receive. A number of factors are thought to determine the level of savings at any one time. Interest rates obviously influence the saver's decision since they represent the return on his or her savings. Many economists believe that decisions to save are taken in response to periods of economic uncertainty: the more worried people are about interest rates, job security and so on, the more they are likely to save. Alternatively, there is evidence that when money is losing value quickly, as in a period of inflation, people tend to purchase consumer durable goods such as televisions and washing machines.

Another factor is social change. Previous generations placed great store by saving in order to carry out major purchases; this is less common today perhaps due to the ready availability of credit.

IMPORTS

You will note that expenditure by UK inhabitants on goods and services imported from abroad will remove those funds from the domestic circular flow and will cause a decrease in the level of economic activity. Periodically, the UK has spent too freely on imports and earnings from exports have been insufficient to cover this. Many factors encourage us to purchase imports: some are favourable to the economy in the long term, whilst others are harmful. If imports of raw materials increase due to the growth of a domestic industry, then this indicates an expanding economy which should sell more exports in the future in order to pay for the increased expenditure. However, if the imports are the consequence of UK citizens preferring foreign goods on grounds of, for example, price or quality, then the impact may be harmful as jobs are lost in domestic industries.

TAXATION

Funds are withdrawn from the circular flow in the form of taxation by the government. It levies two types of tax:

- Direct taxes, such as income tax, corporation tax (on profits) and other taxes on income or wealth
- Indirect taxes, such as VAT and customs and excise duties, which are levied on spending by all of us

If the authorities withdraw funds through taxation and then fail to spend this tax revenue, the circular flow will reduce the level of activity in the economy.

Taxation policy has been substantially altered by the Conservative government in the 1980s and early 1990s. It has reduced direct taxes because of the belief that taxation of this kind reduces the incentive to work and so dampens the spirit of enterprise in the economy. Indirect taxes, such as VAT, have been increased to make up for some of the revenue lost from direct taxes. The government has thus transferred the tax burden from direct to indirect taxes. The total burden of taxation has hardly altered.

Conclusions From the Circular Flow Model

We can draw some important conclusions about the operation of the economy by reference to the model we have developed:

- Any actions which increase the levels of government expenditure, exports or investment tend to increase the level of economic activity
- Similarly, activities which increase savings, imports or taxation will lower the level of economic activity
- A lowering of the level of economic activity will result, for most businesses, in less sales as unemployment in the economy rises and the amount people spend either increases less quickly or falls

ACTIVITY 2.1

Imagine that you are the managing director of a leisure centre which offers a wide range of sports facilities to the local community. The media tells you that the government is raising taxes and reducing its expenditure.

What would you expect the impact of this to be on the level of economic activity and, hence, on your business? Explain your answer. What might lessen or increase the impact?

The government in its management of the economy will seek to alter the level of activity so as to fulfil, as far as possible, its economic objectives. Alterations in the level of activity, whether induced by the government or caused by other factors, will have significant implications for all businesses since they help to shape the environment in which they operate. It is this aspect of the behaviour of the economy which is of most interest to us.

The Government and the Economy

There are a number of groups in society which can influence the level of economic activity. These groups include consumers, trade unions and other pressure groups, major companies, international bodies (such as the European Community) and the domestic government. At present, the government is the most influential by far. We introduced the significance of other

---

KEY POINTS 2.2

- **Economists develop models of the economy to forecast the future in the light of current changes and to help businesses and governments take decisions**
- **The government can adjust the level of activity in the economy in a number of ways**
- **The level of economic activity depends broadly upon injections and withdrawals. This has important implications for businesses**

external parties in Chapter One and have developed these themes as the basis of other chapters later in the book.

Why Does the Government Interfere in the Working of the Economy?

As this century has progressed governments have accepted greater responsibility for the effective operation of the economy. By 1945 the government had established economic objectives which still broadly apply today. These objectives are:

- Steady and sustained economic growth
- A low rate of unemployment
- Price stability
- A balanced balance of payments avoiding long-term deficits and surpluses

It is in pursuing these objectives that the government performs a key role in shaping the economic environment in which businesses have to operate. In this section we shall discuss the objectives of government and the relationship businesses have with these objectives. In the following chapter we shall review the policy options open to the government in its management of the economy. We shall also discuss how the implications of these policies affects firms. Finally, we should be able to decide whether the cure is worse than the disease itself!

Various objectives have assumed importance at different times since 1945. For example, recent Conservative governments have managed the economy with the additional objective of reducing the role of the public sector in our economic system. However, the four objectives set out above have remained relatively unchanged as administrations have come and gone. Equally, the overall aim of improving the standard of living for everyone is unaltered. The ways in which varying administrations have attempted to attain these objectives have altered as the political beliefs of the governments have changed.

Most governments have found the simultaneous attainment of all of these objectives nearly impossible. For example, policies such as increasing government expenditure raises injections and lowers the level of unemployment, but can also cause inflation. Governments have thus given priority to different objectives at particular times. Undoubtedly, the prime economic objective in the UK over the last decade or so has been that of the reduction of inflation and, hence, price stability.

The Economic Issues: Inflation

Inflation is generally defined as:

a persistent rise in the general price level with

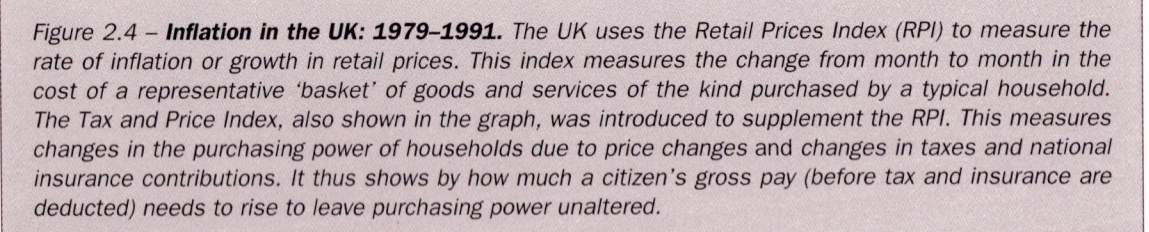

*Figure 2.4 – **Inflation in the UK: 1979–1991.** The UK uses the Retail Prices Index (RPI) to measure the rate of inflation or growth in retail prices. This index measures the change from month to month in the cost of a representative 'basket' of goods and services of the kind purchased by a typical household. The Tax and Price Index, also shown in the graph, was introduced to supplement the RPI. This measures changes in the purchasing power of households due to price changes and changes in taxes and national insurance contributions. It thus shows by how much a citizen's gross pay (before tax and insurance are deducted) needs to rise to leave purchasing power unaltered.*

Source: CSO

no corresponding rise in output, which leads to a corresponding fall in the purchasing power of money.

In this section we shall look briefly at the problems that inflation causes for business and consider whether there are any potential benefits for an enterprise from an inflationary period. Later in Chapter Three we shall also consider the government's likely response to inflation and the implications of their anti-inflationary policies for business.

Inflation varies considerably in its extent and severity. Hence, the consequences for the business community differ according to circumstances. Mild inflation of a few per cent each year may pose few difficulties for business. However, hyperinflation, which entails enormously high rates of inflation, can create almost insurmountable problems for the government, business, consumers and workers. In post-war Hungary, the cost of living was published each day and workers were paid daily so as to avoid the value of their earnings falling. Businesses would have experienced great difficulty in costing and pricing their production while the incentive for people to save would have been removed.

Economists argue at length about the causes of, and 'cures' for, inflation. They would, however, recognize that two general types of inflation exist:

- Demand-pull inflation
- Cost-push inflation

Demand-pull Inflation

Demand-pull inflation occurs when demand for a nation's goods and services outstrips that nation's ability to supply these goods and services. This causes prices to rise generally as a means of limiting demand to the available supply.

An alternative way that we can look at this type of inflation is to say that it occurs when injections exceed withdrawals *and* the economy is already stretched (i.e. little available labour or factory space) and there is little scope to increase further its level of activity.

Cost-push Inflation

Alternatively, inflation can be of the cost-push variety. This takes place when firms face increasing costs. This could be caused by an increase in wages owing to trade union militancy, the rising costs of imported raw materials and components or companies pushing up prices in order to improve their profit margins.

The Impact of Inflation on Business

Inflation can adversely affect business in a number of ways:

a Accounting and financial problems

Significant rates of inflation can cause accounting and financial problems for businesses. They may experience difficulty in valuing assets and stocks, for example. Such problems can waste valuable management time and make forecasting, comparisons and financial control more onerous.

b Falling sales

Many businesses may experience falling sales during inflationary periods for two broad reasons. Firstly, it may be that saving rises in a time of inflation. We would expect people to spend more of their money when prices are rising to avoid holding an asset (cash) which is falling in value. However, during the mid-1970s, when industrialized nations were experiencing high inflation rates, savings as a proportion of income rose! It is not easy to identify the reason for this, but some economists suggest that people like to hold a relatively high proportion of their assets in a form which can be quickly converted into cash when the future is uncertain. Whatever the reason, if people save more they spend less and businesses suffer falling sales. The economic model we developed earlier predicted that, if savings rose the level of activity in the economy would fall. Clearly, if this happened we would expect businesses to experience difficulty in maintaining their levels of sales.

Businesses may be hit by a reduction in sales during a time of inflation for a second reason. As inflation progresses, it is likely that workers' money wages (that is, wages unadjusted for inflation) will be increased broadly in line with inflation. This may well take a worker into a higher tax bracket and result in a higher percentage of his or her wages being taken as tax. This process, known as fiscal drag, will cause workers to have less money available to spend on firms' goods and services. The poverty trap has a similar impact. As money wages rise, the poor may find that they no longer qualify for state benefits to supplement their incomes and at the same time they begin to pay income tax on their earnings. Again, this leaves less disposable income to spend on the output of firms. Finally, it may be that the wages of many groups are not index-linked and so they rise less quickly than the rate of inflation, causing a reduction in spending power and demand for goods and services.

Once again, our economic model can be used to predict that increases in the level of taxation will increase withdrawals, lowering the level of economic activity and depressing firms' sales.

Not all businesses will suffer equally from declining demand in an inflationary period. Those selling essential items, such as food, may be little affected whilst others supplying less essential goods and services, such as foreign holidays, may be hard hit.

c High interest rates

Inflation is often accompanied by high interest rates. High interest rates tend to discourage investment by businesses as they increase the cost of borrowing funds. Thus, investment may fall. Businesses may also be dissuaded from undertaking investment programmes because of a lack of confidence in the future stability and prosperity of the economy. This fall in investment may be worsened by foreign investment being reduced as they also lose some confidence in the economy's future.

Such a decline in the level of investment can lead to businesses having to retain obsolete, inefficient and expensive means of production and cause a loss of international competitiveness. Finally, as we noted earlier in our economic model, a fall in investment can lower the level of economic activity, causing lower sales, output and so on. Thus, to some extent, businesses can influence the economic environment in which they operate.

d Higher costs

During a bout of inflation firms will face higher costs for the resources they need to carry on their business. They will have to pay higher wages to their employees to compensate them for rising prices. Supplies of raw materials and fuel will become more expensive as will rents and rates. The inevitable reaction to this is that the firm has to raise its own prices. This will lead to further demands for higher wages as is called the wage-price spiral. Such cost-push inflation may make the goods and services produced by that enterprise internationally less competititive in terms of price. An economy whose relative or comparative rate of inflation is high may find that it is unable to compete in home or foreign markets because its products are expensive. Our economic model tells us that a situation of declining exports and increasing imports will lower the level of activity in the economy with all the consequent side-effects we discussed earlier.

Can Inflation be Beneficial?

We would be simplifying the impact of inflation on business if we suggested that all the effects were unfavourable. There is a school of thought which argues that a low and stable rate of increase in the price level can be beneficial. It believes that a steady rise in money profits produces favourable expectations and induces investment as firms seek to expand. This action expands the economy as a whole. Paradoxically, inflation can also reduce the costs of businesses in the short run. Many enterprises incur costs

---

CASE STUDY

Wage Rises Exert Pressure on Costs

Britain faces a severe recession unless employers control pay increases running at an average 9.2 per cent for industrial workers and 10.6 per cent for clerical staff.

The warning comes today in a Reward Group survey covering 700 000 employees, which reveals that basic salary increases for 16-year-olds averaged more than 16 per cent last year.

The Reward Group warns: 'Our competitive edge is wasting away and has only been maintained for exports by the recent drop in the exchange rate.

'The indications are that the spurt in pay must now be stabilised and then gradually pulled back. Failure can only lead to a severe recession as our prices become unacceptable and profit margins become so low that investment is curtailed.'

Source: *Independent*, 5 February 1990

QUESTIONS

1 What happens to an economy when it enters a recession? Write down as many features of a recession as you can.

2 What UK products do you think would still sell well even if their prices rose?

3 What can companies do to hold down their labour costs in times of inflation? Make as many suggestions as you can. Which do you think is the most likely to succeed?

which are fixed for some period of time – for example, the rent of a factory may be fixed at a particular figure for a few years. At a time when the selling price of the firm's product, and hence its sales income, is rising this cost will be falling in real terms and thus stimulating the business.

There is a further argument that firms may be persuaded to borrow heavily in a period of inflation since the burden of repaying loans is reduced by inflation. If inflation is running annually at 10 per cent, for example, then the real value of the repayments of the loan will fall by approximately that amount each year. This may serve to encourage investment which, since it is an injection into the circular flow, will promote the level of activity. However, in these circumstances interest rates are likely to be high.

Governments will accept that low rates of inflation are likely to exist in many economies. Inflation rates of 5 per cent or below are not considered to be too great a problem, especially if competitor nations are suffering similar rates.

In spite of the above paragraphs, we must draw the conclusion that inflation is, in general, harmful to business and its environment. Indeed, many economists would contend that inflation is the fundamental evil as its presence leads to lack of competitiveness and therefore relatively high unemployment and low rates of growth. This viewpoint has gained in credence in government circles over the last few years. It is for this reason that its control has been a major objective of government economic policy throughout the 1980s and early 1990s.

Employment

Labour is a major resource in any enterprise and it is vitally important that a sufficiently large, flexible and well-trained workforce is available. Governments seek to minimize the rate of unemployment. Workers will buy at least some of the

Figure 2.5 – *Unemployment Graduates*

Degree of despair for children of the slump

THE class of '91 are the students who applied for university at the height of an economic boom and graduated into a recession. Three years ago, when they won their places at Kent University, interest rates were at their lowest for a decade, inflation was just over 4% and unemployment, already at its lowest since 1981, was still falling.

Today, anxiety has tarnished the optimism and ambition that launched the thirty-seven 'freshers' on their studies at Keynes College, one of Kent's four halls of residence. Only eleven of those who were reunited at their graduation last week have secured a permanent job. Sixteen are still looking for work, or have found temporary employment, while the other ten intend to continue with their studies.

Last week a report by some of Britain's biggest employers revealed a record slump in the graduate jobs market, with a 20% cut in vacancies and a virtual freeze on salaries.

Like many of the 135 000 graduates leaving College this year, Caroline Kirk, twenty-one, was disheartened. In spite of a good second-class honours degree in history, she has so far failed to find a job after three months of searching and fifty applications.

'The idea of going to university was to improve your chances of being chosen for a good job. It's difficult to keep a positive attitude when you get rejections, but you have to remember that you are one of thousands.'

Source: adapted from the *Sunday Times*, 14 July 1991, Charles Hymas.
© Times Newspapers Limited 1989.91

KEY POINTS 2.3

- **Inflation is generally defined as a persistent rise in the general price level**
- **Inflation can be caused by a number of factors, the two most common being excess demand and rising costs**
- **Most effects of inflation on businesses are harmful**
- **Inflation can benefit creditors and a low rate can be viewed favourably if it stimulates demand**

*Figure 2.6 – **Unemployment in the UK.** The graphs show how unemployment in the UK fluctuated between 1971 and 1991. Graph (a) gives a comparison of male and female unemployment rates between 1971 and 1990. Can you think why female rates are consistently lower? Is it what you expected as the proportion of females in the labour force grows steadily? The lower line in graph (b) gives figures for vacancies. These represent jobs available that are notified to the Department of Employment.*

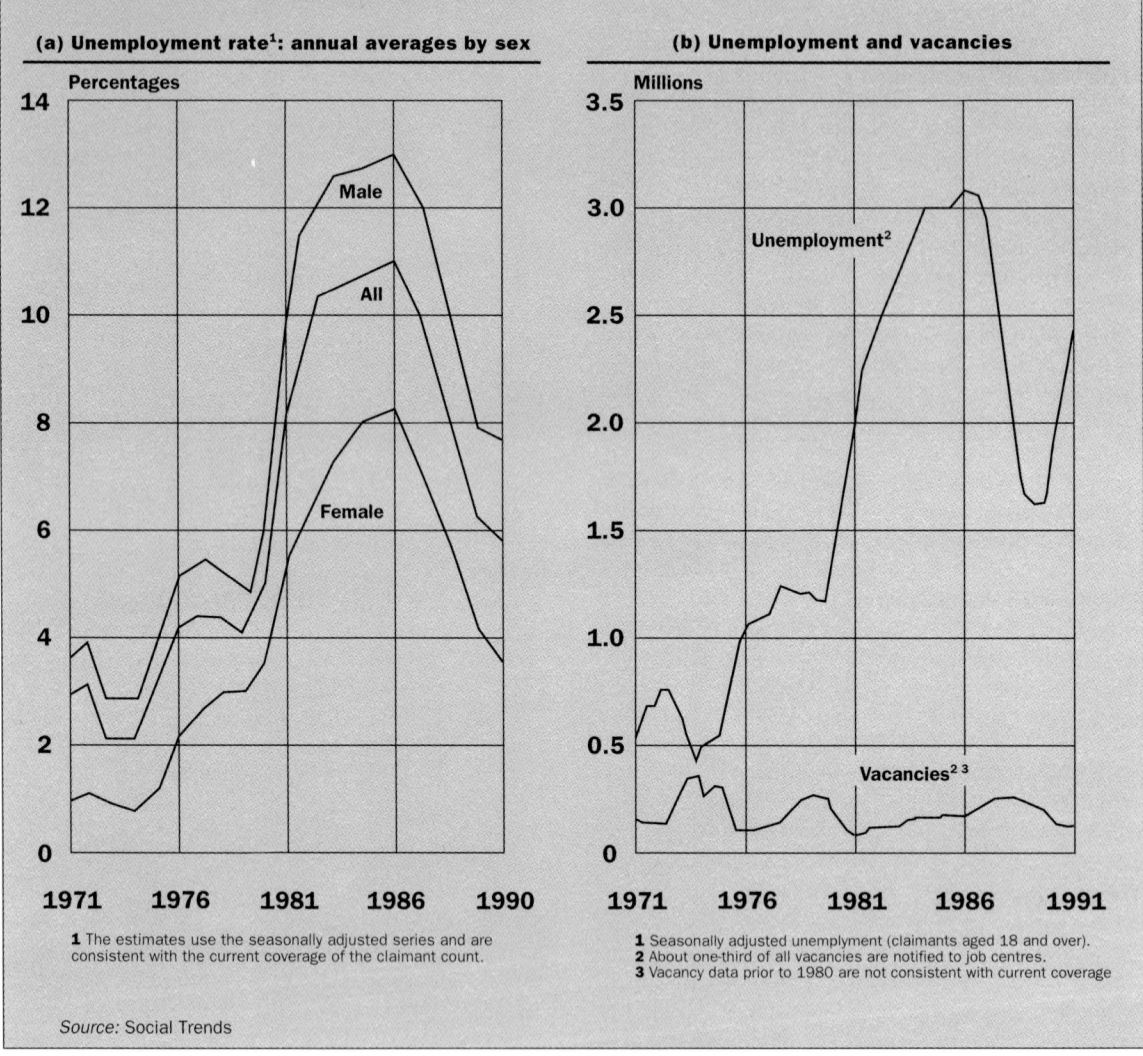

(a) Unemployment rate[1]: annual averages by sex

[1] The estimates use the seasonally adjusted series and are consistent with the current coverage of the claimant count.

(b) Unemployment and vacancies

[1] Seasonally adjusted unemployment (claimants aged 18 and over).
[2] About one-third of all vacancies are notified to job centres.
[3] Vacancy data prior to 1980 are not consistent with current coverage

Source: Social Trends

output of business and so it is important that they are in work to allow them to purchase the economy's output. Unemployment also poses an enormous social and economic cost to any nation.

The social cost is that the unemployed feel degraded and of no value since our society places great emphasis on having a job. Unemployment may result in depression, stress or, in some cases, crime. After long periods of unemployment, some people experience severe difficulties in rejoining the workforce.

In economic terms the cost of lost output is immense. A 10 per cent rate of unemployment means that the potential output of one-tenth of the workforce has been lost to our society. In addition, those in employment are paying taxes to support those out of work and the government has lost tax revenue from the unemployed – a double blow.

The article in Figure 2.5 (previous page) shows how unemployment worsens during a recession and how it affects all type of workers – young and old, skilled and unskilled. This is clearly a waste of resources as these young people remain unused. Some may emigrate to seek employment and be lost permanently to the UK.

There is no single measure of unemployment used by governments to assess the proportion of their workforce which is not in work. Indeed, most nations alter the way in which they measure this key statistic from time to time – in this respect the UK is no different. You may be aware that over recent years the government has introduced a number of changes regarding who should be included in the unemployment total. All but one of these changes have lowered the total. For example, a recent decision was taken to exclude those aged between sixty and sixty-five from the unemployment register.

Predicting the impact of unemployment and controlling it are made more difficult by the fact that various types of unemployment occur. Some types of unemployment pose far more of a threat to economic stability and hence threaten the environment of business.

FRICTIONAL UNEMPLOYMENT

We should not be too surprised that the business community expresses little concern about frictional unemployment. This type of unemployment is caused when people move between jobs. For example, a bricklayer may be unemployed for a few weeks while waiting for a suitable vacancy to appear. A healthy economy will always exhibit some of this unemployment as workers move from one job to another. Businesses favour such flexibility as they search for suitably skilled and qualified labour. This unemployment offers little threat to their well-being unless the interval between jobs becomes prolonged. Equally, the government only seeks to minimize the time spent searching for, or transferring to, the new place of employment.

SEASONAL UNEMPLOYMENT

Like frictional unemployment, seasonal unemployment is not regarded as a major problem on a national level. It regularly rises in the winter before declining again the following summer. For some local communities this can be a serious problem. Both business and government are prepared for it and its small scale and regularity mean that it poses little or no problem.

STRUCTURAL UNEMPLOYMENT

Of some concern is structural unemployment, which is the result of fundamental changes in the economy. It may occur because machinery replaces workers as has recently occurred with print workers in the newspaper industry. Alternatively, it could be the result of consumers no longer wishing to buy certain products which are obsolete or out of fashion.

ACTIVITY 2.2

Imagine that you are the managing director of a medium-sized manufacturing plant. You become aware that technology is available which could replace some of your shop-floor workers. Note down the arguments for and against introducing technology. What other information would you want before reaching a final decision? When you have finished reading the section on unemployment, consider your answer again.

Structural unemployment has considerable implications for businesses. Firstly, it may mean that some of the workers available have outdated skills which will necessitate expenditure on retraining. Secondly, such workers often take some time to recognize that the type of job they used to do is no longer available. Thus, they are unlikely to be spending as much as before and firms in areas of high structural unemployment will probably experience falling sales. Such unemployment will usually cause the government to introduce policies to alleviate the problem. These may be specific, such as support for a declining industry as in the case of the Lancashire textile industry, or general to increase the level of economic activity and thus the demand from firms for labour. We shall discuss such policies later in Chapter Three on managing the economy.

CYCLICAL UNEMPLOYMENT

Over time, all economies move through cycles during which the level of business activity fluctuates. Boom, with high spending, low unemployment and general prosperity, is followed by a slump in which prosperity declines and the level of unemployment rises. The intensity of such fluctuations in business activity may vary, but the general pattern continues.

Such cyclical unemployment is a major target of the government's employment policy as it seeks to maintain a steady growth in the economy. Businesses find that such fluctuations in unemployment have a considerable impact on their production and sales and make forward planning more difficult. The intensity and lengths of these cycles differ. As a recession begins, firms may be unsure as to how to adjust their output plans when they do not know the extent of the slump in demand. To some degree, the decisions that they take in these circumstances help to determine future demand and sales.

REGIONAL UNEMPLOYMENT

Some parts of the UK are considerably more prosperous than others. Most of us would guess that the South East, including London, would top a regional prosperity table; whilst others, for example, Northern Ireland, would appear at, or near, the bottom of the league. An indicator and cause of this regional variation is called regional unemployment. Causes of such unemployment are complex and difficult to eradicate, but in many

*Figure 2.7 – **UK Employment and Income Patterns.*** *Map (a) shows unemployment rates for the standard industrial regions of the UK. Map (b) shows how this level of unemployment has changed in recent years. You will see from map (c) that the level of disposable income (i.e. income that is left in the pay-packet after deductions) varies considerably throughout the UK. You should be able to identify those regions where sales may be highest and those regions where firms will face the highest costs.*

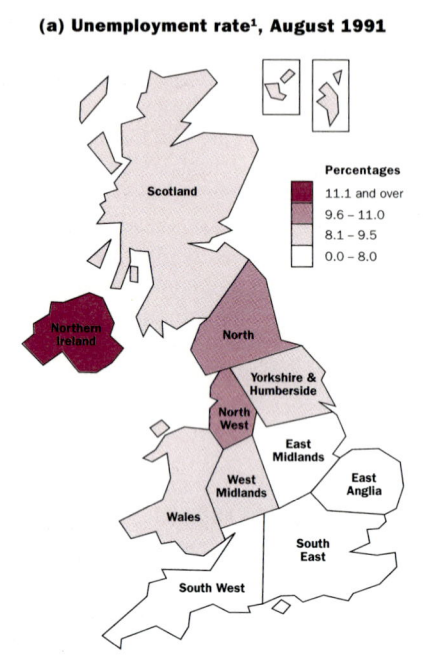

(a) Unemployment rate[1], August 1991

Percentages
- 11.1 and over
- 9.6 – 11.0
- 8.1 – 9.5
- 0.0 – 8.0

(b) Change[2] in previous 12 months

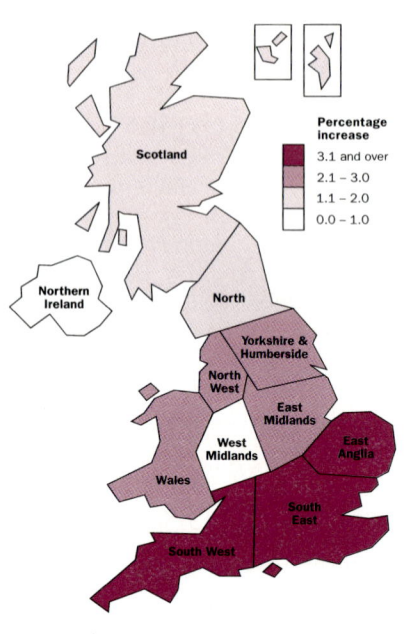

Percentage increase
- 3.1 and over
- 2.1 – 3.0
- 1.1 – 2.0
- 0.0 – 1.0

[1] Seasonally adjusted
[2] Percentage point change in unemployment rate between August 1990 and August 1991

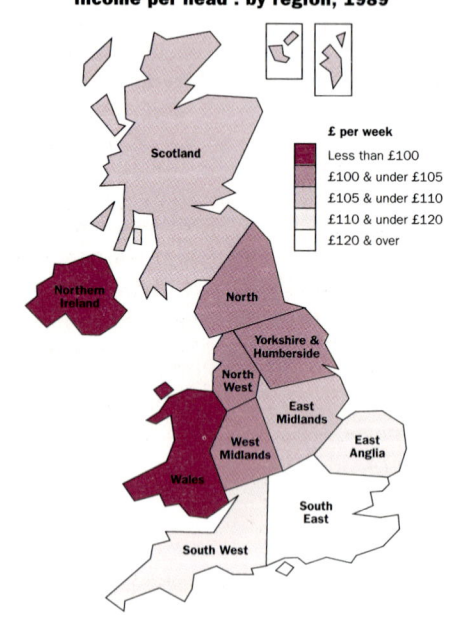

(c) Average weekly household disposable income per head : by region, 1989

£ per week
- Less than £100
- £100 & under £105
- £105 & under £110
- £110 & under £120
- £120 & over

Source: Social Trends

areas they are linked to structural change in the local economy. All post-war governments have operated regional policies in an effort to even up regional prosperity. Businesses are affected by such variations in prosperity. They tend to locate in the more prosperous regions in order to be near to their most important market. The consequences of this crowding together can be costly: higher rents, salaries and the costs associated with congestion (such as increased transport costs).

It is often difficult to distinguish between types of unemployment. However, it is important for both firms and governments to appreciate the nature of unemployment in order that they can take actions appropriate to the situation.

Frictional unemployment might, for example, require improvements, initiated by the government, in the ways in which employers with vacancies are able to communicate with unemployed workers. On the other hand, structural unemployment might involve a different response involving public investment in new factories and retraining schemes. Frictional unemployment might not inconvenience firms too greatly beyond some extra difficulty in recruiting. Structural unemployment, on the other hand, can mean loss of markets as firms close and the income levels in the locality decline.

In the next section we shall discuss how firms might react to changing levels of unemployment.

Business and Changing Employment Levels

Businesses react in varying ways to significant changes in the level of unemployment. It is impossible to predict precisely the response of any organization to changes in the level of unemployment since this will depend upon the firm in question and its circumstances. Any actions taken by a firm will impinge upon all sectors of the organization. A well managed firm will be acting in advance of changes rather than reacting to events.

A forecasted rise in unemployment levels will have serious implications for a firm's production activities. Sales are likely to fall and unless the firm is willing to increase stocks or can find alternative markets, production may have to be reduced. Firms will be forced to reassess their targets and to set new ones. They may seek to reduce output through redundancy and rationalization: firms may close branch plants and shed labour as a result of the introduction of new technology in an effort to cut costs. Firms generally tend to reduce their stocks of finished goods at such times. This action improves a business's financial position because firms have paid to produce the stocks but have not yet received any revenue from the sale of these stocks. Reducing stocks increases the flow of money into the business with little additional cost to the firm. Research and development plans are likely to be postponed or abandoned, and planned investment may well be reduced.

The marketing department is also likely to respond to rising unemployment by altering its plans. It may adjust its strategy to stress the reliability of its product and the value for money that its goods or services offer. It could also rationalize the range of goods or services that it makes available in order to cut costs. It might adopt a new, lower pricing policy in an effort to maintain its sales at an acceptable level. Certainly it will consider entering new markets, possibly overseas where sales may be more buoyant.

The board of directors are likely to review the company's overall position and objectives in the light of the new circumstances. They may consider diversification to provide goods or services which are essential in nature and less susceptible to cyclical fluctuations in demand – for example, foodstuffs or children's clothing. Alternatively, the directors may contemplate merging with another firm in order to produce a range of products to allow them to ride out an economic downswing.

At times when unemployment is falling and the level of economic activity is rising, firms will pursue expansionary policies roughly opposite to those outlined above.

It is impossible to exactly predict the actions of firms at a time when unemployment levels are changing. It will depend upon a number of other factors, including:

- Management awareness of the changing economic environment
- Management skills and attitudes and their ability to deal with changing circumstances
- The organization's size and product range and its financial resources
- Whether the firm operates in an area (geographical or otherwise) that is going to suffer the worst of the rising unemployment
- Their belief in the accuracy of the prediction

Economic Growth

As a nation's economy grows it is able to produce more goods and services each year. You should recall from earlier in this chapter that the value of national output is measured by the national income. Therefore, economic growth is usually termed as the rate at which the national income of a country grows in real terms. This means the rate of growth of national income, after allowance has been made for inflation. Governments seek the fastest possible economic growth without incurring undesirable side-effects such as inflation.

We also noted earlier in this chapter that increases in those factors which create injections into the circular flow (export sales, investment and government expenditure) increase the level of economic activity which, if sustained, leads to economic growth. It follows from this that governments can help promote economic growth by increasing their own expenditure when appropriate. They can also do so by attempting to create an environment whereby exports can flourish and businesses consider investment worthwhile.

Such economic growth is a major objective of governments since a rise in the standard of living of the country's people should follow. This is, however, only true if national income has risen even when inflation has been allowed for, otherwise it means that the price of the nation's output has increased rather than the quantity. It is also important that the growth of the population has not exceeded the growth of national income, otherwise the additional output will have been swallowed up amongst the extra people. It is necessary for real national income per head to rise to increase the general standard of living. And even under these circumstances some groups in society (for example, pensioners) may not share in the increased prosperity because their incomes rise less quickly than those of other groups, notably those in full-time employment.

A growing economy means a developing economy: change is an integral part of growth. Some firms will decline as their products become obsolete or go out of fashion whilst others thrive as their goods or services become popular and as they innovate new advanced ideas. Opportunities are regularly thrown up as markets are created by the additional spending power that is placed in the hands of the public. Talented and perceptive managers can take advantage of the chances created – growth provides a framework for success.

As with all opportunities, some businesses will benefit more than others from the favourable economic environment. All products have a life cycle, though the length of the cycle may vary. Firms with products at the end of their cycle may benefit little from rising sales. In contrast a new product which coincides with a strong period of economic growth has a distinct advantage. It is this factor which partly explains the rapid increase in popularity and sales of Compact Disc players in the late 1980s.

Most businesses prefer periods of economic growth not only because of buoyant sales but also because tax rates can fall. Since governments have to support less unemployed at a time when tax revenues are booming, they can afford to cut rates. It also offers the opportunity to improve the infrastructure of the economy by building new roads, rail links, airports, etc. Both factors can encourage the development of all businesses.

Privatization

One of the most controversial areas of government economic control throughout the 1980s and early 1990s has been the privatization issue. We can simply define privatization as:

> selling, in whole or part, publicly owned industries, or other assets, to the private sector.

This, however, does not reflect the full extent of the initiative. We can devise three categories of privatization:

a Change in ownership of an enterprise
This is what many people understand by the term 'privatization', but it is an incomplete definition. This type of privatization involves the state selling an enterprise into the private sector. Complete enterprises (such as Cable & Wireless and British Gas) have been sold as well as partial sales (such as British Rail's hotel division).

b Deregulation
This involves opening markets which were previously dominated by a statutory state monopoly. The first Thatcher government (1979–83) undertook such liberalization in both the inter-city coach and telecommunications markets. In each case private competition was allowed to challenge the state monopolies (National Express and British Telecom) in at least some of their activities.

c Private provision
This is also known as franchising. Here the state employs private sector organizations to carry out duties which were previously operated by the state itself. Recent examples include the privatization of hospital and school catering and the cleaning of many public buildings. Private firms are now cleaning your school, college or local hospital.

The Privatization Debate

Privatization is an issue which provokes strong feelings in many people. The various Acts of

---

KEY POINTS 2.4

- Several different types of unemployment exist

- Regional prosperity differs greatly throughout the UK and this has considerable implications for costs and sales of businesses

- Businesses will react differently to unemployment according to its type and the nature and market position of the business

- A growing economy will have more prosperous citizens, though not all groups in society will have more money to spend

*Figure 2.8 – **Privatization Sales.** This shows the major privatization sales that have taken place since 1981. This list refers only to the sales of assets and not to the other types of privatization we identified earlier. Can you add any more recent sales to the list to bring it fully up to date?*

Company	Date of privatization
British Aerospace	1981
North Sea Licences	1981
British Sugar Corporation	1981
Cable & Wireless	1981
Amersham International	1982
Britoil	1982
Associated British Ports	1983
British Telecom	1984
Enterprise Oil	1984
British Gas	1986
British Airways	1987
Royal Ordnance	1987
Rolls Royce	1987
BAA	1987
British Petroleum	1987
British Steel	1988
Water	1989
Electricity (regional companies)	1990
Electricity (generators)	1991

Parliament which have been necessary for the privatization programme have caused stormy scenes and passionate speeches on both sides in the Houses of Parliament. We shall look briefly at the major arguments on each side.

The Case For Privatization

a   It rids the economy of monopolies
The advocates of privatization argue that it rids the economy of monopolies which can be inefficient and charge high prices for products of dubious quality. All their customers (many of which are businesses) suffer from these disadvantages: their costs rise and their international competitiveness declines. Those in favour of privatization have pointed to the success of liberalization or 'deregulation' of markets as indicators of how efficiency can be improved. The inter-city coach market is, they argue, a good example of the success of the policy. Fundamentally, the policy is based on an unshakeable belief in the superiority of the private sector over the public sector.

b   It results in a better-run industry
A further reason for privatization was that the government considered that it did not have effective control of nationalized industries under the system whereby a board of directors took charge on a day-to-day basis with a government minister having overall control. Arguments between the minister and the chairperson of the board were frequent and not conducive to a well run industry. The government felt such industries needed more positive and single-minded management.

c   It enables tighter financial control
The control of the finances of nationalized industries was also a matter of some concern to the government. Since they would not be allowed to go bankrupt the industries' investment appraisal was not as effective as it might have been. Furthermore, industries such as British Steel kept open uneconomic plants. The government felt that finances should be more tightly controlled.

d   It enables long-term planning
In spite of a series of White Papers dating back to 1967 the nationalized industries had not established clear objectives. Initially they were required to break-even and later to charge prices so as to maximize their value to society (which meant incurring losses) and finally, in recent years, to reduce their dependence upon the Treasury. It was felt that these policies were not creating an environment in which the industries could create long-term strategies.

e   It provides revenue for government
Privatization has raised huge sums of revenue for the government. This has given them the short-term financial freedom to cut taxes and to create an economy in which enterprise is rewarded without the penalty of heavy taxes. In the period 1979/80–1988/89 the government received nearly £22 billion from its privatization activities.

f   It aims to increase public shareholders
Privatization has also been carried out with the aim of increasing the number of shareholders amongst the general public. At least nine million individuals have bought shares during the programme.

The Case Against Privatization

a   It does not lead to greater efficiency
The critics of the policy have argued strongly that the privatization programme will not result in greater efficiency. Indeed, they contend that the selling of state monopolies to the private sector, where they will continue to act as monopolies, could result in them abusing their market power at the expense of their customers. It is felt in some quarters that the bodies set up to watch over the newly privatized companies (for example, OFTEL and OFGAS) lack teeth and may not be able to protect the interests of private monopolies's customers.

b It's like 'selling the family silver'

As we noted earlier, the government has had a huge inflow of funds which has eased its current financial position. But its critics argue that it is gaining a current benefit at the expense of a stream of future earnings. In a famous speech in the House of Lords, a former Conservative Prime Minister, the late Lord Stockton, likened privatization to 'selling the family silver'.

c Assets were undervalued

A much voiced complaint of the programme is that the state undervalued the assets that it has sold. In order to guarantee a successful sale, the opponents argue, the authorities underpriced the share issues. As a result, most share issues were heavily over-subscribed. That is, individuals and institutional investors (such as building societies and pension funds) applied to buy more shares than were for sale. Some form of rationing had to be used in most of the privatization issues. The government had ten applications for each British Telecom share for sale, for example, and the shares rose in value by 90 per cent as soon as they were traded on the Stock Exchange.

d It threatens the long-term well-being of the organization

Some economists and financial experts fear that a large rise in the number of private individuals holding shares might not be a good move. They argue that it may lead to firms concentrating on short-term profits (in order to retain shareholders who are interested in a quick return) at the expense of the longer-term well-being of the organization.

How Successful Has Privatization Been?

It is difficult to assess the success of the privatization programme at this early stage. If it is to meet the government's objectives, then not only will the individual concerns have to improve efficiency and profitability but also they should act as a stimulus to the rest of the private sector.

In the short term, it appears that the industries are proving profitable. Jaguar and British Telecom have reported large profits, as has British Gas. However, this may merely reflect an abuse of monopoly power in the cases of the ex-public utilities. It could also indicate that the industries concerned have taken a short-term, profit-maximizing view as opposed to a long-term one.

It is important for all business in the UK that such important industries trade with the utmost efficiency since most organizations require telephone services and gas supplies. In turn, those industries will not prove to be internationally competitive if their costs are higher than those faced by foreign competitors. This has particular relevance in view of the Single European Market which has operated since the end of 1992.

It would be more appropriate to allow the new private sector organizations to trade for a number of years in order to be able to properly and fairly assess their contribution to the well being of business in the UK. Even then, each case will need to be judged on its merits: a single judgement could prove to be a gross simplification.

The Balance of Payments

The UK economy is becoming increasingly international. This means that the UK economy is becoming more reliant upon the economy of the rest of the world. The rest of the world supplies the UK with a huge range of goods and services and is a vital market for UK products. The UK purchases raw materials and components from abroad and also employs many foreign workers. Thus, the UK's economy is becoming integrated with the economy of the rest of the world, and this trend is likely to accelerate during the remainder of the 1990s. The success of the UK economy in terms of employment levels, standards of living and the profitability and growth of businesses will increasingly depend upon the international environment. The government plays an important part in creating a suitable environment in which business can flourish. Furthermore, it attempts to encourage trade by guaranteeing exporters against bad payers, promoting UK goods abroad, supporting industrial research and so on.

We noted earlier in this chapter that the balance of payments is

> made up of the exports and imports of goods and services which comprise the current account and the flows of funds not associated with the purchase or sale of goods and services which make up the capital account.

Examples of capital flows could be French investment in the UK water industry or a UK government loan to an underdeveloped nation.

It is the balance between exports and imports which helps to determine the level of economic activity in an economy. As we saw in our model of the economy, expenditure on imports represents a withdrawal from the circular flow – funds find their way out of the domestic economy into foreign economies. Similarly, exports are an injection, in that they are a boost into our circular flow from abroad. The balance between these two helps to determine the level of activity in the economy.

If the UK enjoys a surplus on the current account, then it should be clear to you that international trade, at least, will boost the level of activity in the economy since injections exceed withdrawals. Why, you might ask, doesn't the government attempt to achieve the largest possible surplus on the balance of payments so as to boost the domestic economy? The simple answer is that such a policy would be counter productive in two ways. It could lead to retaliation by other governments because a UK balance of payments's surplus means a deficit elsewhere. Also, in some circumstances, such a policy could prove inflationary.

Some governments have used such arguments as an excuse for protecting their domestic industries by limiting the amount of imports entering the country. They do this by imposing taxes, known as tariffs, on imports or by imposing quotas, which are a limit on the number of units of a good that can be imported into a country. They believe that in this way they improve the standard of living and business confidence by maintaining domestic employment. They seek to protect some domestic industries from more competitive foreign industries. Such a belief was widespread in the 1930s, when international trade slumped as many advanced nations sought to restrict imports. Few, if any, economies benefited from such an approach.

A more modern view (which was also prevalent in the nineteenth century for different reasons) is that trade should be relatively free. Governments should allow industries to decline as more efficient foreign industries out-compete them. The resources of labour and capital that were employed in this industry will, it is argued, find their way to another industry and be used efficiently. The people of that nation should not be denied cheap imports since to do so would reduce their standard of living. Many economists advise their governments that greater international specialization will improve their nation's standard of living. This appears to be contradicted by the fact that much trade between advanced Western economies is in similar consumer durables such as cars, televisions, refrigerators, etc.

In creating the best possible environment for their businesses, many modern governments tend towards the latter view. However, there are problems associated with such an approach. The decline of an industry and the consequent unemployment can be politically embarrassing, especially if it is centred upon one locality. For this reason, the UK government protected the textile industry from the full rigour of foreign competition for many years so as to slow its decline. Equally, the debate over the closure of many of the UK's coal mines in 1992, due partly to the presence of cheap foreign coal, shows the degree of embarrassment a government can suffer.

This approach also assumes that resources (especially labour) move freely to their new use as the economy adjusts. This may not occur because the labour has the wrong skills or is located in the wrong part of the country. You should be aware that many of the recent job losses in the UK have been in manufacturing industries in the North, whilst much new work has been created in tertiary industries in the South. Such problems must be addressed if the right economic environment is to be available for industry to succeed. In the next chapter we shall see how governments attempt to create such an economic environment.

We could argue that many governments are losing some of their ability to shape their domestic environment as regards foreign products. Increasingly, multinational firms are siting factories abroad. Multinational firms are those such as General Motors which operate in more than one country. The UK has been a popular location for such firms over the years, with Ford, and recently Nissan, being examples of major manufacturers moving here.

International monetary flows also affect the level of activity in the UK economy. If foreign

KEY POINTS 2.5

- **Privatization has been a major feature of the UK economy over the last decade and can take several forms**

- **The proponents of privatization believe it promotes industrial efficiency as well as providing funds for the government**

- **Privatization's critics argue that private monopolies may overcharge consumers and that the industries were sold too cheaply**

- **Rises in exports generally improve the business environment, while increases in imports can boost the UK economy or provide extra competition for UK products**

investment in the UK exceeds UK investment overseas, then a net inflow of funds exists and this should stimulate UK economic activity. This is because the net inflow will act as an injection into the circular flow of income.

The government can influence the net flow of funds into and out of the economy in a number of ways. It could raise interest rates, although this may penalize firms in a number of ways, including higher borrowing costs, less credit sales, higher personal saving and so more withdrawals from the circular flow. However, the returns from high interest rates are attractive and persuades foreign investors to lodge their funds in the UK. These funds may well become available to UK businesses. By successfully pursuing its other economic objectives, such as low inflation and minimal unemployment, the government creates a stable and confident business environment which encourages foreigners to invest their funds in the UK economy.

In the next chapter we shall look at how governments use the economic weapons available to them to try and attain their economic objectives, and the implications of these policies for businesses.

EXAM PREPARATION

SHORT QUESTIONS

1. Why might industrialists oppose import controls?
2. Give two examples of multinational firms that operate in the UK.
3. Give one example of organizations from each of primary, secondary and tertiary sectors which have been privatized.

BTEC ASSIGNMENT

You are employed as a freelance researcher by the government of an Eastern European state which has recently overthrown a communist regime. The new, democratic government is interested in privatizing many of its state-controlled industries as part of its economic reforms.

It is interested in the UK experience of privatization and has hired you to research the social, business and economic implications of privatizing major businesses.

Your brief is to choose an example of a business which has been recently privatized and to analyse the advantages and disadvantages which can be expected to result from this privatization. Aspects which should be considered include: wages, conditions of employment, levels of employment, range and quality of product and/or service, pricing policy and investment programmes. Your client would expect you to contact the business(es) concerned for information as well as political parties and interested pressure groups. It is important that you have balanced sources on which to base your report.

Your report should be structured formally and should be supported by statistical data as necessary.

ESSAYS

1. Examine how an enterprise might alter its plans if a prolonged period of unemployment is predicted. (AEB 1988)
2. 'Privatization, through the profit motive, ultimately maximizes consumer satisfaction. Certain industries are too important to be left in private ownership.' From your study of business, how far can you reconcile these two views? (AEB 1988)

CHAPTER 3
Business and Economic Policy

> ▷ ▷ **QUESTIONS FOR PREVIEW** ▷ ▷
>
> 1. How can the government use changes in taxation and adjustments in public spending to alter the level of economic activity?
> 2. How do changes in interest rates and the availability of credit affect the economy?
> 3. What impact does government use of economic controls have on businesses?
> 4. In what ways do the activities of businesses themselves affect the economic environment in which they work?

THE GOVERNMENT has the duty to manage the economy so as to give the highest possible standard of living to the country's people – and this includes providing a prosperous environment for its businesses. It manages the economy so as to achieve as far as is possible its objectives outlined in Chapter Two. Its stewardship of the economy will aim to create the best possible environment for business in order to promote the development and growth of new and existing enterprises. Success in shaping such an environment will help promote employment and economic growth as businesses thrive in a positive atmosphere.

As discussed in the previous chapter, governments pursue a number of economic objectives which may conflict with one another. This may involve the government in 'trade-offs' – attaining one objective at the expense of another. For example, some economists believe that if the government introduces policies designed to reduce the rate of inflation it may have to accept rising unemployment as a side-effect.

In this section we shall review the policies available to the government and analyse how the use of such policies may affect businesses in the short and long run. We shall look at the government's activities within three categories:

- Fiscal policy
- Monetary policy
- Other controls

Fiscal Policy

Technically, fiscal policy can be said to refer to a policy based upon taxation. However, we shall use the term in its broadly accepted meaning of policy relating to the management of taxation and government expenditure. The possibility of controlling the economy by such means was only fully appreciated in the years immediately preceding the Second World War following the revolution in economic thinking brought about by the work of John Maynard Keynes.

Britain's taxation system has evolved steadily over the last two centuries. We already know that our current taxes can be split into two broad categories: direct taxes on income and capital, such as income, corporation and inheritance taxes; and indirect taxes on expenditure, such as VAT and excise duties.

Expenditure by the government can be classified. The main items are expenditure by central government on items such as social services, defence and the National Health Service. There is also substantial expenditure by local authorities to provide education, libraries and many other services. The details of the government's expenditure plans for 1992–93 are set out in Figure 3.1 (on page 39).

How Does Fiscal Policy Work?

In general, a government's fiscal policy is the

JOHN MAYNARD KEYNES
1883–1946

Keynes was born in Cambridge in 1883 where his father lectured at the University in economics and logic. He attended a local preparatory school and gained a scholarship to Eton where he gained a number of prizes for his schoolwork.

Keynes impressed his teachers and peers with his ability and cleverness and won a place at King's College, Cambridge to read mathematics. As a University student at Cambridge he led a full life. He was President of the Union and President of the University Liberal Club as well as a member of the Apostles, a select debating society. He achieved a first class degree in mathematics.

In the two years after receiving his degree, Keynes entered the civil service and began to study economics intently. He spent his time as a civil servant working in the India Office but found the work routine and tedious. In 1908 he returned to Cambridge as a lecturer in economics. In due course he became a fellow at his old College of King's and he remained in this post for the remainder of his life.

Keynes became editor of the *Economic Journal* and in this he wrote extensively on economics. During the First World War Keynes entered government service as an economist for the first time. During the war he rose rapidly through the Treasury and ended up overseeing the management of the UK's reserves of foreign exchange. He knew many of the premier figures of the time and worked hard on behalf of his country, even though he held reservations about the slaughter that was taking place on the battlefields.

Keynes opposed the policy by which the Allies forced the Germans to pay huge reparations for war damages. He wrote pamphlets on these reparations and on the economic consequences of the peace. In 1930 he published a lengthy work on money and was appointed as chairman of a panel of economists set up to advise the government.

It was during this post-war period and through these writings that Keynes began to shape his views which were eventually expressed in his *General Theory of Employment, Interest and Money* in 1936. This revolutionary text advocated a central role for the government in the management of the economy. He argued for the government's management of the economy through controlling the level of spending of individuals and the government itself. After the Second World War, his ideas on economic management were adopted in most democratic nations and heralded an unprecedented period of low unemployment and economic prosperity.

Keynes's public service continued throughout the Second World War, though his health began to fail him after he suffered a severe heart attack in 1937. Throughout the war Keynes acted as an advisor to the Treasury and wrote on 'How to pay for the war'. In 1942 he was given a peerage and became Lord Keynes. His prime role during this conflict was to negotiate with the Americans on financial matters. He arranged for the Americans to make loans and was involved in establishing the International Monetary Fund in 1944.

He died in 1946 as a result of another heart attack, but left a legacy of a greater understanding of the economic system and how it could be harnessed to the well-being of nations.

(*Photo*: The Hulton Deutsch Collection)

---

relationship between the level of government expenditure and the amount raised in taxation in any given fiscal year. The fiscal year runs from 6 April to 5 April the following year. If the government spends more than it raises in taxation (known as a budget deficit) then, as we noted when developing the model of the economy, injections into the circular flow will exceed withdrawals from it and the level of activity should increase. You should be aware that this might lead to rising employment rates but also to the danger of inflation and increases in imports. On the other hand, a surplus of taxation (as in the UK in the late 1980s) will reduce the level of economic activity. This is termed a budget surplus, and might result in an increase in unemployment.

This balance between taxation and government expenditure is determined annually when

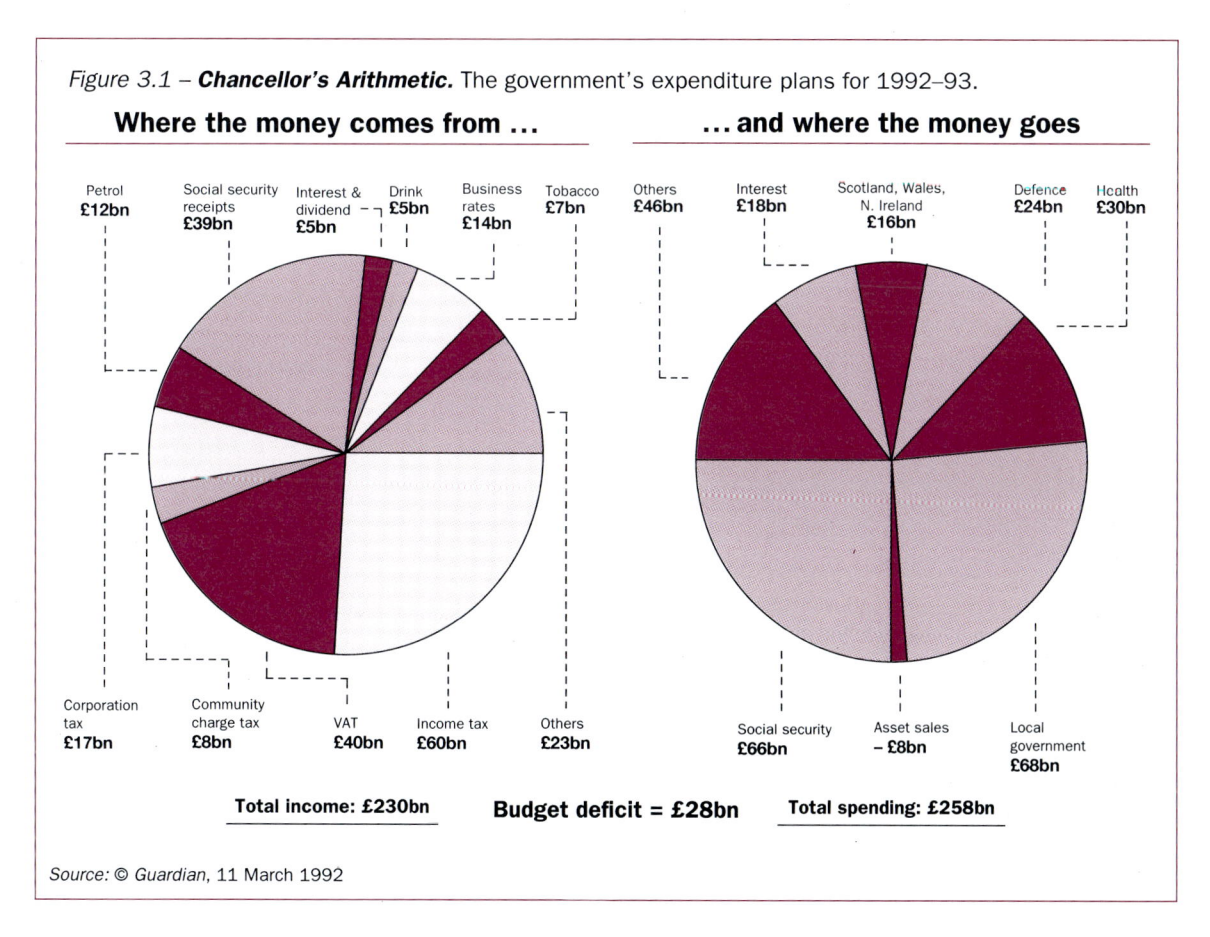

*Figure 3.1 – **Chancellor's Arithmetic.** The government's expenditure plans for 1992–93.*

Where the money comes from ...

- Petrol £12bn
- Social security receipts £39bn
- Interest & dividend £5bn
- Drink £5bn
- Business rates £14bn
- Tobacco £7bn
- Corporation tax £17bn
- Community charge tax £8bn
- VAT £40bn
- Income tax £60bn
- Others £23bn

... and where the money goes

- Others £46bn
- Interest £18bn
- Scotland, Wales, N. Ireland £16bn
- Defence £24bn
- Health £30bn
- Social security £66bn
- Asset sales – £8bn
- Local government £68bn

Total income: £230bn   Budget deficit = £28bn   Total spending: £258bn

Source: © Guardian, 11 March 1992

the Chancellor of the Exchequer, as the UK's minister of finance is known, announces the annual budget. Proposals have been made to move the budget to the late autumn to tie in with the setting of the government's expenditure plan. This confirms the government's spending plans for the forthcoming fiscal year and identifies the taxes which will provide the necessary funds.

All governments have a fiscal policy even if they do not regard it as a key policy in their management of the economy. This is true because all governments spend money and raise taxes and, therefore, some balance – or imbalance – must exist between the two.

We cannot predict the precise impact of fiscal policy on the business environment by simply considering the relationship between government spending and taxation revenue. The exact economic consequences will depend upon the types of tax which are altered and the state of the economy prior to the changes being implemented. In general, however, the table in Figure 3.2 (next page) summarizes the causes and effects of fiscal policy.

The effectiveness of fiscal policy is a matter for some considerable dispute among economists, but that debate is beyond the scope of this book. We can safely assume that fiscal policy does have the general economic effects outlined above at least in the short term, though the extent and speed of the effects may be open to argument. It is the taxation aspect of fiscal policy that we shall consider first.

Measures Aimed at Consumers

The government levies two categories of taxes: direct taxes (for example, income tax and capital gains tax on citizens's income and wealth) and indirect taxes (for example, VAT upon consumers's spending).

CHANGES IN DIRECT TAXES

The government can alter the rate of income tax and predict fairly accurately the consequent effects on spending by consumers and, therefore, the level of activity in the economy. The exact impact, however, will be determined by a number of factors.

The extent to which taxpayers adjust their spending will depend upon the goods and services in question. We should not be surprised that spending on essential items, such as food and housing, will remain fairly constant when taxes are changed. Alternatively, spending on luxury goods and services, such as foreign holidays, may

Figure 3.2 – **Budget Policy and Economic Activity**

Level of economic activity

	RISING	**FALLING**
Caused by	Cuts in taxes or increased government spending	Increase in taxes or reduced government spending
Likely effects	Falling unemployment, inflation may increase and imports rise, worsening the balance of payments	Rising unemployment, inflationary pressures lessen and imports decline
Impact on business	Demand rises, so too may costs. Skill shortages, more competition from overseas	Falling demand, stocks increase. Possible redundancies. Rise in bankruptcies

decline fairly sharply in the event of an increase in taxes. Similarly, a cut in taxation will increase demand for luxury goods and services. Goods and services whose demand fluctuates with income are termed income elastic; those that do not are income inelastic. We will discuss more fully the principles behind the concept of income elasticity in Chapter Four.

ACTIVITY 3.1

Make a list of the major items on which your family spends its income. (You may need to consult other members of your family.) On this list mark those items which you would buy less of if your income fell significantly, or which you would buy more of in the event of a substantial rise in income. These are income elastic goods – that is, expenditure on them is sensitive to income changes. The rest are most probably income inelastic – that is, not sensitive to changes in income.

The implications of a change in income tax will vary according to the types of good or service firms produce, but even firms selling income inelastic goods will suffer some decline in sales as the level of economic activity lessens. We can imagine that in the case of rising taxes, even a major food retail chain such as Sainsbury's will find that its sales suffer some decline as the level of economic activity slackens.

Rises in income tax may lessen economic activity because high tax rates can act as a disincentive to working. Very high rates might lead to workers refusing to work overtime or, in some cases, preferring to become unemployed. Such high rates may also lead to the so-called 'brain drain', as highly qualified workers move to nations with lower tax rates – and possibly higher salaries. The free movement of labour within the European Community since December 1992 may exacerbate this effect. These disincentive effects of high direct taxes will obviously dampen the level of activity in the economy. This is a major reason why income tax rates have been reduced in recent years by Conservative governments. Opposition parties and many economists do not agree with this analysis and would use fiscal policy more freely without worrying about such 'disincentives'.

CHANGES IN INDIRECT TAXES

Changes in indirect taxes and especially VAT usually work quickly but their effects are difficult to predict. A rise in VAT will cut consumer spending, reducing demand for goods and services and eventually lowering output. However, the extent of the fall in demand will depend upon the price elasticity of demand of the items in question. This means that some products suffer large falls in demand if their price rises and significant increases in demand if their price is cut, whereas others will see only small changes. This concept is developed more fully in Chapter Four. In spite of this theory, it is difficult to calculate accurately the effect on the quantity demanded of a product when its price changes. This means that the government cannot be sure of the exact impact upon demand and, hence, the sales figures of businesses if it alters, say, the base rate of VAT. Neither can it be certain how much extra – or less – revenue it will raise.

Increases in indirect taxes (which may be used to cut the level of economic activity and hence inflation) are inflationary themselves. Anything that adds to the general level of prices reduces the purchasing power of money. Rises in these taxes add to the prices of goods and so, in the short term at least, fuel inflation. In the long term, they should reduce the level of economic activity by an unspecified amount.

Recently, governments have transferred the burden of taxation from direct to indirect taxes. In 1979, the basic rate of income tax was 35 per cent and VAT was levied at 7½ per cent. In 1992, the comparative figures were 25 per cent (with an introductory band of 20 per cent) and 17½ per cent respectively. This means that taxpayers in lower income brackets pay more of their income in tax. This is a direct result of the weakening of the link between the level of income earned and the amount of tax that is paid. This change has provided increased sales and opportunities for firms supplying goods and services to better-off members of the community.

Effects on Producers

Corporation tax, which is levied upon company profits, has the greatest impact upon producers. Profits, as we saw earlier, are a major source of investment funds. Increases in corporation tax on firms' profits will lower economic activity because they will leave firms with less funds to invest and so will prevent their output rising. Indeed, if firms decide not to invest and replace worn out capital equipment, their capacity to produce may even fall. Furthermore, firms may pay shareholders smaller dividends (or none at all!) and this will cut consumer expenditure and, hence, demand for goods and services.

Businesses will reduce their investment (which, remember, is an injection designed to boost economic activity) if they believe the government is trying to cut the level of spending in the economy. Rises in any taxes would be a clear signal that this is what the government is trying to do.

Most governments have found that changes in corporation tax are a slow way to influence the level of activity since investment plans take time to come to maturity and so have no impact upon the level of economic activity for years. For similar reasons, any expansionary impact from tax cuts will be delayed. Often, changes in the level of public investment (on roadbuilding, schools, etc) can have a quicker effect. This is because governments can commit their funds to projects such as these almost immediately, whereas consumers and businesses may be more cautious before they increase their expenditure. Businesses may wish to reduce their debts or see rising sales before increasing levels of investment.

ACTIVITY 3.2

Imagine that the government has decided to build a new bridge across a large river near your home. Make a list of the types of business which could benefit from this decision. Add to your list those goods and services which are likely to be supplied by local businesses and those which may be supplied by foreign firms or those from other parts of the country. Can you think of disadvantages that may be suffered by local businesses as a result of the decision to build the new bridge?

Government Expenditure

This is the other half of fiscal policy. Not all spending by the public authorities has the same effect on the economy. We can identify two main categories of expenditure which influence the economic environment in different ways. The following are examples of these categories:

a Transfer payments

These comprise expenditure on unemployment benefit, pensions and other social security payments. Changes in expenditure on these items have a rapid impact upon the economy since the recipients are generally not well off and immediately spend the increases or cut back to take account of reductions. This effect is emphasized by the fact that the taxpayers who provide the funds for redistribution via transfer payments may be well off and so may not have spent all of the money which was transferred. Hence, the change in spending will be considerable. An increase in transfer payments will often lead to substantial increases in demand for basic goods such as food, clothes, public transport, electricity, gas and so on.

b The infrastructure

This is spending on railways, housing, roads, bridges, etc, which improve the economic environment in which businesses operate. Investment in these areas can boost the economy by providing work for construction firms and others. It can also assist existing businesses to lower costs by providing cheaper transport and improved services. As we noted earlier, altering the level of investment – even public investment – is a slow method of controlling the economy.

More directly, the government can influence the level of investment by private firms through the tax reliefs and investment grants it offers. It allows businesses to deduct depreciation from profits before corporation tax is levied. In certain circumstances (for example, to encourage industry to locate in economically depressed regions) the government may offer grants towards investment in an attempt to create employment. Clearly, changes in grants or tax allowances can be used to encourage or reduce investment.

42 **The Business Environment**

*Figure 3.3 – **The Assisted Areas.*** The maps show those areas of the UK in which the government pays grants to persuade industry to locate there, as well as proposals to redraw the areas that receive such benefits.

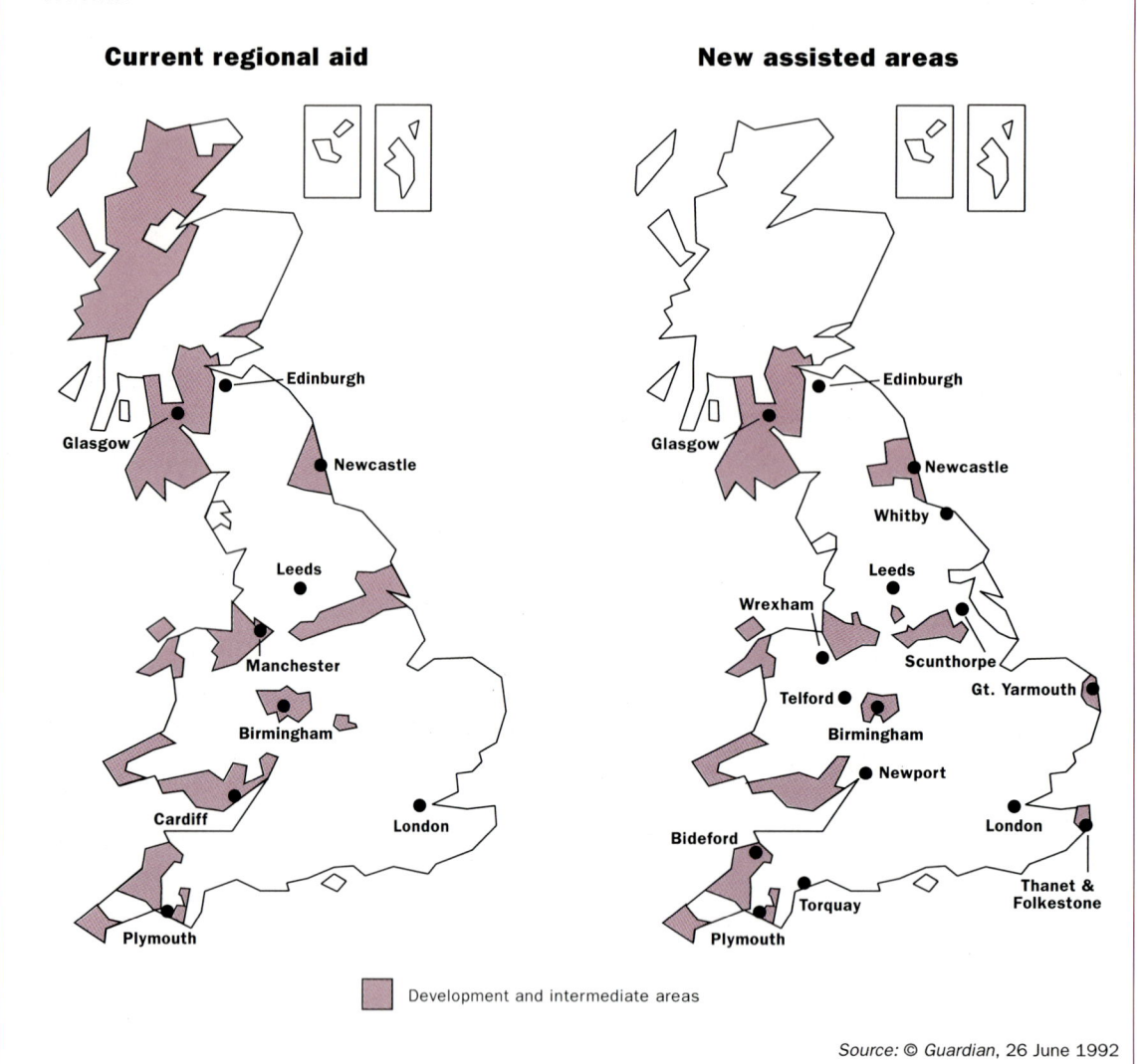

Current regional aid

- Edinburgh
- Glasgow
- Newcastle
- Leeds
- Manchester
- Birmingham
- Cardiff
- London
- Plymouth

New assisted areas

- Edinburgh
- Glasgow
- Newcastle
- Whitby
- Leeds
- Wrexham
- Scunthorpe
- Telford
- Gt. Yarmouth
- Birmingham
- Newport
- London
- Bideford
- Torquay
- Thanet & Folkestone
- Plymouth

▨ Development and intermediate areas

Source: © *Guardian*, 26 June 1992

KEY POINTS 3.1

- Fiscal policy determines the balance between taxation and government spending
- A budget deficit will expand the level of economic activity while a surplus will have the opposite effect
- Fiscal policy can affect the level of economic activity but it is arguably slow and imprecise in its operation, though it depends upon the precise policy employed

1992 and Taxation

The creation of the Single European Market required a greater uniformity of taxes among EC members. This was not simply a matter of bringing VAT and other expenditure taxes into line. Any significant variations in direct taxes could cause firms to relocate to find the site of least taxation. Highly taxed economies could therefore suffer a decline in their industrial base.

Fiscal policy is often criticized for being slow to operate and imprecise in its effects. In spite of these weaknesses, it was a major weapon in the economic armoury from the late 1940s until the mid-1970s. A significant and influential group of economists, known as 'Monetarists', now believe that fiscal policy is uncontrollable and even damages the economy. Thus, they advocate a neutral fiscal policy (where taxation receipts equal government expenditure) and the use of other methods of monetary control – most notably monetary policy. It is to monetary policy that we now turn our attention.

Monetary Policy

This method of controlling the economy centres on adjusting the amount of money in circulation in the economy and so the level of spending and economic activity. This may involve the manipulation of the money supply, interest rates or exchange rate.

A first difficulty here is to decide exactly what comprises money. We should agree that it is notes and coin, and perhaps the money in our current accounts at the bank, but should we include our savings and deposit accounts? And what of specialist forms of money held by financial institutions? Owing to the complexity of this issue, several definitions of money exist and the government's official measure has altered over the years. Part of the difficulty in assessing the effectiveness of monetary policy is the doubt concerning what exactly is covered by the term money.

Monetary policy was first employed as a means of control in the 1950s, but has been more widely

*Figure 3.4 – **The Bank of England.*** This is the UK's central bank. Established in 1694, it plays a key part in implementing the government's monetary policy. It ensures that interest rates are at the level desired by the government of the day and oversees the printing of notes and coin. It has wider responsibilities in managing the nation's debt and holding its reserves of foreign currency and gold. Thus, it holds responsibility for the country's monetary policy and its financial relations with other countries.

(*Photo:* The Hulton Deutsch Collection)

MILTON FRIEDMAN
b. 1912

Milton Friedman was born in Brooklyn, New York, in July 1912 the son of Jewish immigrants. He immediately attracted attention as a brilliant student and received a number of state scholarships. He studied at a number of American universities, eventually being awarded a doctorate by Columbia University. Since then Friedman and his academic achievements have been honoured by a considerable number of honoury degrees from universities worldwide.

In 1948 at an early age, Friedman was appointed Professor of Economics at the University of Chicago, a post he held until his retirement in 1977 aged 65. Friedman soon began to attract attention for his criticisms of all forms of government intervention in the economy. This brought him into direct conflict with the ideas of Keynes and his supporters, such as Friedman's great rival John Kenneth Galbraith. His free market views extended to criticizing many aspects of the welfare state and even public education – from which he had so clearly benefited.

Friedman was at the height of his powers and popularity in the 1960s and 1970s when he was undisputed leader of the Chicago School of Economics. This group of liberal economists advocated the extending of free market economics and the reduction of the role of the state in managing the economy. Friedman's ideas had their origins in the work of earlier economists, but he expressed his ideas with originality. Many of his views have attracted considerable controversy. For example, he contends that government economic intervention in the form of imposing minimum wages has an undesirable side effect, in that it creates unemployment as firms hire less of the now more expensive resource. This, Friedman argues, lessens the welfare of those whom the government sought to protect.

Monetarism may not be Friedman's most important contribution to economic thought, but it is the idea with which he is most closely identified. Monetarist economists believe that the sole cause of inflation is increases in the money supply. Friedman is credited with saying that 'inflation is always and everywhere a monetary phenomenon'. Friedman's leadership of the Chicago School coincided with the rise of inflationary pressures throughout the Western world alongside the apparent demise of Keynesian economics.

Friedman explains the failure of monetarist policies in the UK and US by arguing that the governments concerned did not wholeheartedly adopt monetarist philosophies. They did not, he contends, single-mindedly adopt the growth of the money supply as their prime economic target. Unlike Keynes, Friedman has survived to see the overthrow of his ideas and their replacement by new schools of economic thought. Nevertheless, his impact on economic thought has been immense and his work was recognized by the award of the Nobel Prize for Economics in 1976.

Now in his 80s, Milton Friedman is in semi-retirement. He still writes for the American magazine *Newsweek* and carries out research at Stanhope University. He remains an articulate and ardent spokesperson for monetarism and is currently working on an autobiography in which he will undoubtedly continue to espouse his monetarist philosophy.

(*Photo:* The Hulton Deutsch Collection)

used since the 1970s. In 1976, the International Monetary Fund (IMF) only granted the UK a loan on the condition that it made greater use of monetary methods in its management of the economy. In 1979, the Conservatives were elected to office with a commitment to control inflation through the restriction of the money supply. Their Medium Term Financial Strategy remained a central feature of economic policy until 1986.

As the caption to Figure 3.4 (previous page) shows, the central bank plays a major role in the implementation of a nation's monetary policy. In some countries (for example, Germany) the central bank operates monetary policy independent of government policy. However, the UK's central bank, the Bank of England, implements monetary policy on behalf of the government. Monetary policy has three main aspects:

- Controlling the supply of money
- Controlling the rate of interest
- Managing the exchange rate

Controlling the Supply of Money

The aim of the authorities when controlling the money supply is to limit the amount borrowed, and hence spent, by businesses and individuals. It is hoped in this way to limit the level of overall demand in the economy and thus to remove or reduce inflationary pressure.

A variety of policies are available to restrict the money supply:

a By influencing bank lending

Banks have to hold a proportion of their assets as a reserve in case customers demand repayment of their deposits. This reserve has to be in a liquid form, that is easily convertible into cash. Many banks indeed hold a significant proportion of this reserve as notes and coin either in their vaults or at the Bank of England. Either by altering the amount that has to be held as a reserve or by taking away some of the reserve, the Bank of England can force the high street banks to adjust their lending levels. This in turn affects the amounts borrowed and spent and so the level of economic activity will change according to changes in demand. Clearly, if consumers are buying less products then firms will ultimately recognize this and produce less. What decision do you think the firm will need to take under these circumstances?

b By controlling the issue of notes and coin

The government controls the issue of notes and coin via the Bank of England and the Mint respectively. These make up a small proportion of all the money we spend, but an increase in these issues could be used to give a small boost to economic activity.

c By credit restrictions

The authorities can make credit less available by requiring higher deposits and faster repayments for goods which are purchased through loans. On occasions, the government has enforced the repayment of hire purchase (HP) loans on cars within two years. At other times no restriction has been in force. Tighter restrictions should limit certain types of spending, while a looser policy allowing lower deposits and longer repayment periods would have the opposite effect.

d By qualitative and quantitive controls

Under this approach the government has, on occasions, directed the amount that banks can lend and to whom the money should be lent. Neither policy has been much used in recent years.

HOW EFFECTIVE IS CONTROLLING THE MONEY SUPPLY?

Many economists have expressed doubts about the effectiveness of managing the economy by controlling the money supply. They argue plausibly that businesses and consumers will simply find alternative sources of loans. In recent years, many companies, and particularly high street retailers, have offered credit to consumers. There

Figure 3.5 – Controlling the Money Supply

Bundesbank monetary policy criticised

GERMANY lurched into recession partly because the Bundesbank has made wrong monetary policy decisions, the DIW institute in Berlin claimed yesterday. Unless the central bank cuts interest rates quickly, the economy will weaken further until well into this year and the Europe-wide slump will drag on into 1994, it warned.

Continuing decline, underlined yesterday by news that west German industrial output in November was almost 6 per cent down on a year earlier, was unavoidable, the institute said.

The Bundesbank, which controls German monetary policy, caused widespread dismay in July when it raised its discount rate from 8 per cent to 8.75 per cent. It responded to the European monetary crisis in September with a reduction to 8.25 per cent and a disappointing 0.25 per centage point cut to 9.5 per cent in the internationally sensitive Lombard rate.

The institute's criticism came as Mr Helmut Schlesinger, president of the central bank, repeated that it would be wrong to change tack too soon to help resolve 'short-term' economic problems, either in Germany or elsewhere.

Monetary policy had to continue its role as a brake on inflation, he said.

There has been growing domestic as well as international pressure on the Bundesbank to cut rates. German industry has been more openly critical of higher interest rates recently. Bonn has made no secret of its desire to see rates reduced although ministers and officials are anxious not to be seen to put any political pressure on the Bundesbank.

Source: Financial Times, 7 January 1993

is some evidence from the recent financial history of the UK to suggest that this is the case. Indeed, the UK government moved away from control via the money supply in the mid-1980s because of such doubts. It had made its task more difficult by allowing financial markets to operate more freely, thus giving people and firms more possible sources of funds. Charles Goodheart, a Bank of England official, expressed the government's difficulties succinctly. He believes that the amount of money in the economy is a good indicator of the level of economic activity so long as no attempt is made to control it. Once it becomes a policy target and is controlled, people begin to use forms of money which are not within the definition (for example, store credit cards) and so it is no longer any use as a predictor.

It is these difficulties that led the Conservative government of the 1980s to adopt the rate of interest as the main instrument of monetary policy. They supported their interest rate policy with a neutral fiscal policy. That is, they sought to avoid a budget surplus or deficit by planning to match tax revenue with government expenditure.

Limits on the amount of money available within the economy can arise from other sources. There has recently been considerable criticism of banks for operating a lending policy which discriminates against small firms who, banks believe, represent a greater risk. Such limitations can damage the cash flow of small enterprises and increase the number of business failures.

The Effects of Controlling the Money Supply on Business

If the authorities restrict the money supply, then firms will find that it has implications for their working capital. Businesses may find financial institutions less able and willing to lend funds. Firms (and especially small firms with lesser resources) may experience difficulties in paying their workforce and suppliers as credit becomes scarcer and more expensive. Certainly, recent Conservative governments have relied upon such a policy and sought to increase its impact through regular publicity. It was believed that such a policy would dissuade firms from high pay settlements.

Controlling the money supply also affects the sales revenue of businesses. Consumers will also find credit difficult to come by and so their expenditure (and hence firms's incomes) may decline or grow more slowly. We mentioned earlier that consumer durables (cars, washing machines, televisions, etc) are extensively purchased on credit. Thus, businesses supplying this type of product will find their sales are sensitive to the availability of credit. The motor vehicle and similar industries have been hard hit by alterations in the regulations relating to hire purchase which have provoked dramatic surges and declines in demand for their products. This caused other forms of financing the purchase of vehicles to emerge (for example, leasing).

Governments can, of course, relax monetary policy by making money more freely available to businesses and citizens. This should increase expenditure and output and, depending upon the level of demand, raise the level of economic activity.

Interest Rate Policy

The interest rate is quite simply the price of borrowed money.

The Bank of England currently has unpublished bands of rates which it considers appropriate to the economic situation. It pursues the attainment of these rates by its dealings in the London money markets. Through complex actions the Bank of England influences all rates of interest and most notably the high street banks's base rates. It can encourage a fall in interest rates by making more funds available to borrowers, whilst restricting the quantity of money available will tend to push up interest rates. A major determinant of interest rates is the balance between the supply of funds from savers and the demand for funds from businesses and other investors. If there is a 'shortage' of funds, then interest rates will rise, representing a rise in the 'price' of money. A glut of funds would have the opposite effect.

Interest rate policy has been extensively used in the management of the economy recently. Rises in the rate are designed to cut economic activity by curbing public and private investment and consumers's purchases on credit. Firms base their investment decisions on the current and predicted interest rates and they discount expected earnings at the appropriate rate to determine whether the investment is worthwhile. Surveys of firms suggest that other factors influence investment decisions, primarily expectations concerning the future health of the economy. Many firms invest from retained profits rather than by borrowing. For these reasons changes in interest rates may have less of an impact on investment, and thus on the economic environment, than some people imagine.

High rates of interest will, however, affect business behaviour in other ways. Firms may reduce stock levels in order to reduce the money tied up in this way. The money can then be released for working capital rather than having to use overdraft facilities. This may mean they produce less and so require less employees and less supplies. Most firms will face higher costs of production as they face more expenditure on servicing existing debts. Moreover, suppliers, facing similar pressures, may be forced to raise their prices. Such higher costs may be passed on to the consumer in the form of higher prices. These higher costs may also reduce the international competitiveness of firms.

Firms may find that bad debts put pressure on their liquidity position as costs rise and revenues decline. Firms may be forced to seek new markets. These could be overseas or perhaps a different market segment in the home country. For example, firms may adjust the marketing mix to put more emphasis on price and produce more basic models.

Firms are likely to face falling demand when interest rates rise, especially if consumers often purchase their products on credit. Equally, demand for luxuries will decline. Demand for these goods might be sensitive even to small changes in interest rates. The level of demand for more essential products can also fall as consumers postpone purchases until circumstances are more favourable.

As we saw in the Case Study on page 17, it is small firms that bear the brunt of high interest rates as they have less reserves and a relatively greater need for borrowing. Often, because they pose a greater risk, small firms have to pay a higher rate anyway. The National Federation of Self Employed and Small Businesses estimate that every 1 per cent rise in interest rates costs the UK's 1.5 million small firms an extra £200 million in interest payments. They argue that rises in bankruptcies follow rises in interest rates.

Rises in interest rates strengthen sterling as it offers overseas investors a greater return on their money, causing an inflow of foreign investment funds. To invest in the UK, foreigners must buy sterling, and this extra demand pushes up the price – or exchange rate – of sterling. The rise makes it more difficult for UK firms to be price-competitive in domestic and foreign markets because exports prices rise and import prices fall. (We will consider this more fully in Chapter Seven.) The consequent fall in exports and loss of home sales to imports will depress the level of economic activity further. Obviously, a fall in interest rates would have the reverse effects. We shall consider this further when we look at exchange rate policy.

Consumers will be affected by changes in

Figure 3.6 – **New Cars and Interest Rates**

New car sales race to record level

NEW CAR sales hit a record level in August as the introduction of the new number plate took registrations beyond the half-million mark for the first time in a single month.

Despite earlier indications that sales would not beat the previous record set in August 1988, a late surge of buyers in the showroom took sales to a total of 500 112 – 4.8 per cent up on the same month last year.

The record level of sales suggests that the Chancellor's high interest rates policy is having little impact upon the car market.

However, the share of the market taken by imports was slightly down from 61 per cent a year ago to 60.2 per cent. August sales are traditionally dominated by private car buyers – hence the high numbers of foreign cars bought.

Source: adapted from the *Independent*, 7 September 1989

KEY POINTS 3.2

- **Monetary policy can be implemented by either controlling the supply of money or the level of interest rates**
- **It has proved difficult to control the supply of money and this policy has fallen from grace**
- **Interest rate policy is currently a cornerstone of government economic policy**
- **The side effects of interest rate policy can be considerable and undesirable**

interest rates and their behaviour will, of course, alter the economic environment for business. A rise in rates may persuade them to save more and less purchases will be made on credit, adversely affecting firms who produce such goods and services.

The overall impact of changing interest rates will depend upon the size of the change as well as the initial level. A small increase on top of higher rates may have more of an impact than a similar rise at lower rates. Real rates of interest are important, too. We might borrow happily if rates are high so long as a substantial rate of inflation also exists. This means that inflation will reduce the value of repayments over the period of the loan, which is favourable to debtors. Thus, a 1 per cent rise in interest rates to 15 per cent may not have a great impact if the rate of inflation is 20 per cent because the real value of the debtor's repayments is falling by one fifth annually, which more than compensates for the high interest charges.

Other Policies to Control the Economy

A variety of other policies exist to control all or some aspects of the economy. Their popularity has fluctuated over the years as economic understanding has progressed and new ideas have become fashionable.

Exchange Rate Policy

Chapter Seven discusses trading abroad and the significance of the value of the pound to UK business. These factors affect the competitiveness of UK industry and a policy which affects the pound can be employed to control the level of economic activity.

Government-induced falls in the exchange rate tend, in the long run, to expand domestic economic activity as exports (an injection into the circular flow) will fall in price and their sales should increase. You will realize, of course, that not all export sales will rise by a similar proportion. The extent of the rise in sales following the fall in the exchange rate will be determined, amongst other things, by the price elasticity of demand for exports. The effects in the short run may, however, be minimal as orders for UK exports are placed some months ahead. Such a decline or depreciation in the exchange rate will stimulate exporting industries and will also have a 'knock-on' effect on the rest of the economy as the exporting firms place new, additional orders with supplying firms.

A declining or depreciating exchange rate will stimulate economic activity in a second, important way. Imports into the UK will rise in price as the pound falls in value. Although this may have inflationary consequences it does boost the price-competitiveness of some domestic industries. For example, Austin–Rover might experience rising domestic sales because other cars such as Volvo will become more expensive. However, goods and services are not sold in UK markets on price alone: factors such as quality and after sales service matter, too. Firms who import large quantities of raw materials may find that their production costs rise and eat into any gains in competitiveness.

For a time during the 1980s, the UK authorities pursued an exchange rate policy in which they attempted to maintain a stable relationship between the value of the pound and other major currencies. The hope was that this would provide those companies involved in foreign trade with a more stable environment in which to do business. Another objective was to prevent falls in the exchange rate that would fuel domestic inflation. The UK is a very 'open' economy buying and selling over 30 per cent of goods and services to and from abroad. This means that changes in the exchange rate, and hence import and export prices, have significant impacts on domestic inflation.

For most of the last 40 years, exchange rates have been either fixed or determined as a side-effect of other economic policies. The UK's membership of the EC's Exchange Rate Mechanism (ERM) tied the value of the pound to the currencies of most of the other EC members. This was a natural culmination of the government's more informal attempts to maintain a steady exchange rate between sterling and the German deutschmark. However, a series of pressures led to the UK's withdrawal from the ERM in the autumn of 1992 and a return to floating exchange rates. We will look at the ERM in greater detail in Chapter Seven.

Regional Policy

The aim of the UK's regional policy is to remove or lessen the regional disparity between incomes, industry and general prosperity by influencing the location of industry. Traditionally, the North, Scotland, Wales and Northern Ireland have been less prosperous than the Midlands, South and South-East.

The government undertook a major review of regional policy culminating in the White Paper of November 1984. The government now offers a range of investment grants to firms opting to locate in certain areas based on their capital costs and the number of jobs they are likely to create.

Business and Economic Policy 49

*Figure 3.7 – **Unemployment and Expenditure by Region**.* The details below outline the causes and impact of the UK government's regional policy. Are the relationships between the pieces of information what you would expect? Would you expect more regions to receive assisted area status? What other organization might provide regional aid?

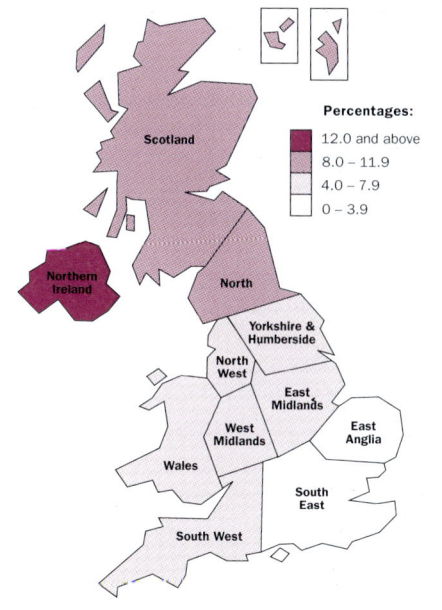

Percentages:
- 12.0 and above
- 8.0 – 11.9
- 4.0 – 7.9
- 0 – 3.9

Regions shown: Scotland, Northern Ireland, North, Yorkshire & Humberside, North West, East Midlands, West Midlands, East Anglia, Wales, South East, South West

Source: Social Trends 1991

Grants are available for both service and manufacturing industries. The areas that receive government support cover 35 per cent of the working population. Government expenditure on regional policy has declined in real terms in recent years.

The success of the UK's regional policy depends upon the relative strength of the government's measures as compared with other location factors (such as the cost of skilled labour, sources of supplies and proximity to markets). The increasing importance of the European Community as a market has attracted industries to the South and East Anglia and successive governments have experienced difficulty in preventing this 'drift south'. Also, the ready availability of gas and electricity as power sources has allowed industries to be more footloose and this has accelerated the trend away from the traditional manufacturing areas of the North.

Further factors limiting the success of regional policy include:

- Some depressed areas have suffered shortages of suitably skilled labour and this dissuades firms from locating in such regions in spite of government incentives
- Some firms remain in the more prosperous regions of the South because their managers and families do not wish to locate in areas with what they consider to be poorer social and leisure facilities

United Kingdom   Percentages and £ per week

Average weekly household expenditure as a percentage of total (1988–89)

	Housing	Fuel, light and power	Food	Alcohol and tobacco	Clothing and footwear	Household goods and services	Motoring and fares	Leisure goods and services	Miscellaneous and personal goods and services	Average expenditure per household (£ per week)
United Kingdom	17.2	4.9	18.5	6.5	6.9	13.2	15.3	13.4	4.2	216.05
North	15.7	5.4	19.5	7.7	7.0	12.7	15.9	12.4	3.6	191.68
Yorkshire and Humberside	15.0	5.5	19.5	7.4	7.7	12.5	15.8	12.5	4.3	188.80
East Midlands	17.2	5.2	18.8	6.8	6.2	12.7	16.1	12.6	4.5	199.39
East Anglia	17.6	4.7	18.2	5.4	6.2	13.0	15.1	15.6	4.2	219.30
South East	18.6	4.1	17.7	5.5	6.8	13.8	14.8	14.3	4.5	250.98
South West	17.0	4.9	18.1	5.9	6.0	13.9	15.8	14.5	3.9	220.11
West Midlands	17.9	5.1	19.1	6.6	6.8	13.0	16.2	11.4	4.0	200.72
North West	16.8	5.1	18.3	7.7	6.7	12.2	14.6	14.2	4.4	205.26
England	17.5	4.7	18.3	6.3	6.7	13.2	15.3	13.6	4.3	219.57
Wales	15.4	5.7	19.2	7.0	7.6	13.1	15.8	11.8	4.2	197.10
Scotland	16.3	5.4	19.6	7.9	8.1	12.4	14.2	12.1	4.0	196.27
Northern Ireland	11.9	7.4	21.0	5.7	9.2	13.9	17.6	9.7	3.7	200.99

Source: Family Expenditure Survey, Central Statistical Office

- Since the election of the Conservative government in 1979, the government has managed the economy with greater emphasis on market forces and less reliance on state intervention. This has resulted in less expenditure and commitment to regional policy

Prices and Incomes Policy

Past governments, the Labour administrations of the 1970s, for example, have imposed periods of wage and price restraint on the whole economy in an effort to squeeze out inflation. These policies have been simple in design. Clear annual limits have been imposed on wage increases either in percentage terms or in cash amounts. On occasions, restrictions on the rate of price increase have accompanied the wage controls.

Prices and incomes policies have fallen from favour in recent years and have been rarely employed in the UK since the late 1970s. However, in 1992 the government did impose a 1 per cent ceiling on public sector pay settlements. This was an attempt to restrain public expenditure as well as a means of controlling inflationary pressures. Critics of these policies argue that they distort the operation of the free market which harms the economy. They also contend that in the long run the policies do not work since implementation is inevitably followed by a catching-up period. Furthermore, it has proved more difficult to impose this type of control in the private sector than in the public sector.

Supply Side Policies

Supply side policies refer to a broad range of policies which aim to improve the working of the economy by encouraging the free operation of markets by offering incentives to firms and individuals. The adoption of such policies in the USA and UK in recent years reflect a major change in economic thinking. These policies can take a number of forms:

a   Limiting trade union power

Attempts to make labour markets operate more effectively have been made by reducing the role of trade unions. Some economists believe that unions have caused excessive wage rises, limited productivity increases and damaged the UK's international competitiveness. The Conservative governments of the 1980s passed a series of Acts of Parliament to limit union power.

b   Reducing labour costs

The government has attempted to reduce labour costs and to allow wages to reflect the firm's market position by removing barriers (such as Wages Councils) to wage reduction. Previously, Wages Councils protected the minimum wages of workers in industries such as catering which traditionally paid low wages. This policy has been reinforced by the government through its introduction of a lower rate of National Insurance contributions for those on low wages. This change has reduced the relative cost to firms of employing low-paid workers.

c   Improving labour mobility

The government has also sought to improve the mobility of labour between regions. For example, it has encouraged people to purchase their council house so that it can be sold if a family wishes to move. This policy has not had much success in this context. The government's efforts have been more than offset by the huge differential in house prices between prosperous and less prosperous regions of the country and the collapse of house prices nationally in the early 1990s.

d   Improving training

The government has argued that much of the poor performance of the UK economy in recent years is due to the workforce being ill-trained relative to those of our major competitors. A variety of reforms have been introduced: for example, the creation of Training and Enterprise Councils which we will consider in detail in Chapter Five.

KEY POINTS 3.3

- **Entry to the European Monetary System limits the use of exchange rate policy**
- **Regional policy aims to even out prosperity between the UK's regions through persuading industry to move to depressed areas**
- **Prices and incomes policies have not been employed in recent years**
- **Supply side measures have become popular recently and concentrate on making markets work more efficiently**

The Influence of Business Upon the Economy

So far in this chapter we have considered how and why the government alters the economic environment in which businesses operate. Clearly, the government is the major influence shaping the environment. However, businesses themselves, by their actions, also shape their own economic environment.

During an economic depression, businesses can alleviate some of the worst aspects of unemployment by holding on to their labour. This can also help to maintain demand for their goods or services. Their motives might be that they believe the depression will be short-lived and that they do not wish to shed skilled labour. This labour might be expensive to replace once the economy shows signs of recovery, particularly if they have to train unskilled workers. It might be that some employers are benevolent and wish to protect the community in which they are located. Family-owned businesses may possess such views.

Equally, during an inflationary period, both public and private enterprises can increase or reduce the rate of price increase through their pricing and wages policies. Excessive wage settlements, as recent governments have often pointed out, merely fuel inflation and lead to loss of competitiveness and later, loss of jobs.

It is equally true that businesses have a major influence on the UK's balance of payments. Their behaviour in importing goods and services and their success in export markets make a major contribution to the external balance. The government may be forced to take some form of corrective action if the imbalance becomes too adverse.

Finally, the extent to which funds are ploughed back into businesses, as opposed to paying dividends to shareholders, can affect the business environment. The will and ability to produce innovative, well-researched products allows an economy to compete successfully in world markets and this has substantial implications for the level of employment, the balance of payments and so on.

CASE STUDY

Burton Group

Burton Group, the fashion retailer, sacked more than 1900 people yesterday in an attempt to streamline its bureaucratic head office, remove under-employed shop assistants, and bear down on its mammoth wages bill.

Burton is dismissing 933 buyers, merchandisers, personnel and financial staff and others employed in central functions in five different locations in the West End of London. They represent 25 per cent of the head office workforce. It is also axing about 1000 full-time shop-floor jobs across all its fashion chains, which include Burton, Top Shop, Top Man, Principles, Dorothy Perkins, Evans and Champion Sport.

Burton will inform shop assistants over the next six weeks. It expects to create up to 3000 part-time jobs instead. Most of the casualties will be offered part-time work.

The cost of the redundancies will be £10–£15 million, Burton said. That cost will be paid back in the current year in savings on wages.

Paul Morris, the store analyst with Goldman Sachs, applauded the streamlining, raising his profits forecast for 1993/94 from £62.5m to £72.5m. 'And it will wash its face in the current year.'

QUESTIONS

1 Describe the impact of Burton's decision on the local economy in the West End of London.

2 What actions could the government take to minimize the impact of the job losses on the local economy?

Source: Independent, 8 January 1993

CASE STUDY

Eastgate Furnishings Ltd

In the late 1970s, Jim Trevelyan had established a firm designing and manufacturing a range of wallpapers on a new industrial estate near Sheffield. Jim had graduated with a degree in fine arts and took great delight in the design side of the business. It soon became apparent that he lacked the commercial expertise and he took a partner, Claire Morris, who injected knowledge and experience into the business. The two worked well together and, after some early setbacks, the firm developed steadily.

Eastgate Furnishings had developed throughout the 1980s. Claire had insisted that a limited company be formed and that a wider product range and market be developed. The company had expanded on its Sheffield site to produce and sell a wide range of products associated with home furnishings. Eastgate manufactured furniture and produced curtains and bedding from material they purchased abroad. By borrowing heavily, the company had managed to invest in new factory space and machinery as well as market its products strongly. The target market had been and continued to be the many thousands of people who were purchasing their own homes for the first time.

In 1988, the company enjoyed a remarkably prosperous year. Sales of furniture, wallpapers and fabrics were buoyant and profits soared. Consumer spending had risen by 6 per cent over the year, unemployment had fallen to 1.5 million and Eastgate had benefited from the general prosperity. Sales in EC countries had risen slowly as the company's name had become known on the continent.

Jim's natural optimism was reflected in his desire to expand the business. Claire was more cautious especially following the receipt of an economic report from the financial director. His report was based on an economic forecast produced by the business school of a local university. It predicted the following trends for the coming four years.

At the board meeting, Jim spoke earnestly about his desire to expand the firm while they had the opportunity. He argued that they should further develop their production capacity at Sheffield. Although he had some support, a number of the other directors spoke against the idea and used the economic forecast to justify their views. Claire expressed concern that the economic climate was unsuitable for expansion: 'What the report does not highlight is the government's likely response to the economic changes. This Chancellor is committed to the use of interest rates in controlling the economy and a rise in interest rates could do us considerable harm.'

	1989	*1990*	*1991*	*1992*
Gross Domestic Product (% change)	2.4	1.1	1.7	3.6
Wage Rates (% change)	8.6	8.8	7.2	6.5
Inflation Rate (%)	8.3	8.5	7.3	5.7
Consumer Spending (% change)	3.9	1.2	2.3	3.1
Balance of Payments (£bn)	–19.9	–13.8	–12.4	–11.1
Unemployment (£m)	1.9	2.1	2.3	1.8

QUESTIONS

1 What policy options are available to the government to reduce the rate of inflation?

2 What does the data in the case tell you about the likely future environment in which Eastgate Furnishings will have to operate until 1992?

3 Why does Claire argue that the consequences of higher interest rates for Eastgate Furnishings could be severe?

KEY POINTS 3.4

- Businesses *shape* as well as *respond* to their economic environment
- Firms that increase their wages too high can fuel inflation
- Businesses can curb unemployment and affect the local economy by their employment policies
- Decisions on suppliers and markets have consequences for the UK's balance of payments

EXAM PREPARATION

SHORT QUESTIONS

1. State and explain ONE effect of an increase in interest rates on a business organization.
2. The government decides to impose tariffs on a range of goods. List THREE reasons why the demand for imported goods may not decline.
3. Give TWO factors which limit the mobility of labour.
4. Give TWO ways in which a reduction in the general level of interest rates may affect a manufacturer of consumer goods.

DATA RESPONSE QUESTION

Toyntons Motor Sales

Toyntons is a private limited company engaged in the sale of motor vehicles. The business has one showroom situated at Derby, from which it sells Fiat motor cars by franchise as well as secondhand motor vehicles.

The business had been growing at a good rate up until the beginning of 1989, with increasing turnover and profits. On the basis of past success, at the end of 1989 the directors of the business were considering expansion by opening a second showroom in another part of the country at the beginning of 1990.

The following economic reports were available to them:

ECONOMIC REPORT: RETAIL PRICES (October 1989)
The annual rate of inflation accelerated to 7.6 per cent in September, somewhat worse than the financial market expectations. If mortgage interest payments are excluded, the rate was 5.8 per cent compared with 5.7 per cent in August. The 0.7 per cent increase in the month reflected increases in the prices of clothing, footwear and food. The figures confirm that there is now little hope of meeting the Treasury forecast of 5.55 per cent inflation by the fourth quarter of 1989. On average independent forecasts expected inflation to be 6.9 per cent in the fourth quarter of 1989.

ECONOMIC REPORT: RETAIL SALES (November 1989)
The volume of retail sales rose by 0.5 per cent in August, and was estimated to have risen by 0.4 per cent in September, making a 2.1 per cent total rise in the year to September 1988. In the third quarter, sales were 0.6 per cent below the

second quarter. The slowdown in retail sales growth implies that consumers are responding to the government's high interest rate policy. A September survey carried out before the latest rise in interest rates suggests the slowdown is likely to continue. Whilst a slight pick-up in sales is indicated for September in both retailing and wholesaling, levels were weak compared with a year ago.

Questions

(a) Choose a location in the UK and explain why it would be a good place for Toyntons to open their second showroom.(20)

(b) Explain the connections between a high interest rate policy and the problem of rising inflation. (10)

(c) In what ways and for what reasons would you expect the information contained in the reports to influence the expansion decision? (20)

(UCLES 1990)

BTEC ASSIGNMENT

You are a small business advisor employed by a high street bank. As part of your duties, you have to advise customers of the bank who are planning to set up in business for themselves.

You have been asked to make a presentation to a group of new business owners to explain the mysteries of economic data and policies and how they might affect small businesses.

In order to complete this task, it is important that you research the latest government statistics for key economic measures, such as unemployment and the balance of payments. You will need to present this data simply in a clear visual format. You will also have to outline the governments economic targets and how policies to achieve these targets may affect small businesses. You should offer some advice on how small businesses might cope with changes in the economic environment.

Your presentation should last about fifteen minutes and be well supported by visual materials and possibly some notes summarizing key points.

ESSAYS

1 What would be the consequences, for industry, of the Chancellor of the Exchequer raising the rates of expenditure taxes? (25) (UCLES 1985)

2 The government is proposing to introduce further credit restrictions.
   (a) How might this policy be implemented? (5)
   (b) What effect would you expect these measures to have on:
      (i) the motor car industry? (5)
      (ii) builders's merchants supplying the DIY trade? (5)
      (iii) the overall level of economic activity? (10) (UCLES 1986)

3 What are the likely effects on a firm producing consumer durables of the government raising interest rates throughout the economy in order to control inflation? (AEB November 1990)

4 (a) How are interest rates determined?

   (b) Explain how and why changes in the rate of interest affect business decisions. (JMB specimen paper)

CHAPTER 4

The Competitive and Technical Environment

> ▷ ▷ **QUESTIONS FOR PREVIEW** ▷ ▷

1. Where do ideas for new business activities come from?
2. What is a franchise?
3. How are new ideas protected?
4. What different market structures exist and how might they affect competition?
5. What is technological competition?
6. What factors influence the demand for a product?
7. What factors influence the supply of a product and how does this interact with demand for a product?
8. What is elasticity and what is its significance for business?

THE COMPETITIVE and technical environment in which businesses operate is an important part of the overall business environment. In some ways firms shape their own competitive and technical environment by creating and developing new ideas. In other ways they have to react to changes in the environment as competitors introduce new technology, change prices or alter their advertising strategy. In all of these matters, change plays a central role.

Some businesses are more subject to change than others. A business involved with the design and manufacture of computer equipment is highly dynamic, whereas a business which is involved with insuring people's lives tends to be less dynamic. However, all businesses, regardless of how dynamic they are, operate in a changing environment and must contend with this.

If the word 'dynamic' implies change, then the most dynamic of businesses is the new business which goes from 'nothing' to 'something' very quickly. However, the start-up business is a special case of change. All businesses have to look for new opportunities for providing products or services in order to maintain growth, replace obsolete or declining products, and keep existing customers happy by offering a wider range of products. We can show these alternatives as a table (see Figure 4.1).

*Figure 4.1 – **Opportunities for Business***

	Existing products	New products
Opportunities with existing customers	More of the same to existing customers	New products or services to existing customers
Opportunities with new customers	Existing products or services to new customers	New products or services to new customers

New businesses obviously do not have existing customers, but they have opportunities either to supply new customers with products or services already available on the market, or to supply new products to a new market. Often, potential customers are slightly suspicious of purchasing products or services from a new supplier who does not have a 'track record'. Many new businesses avoid this problem by arranging to supply well-known products, often with an agreement from a major supplier. This can range from opening a 'corner shop' to retail well-known products to purchasing the rights to be the sole supplier in a defined locality, such as opening a Kentucky Fried Chicken 'take away' in a major town. The latter is an example of a franchise which we shall consider in some detail later.

In this chapter we will look at the methods used to find business opportunities, from generating new ideas to obtaining a franchise. We shall also examine how new ideas for business can be protected to enable the originator to get a fair return for the effort spent.

New Ideas

It is often thought that to be really successful in business it is necessary to design and produce a product or service which has never existed before. As a result of its novelty, customers will 'fall over themselves' in trying to buy it. Sometimes this does happen: the Rubik Cube was a good example of a highly innovative product. This toy had considerable success for a period until the novelty wore off and competition from imitators reduced sales as quickly as they had arisen. However, before the deluge of cheap imitations flooded the market, the Hungarian designer, Professor Rubik, became a millionaire.

At the other end of the scale, the Sinclair C5 electric-propelled bicycle was an unsuccessful attempt to change transportation habits. Although inspired by Sir Clive Sinclair, a successful designer of low-cost computers, and designed by professionals, it failed to attract customers in any significant numbers and a great deal of money was lost.

It is possible that these roles might have been reversed: the Rubik Cube could have been the disaster, and the C5 the success story!

Daydreaming

In the Goldfish Windows Case Study, there is no doubt that Ben has a good imagination, and this quality in any person is very special. Perhaps we all have a brilliant idea at some time in our lives. The problem is that these ideas turn up when least expected and therefore the timing is usually wrong. How many times have you heard people talk about a 'failed' idea, that it was 'ten years too early' or that someone was born 'before his time'.

Employees can prove to be a good source of ideas for businesses, for final products as well as ideas for improving production or administration

---

CASE STUDY

Goldfish Windows

Ben was watching his goldfish one day when he had an absolutely brilliant idea for doing away with curtains! Basically, Ben was a bit lazy in cleaning out the goldfish tank and the water was getting exceedingly murky. So murky in fact that you could not actually see the other side of the tank when you looked in from one side.

That's when the idea hit him. The goldfish could 'retire' by withdrawing to the other side of the tank, where it was no longer visible. Why not, he thought, have windows which contained a liquid, probably heavily dyed water. The windows would comprise three panes of glass. There would be a permanent airgap between the two outer panes, just like conventional double-glazing, but the gap between the two inside panes would be filled, or not, with the dyed liquid.

Instead of 'pulling curtains', all you had to do would be to raise the level of a tank of dyed liquid so that the gap between the two inside panes became opaque. When you wanted to see through the window, you would just lower the external tank, and the window space would empty. Ben was not sure at this stage how the lowering device would work.

Ben's imagination started working at a furious pace. Would it not be possible to use lots of different coloured liquids so that architects could create a 'psychedelic' effect on skyscrapers? Could the liquid inside the window remove heat from the tropical sun and heat up washing water? Could the coloured liquid be a really strong dye so that if any burglar tried to break the glass he would be covered in a very identifiable colour? Was there no limit to Ben's imagination? Could he become a millionaire overnight?

QUESTIONS

1 Do you think Ben's idea has any merit? Give your reasons.

2 Would you lend any money to Ben to develop his idea further? Now review your answer to the first question.

methods. Some employers offer cash incentives in an effort to attract such new ideas. However, UK businesses are frequently criticized for ignoring this valuable source of ideas.

Figure 4.2 – **Suggestion Boxes**

Suggestion boxes 'worth £1 billion'

DAVE ALLEN had a good idea last year. Mr Allen, a works area supervisor for Dexion the furniture maker, suggested that models be produced to help architects experiment with furniture as they designed offices. The UK Association of Suggestion Schemes and the Industrial Society decided this was the suggestion of the year, and sent Mr Allen to Florida for a holiday.

According to the UKASS, up to £1bn a year could be saved by British industry and commerce if all employers adopted employee suggestion schemes. Some of Britain's largest organisations, in both the public and private sectors, are committed to such schemes. Claimed savings include £20m for the Department of Social Security, £7m for British Rail and £5m for Rover.

However, British business has been much less keen to set up schemes than its Japanese and American counterparts, and where they do exist, they have less impact. A survey by Industrial Relations Services shows that while the average British worker in a scheme makes a suggestion once every five years, the average in Japan is a staggering 24 suggestions a year.

Source: Independent, 9 February 1992

The commercial success of Ben's idea of liquid-filled windows or of employee suggestion schemes depend upon many factors:

- Are there potential customers who need the idea?
- Can the product be designed properly so that it works efficiently?
- Will customers pay more for the product than it costs to produce?
- Are there enough customers to make the project financially worthwhile?

If the answer to any one of these questions is 'no', there seems little point in continuing with the idea. Ben returns to daydreaming and watching his goldfish swim in and out of the gloom. Let us hope that it did not cost Ben too much to find out the answers to the questions. However, these are the questions that must be answered as accurately as possible before any progress is made on a new idea. It is essential for all businesses to assess the viability of new ideas before committing large amounts of resources to them.

Even if the answers to the questions above are satisfactory, there will always be a risk in backing any idea for a new product or service. However, if the risks can be clearly defined – in terms of upper and lower estimates of volume of sales, costs of development, production and distribution, and potential profits – it may be possible to find financial support. Different providers of money (or investors) are prepared to back businesses with different risks. But in general, the greater the level of risk the more difficult it is to find help and the higher the interest charges for any money advanced to develop the idea.

Sources of New Ideas

If the idea of making liquid-filled windows represents one end of the innovation scale, then the other end would be making triple-glazed conventional windows. This is not a new idea: countries which have extremely cold winters have used multi-glazing for a long time. But in a more temperate climate, triple glazing would be a new idea. Perhaps the idea could be adopted by an existing double-glazing manufacturer, who adapts the idea to suit its production methods and at the same time improves the design fractionally in order to have a slight 'edge' on any competitor.

Therefore, new opportunities for businesses do not have to be revolutionary. They can be copies of products produced elsewhere, with or without minor adjustments to the design. Later in this chapter we shall examine some of the laws which exist to prevent unfair copying.

Let us imagine that we are running a business which needs to improve profits. We have tried all the ways of reducing costs and improving sales volumes of existing products, and now we must urgently consider supplying new products or services. There are basically two approaches to solving this problem:

- Designing an information gathering system
- Involving as many employees as possible in an idea generation activity – either suggestion boxes, which we mentioned earlier, or brainstorming

GATHERING INFORMATION

It is important that information gathering is done on a regular basis. There are several ways of doing this:

SIR CLIVE SINCLAIR
b. 1940

Sir Clive Sinclair was born at the start of the Second World War in 1940 and attended thirteen schools in Surrey and Berkshire. He left aged seventeen having shown some real ability in mathematics and having developed a keen interest in the then developing field of electronics. Whilst at school he had designed a simple calculating machine and a micro-radio.

On leaving school, he joined *Practical Wireless* as a journalist and a year later became its editor. He held the job for a further two years before setting up his own company to produce the first of his many inventions. These inventions then followed one after the other: micro-radios, small amplifiers, small calculators, and then his well-known computers, the ZX80, the ZX81, the Spectrum and the Z88 laptop.

He was Chairman of Sinclair Radionics from 1962 to 1979 and, since then, has been Chairman of Sinclair Research. He is perhaps best known for inventing and manufacturing the electrical tricycle, the C5. This was a considerable technical achievement, but a commercial disaster with few sales. This contrast reflects Sir Clive accurately: undeniably brilliant at invention, less successful at developing these ideas into commercial and profitable products. Some would argue that it is true of the UK as a whole. The country has a high reputation for research and invention, but other nations and their companies tend to develop and market the ideas.

However, Sir Clive is not daunted! In 1992, he launched his battery-powered bicycle, the Zike. This weighs eleven pounds, is rechargeable within an hour and has been introduced in the middle of a recession. He is not satisfied with this. His ambition is to develop a successful and practical all-purpose electric car. The tradition of the somewhat unworldly, but highly talented, British inventor continues.

(Photo: The Hulton Deutsch Collection)

---

a Research work
Find out if any research work is being undertaken at universities or other research establishments on products or services related to the existing range.

b Trade magazines
Read periodicals and magazines associated with the industry to learn of new products or processes which are being offered by suppliers.

c Exhibitions and trade fairs
3. Visit exhibitions and trade fairs to find out what the competitors are offering, especially with regards to innovative features, product prices and delivery times.

d Customers
Visit customers to find out their requirements for products not yet available or available from a source which is unsatisfactory because of quality, delivery or reliability problems. Survey and research these customers regularly to obtain a view of changing tastes and fashions.

e Conferences
Attend conferences to meet competitors and members of organizations to learn of 'gossip' about activities as yet not officially disclosed. This could range from knowledge of a new, yet to be announced, product to the possible bankruptcy of a major supplier.

f Professional organizations
Become a member of a professional organization, such as the British Institute of Management (BIM), which operates information services for members about all aspects of business, and will assist with obtaining interviews with politicians.

g Newspapers
Read newspapers, especially the Sunday press, which contain business-to-business sections and advertisements featuring 'Opportunities for Business'. Many of these opportunities are for franchises, which are discussed in more detail later in this chapter.

h Other organizations
Join an organization such as the Chamber of Industry and Commerce, a local self-supporting 'club' of businesses which operates with government encouragement. The Chamber runs seminars

on export opportunities, circulates lists of opportunities for business with foreign companies, either importing or exporting, and provides assistance on all types of government aid programme.

If this information gathering is undertaken on a regular basis, a meeting of informed people may well be able to generate many ideas for new business opportunities. Such a meeting should be planned in advance, with speakers giving their ideas in rotation. Clearly, this will involve some costs for the company. This, however, should be covered if the ideas are effective and earn a good return.

GETTING IDEAS – BRAINSTORMING

The generation of new ideas can be achieved through brainstorming sessions. This is where a group of people, usually with a chairperson, concentrate on generating as many ideas as possible in response to a simple question – for example, 'How do we diversify our product range into the catering industry?'

Some ideas, which may be extreme and unsuitable, could well lead to very plausible ideas from other members of the meeting. The ideas are all noted in sufficient detail for future analysis. The chairperson of a brainstorming meeting will try to keep the ideas flowing by encouraging quiet members to participate, and by firmly stopping any comment on the validity of an idea during the meeting. Quantity rather than quality is required at brainstorming sessions. Some brainstorming meetings need 'warming up', like a studio audience at a TV show.

---

*Figure 4.3 – **Glaxo and R & D***

Glaxo invests in '£1bn hot-house' to foster discovery

BRITAIN'S biggest construction project apart from the Channel Tunnel is under way in Stevenage.

The site covers 1.5m sq ft and building alone – excluding fittings – will cost £500m. But it is not a retail park, or a Canary Wharf-style office development. It is a new research facility for Glaxo, the world's second largest pharmaceutical company. When it is completed in 1994 it will house 1,400 of the group's research and associated support staff.

The project marks the culmination of a period of dramatic expansion in R & D for Glaxo. In 1986, it had 1,700 people researching and developing new drugs; now it has 7,500. Then, its facilities were almost exclusively in the UK – at Ware, 10 miles from the Stevenage site, and Greenford, West London. Now, it has operations in Italy, Spain, France, Japan and the US – most of them opened, or significantly extended, within the last two years.

Stevenage is by far the biggest project but the other facilities have also absorbed significant sums. The Girolami Centre in North Carolina, named after the group's chairman, Sir Paul Girolami, cost $350m; the Japanese facility £80m. In total, the group estimates that half its £2.1bn of capital spending over the last five years was on building and equipping research facilities, and it is budgeting to spend a further £1bn in the next five.

That investment has been aimed simply at creating the best possible environment for Glaxo's scientists to work in; far more is spent each year on actually researching compounds and developing them into marketable drugs. Last year Glaxo spent £475m on R & D, bringing the total for the past five years to £1.6bn. This year, spending will be about £600m and by 1995 it could reach £1bn.

The huge sums underline how vital R & D is to Glaxo. Discovery is the life-blood of the company; only by finding new and better drugs can it continue to prosper. That means it has to attract the best scientists – and, it hopes, offering modern, well-equipped facilities will give it an advantage.

Richard Sykes, head of R & D at Glaxo, said: "You have got to be innovative to keep people motivated. Most important is to keep the job interesting – money (as salaries) is not critical to scientists. It is more important to build new, modern laboratories, to give them the equipment they need, to have outstanding relationships with academic institutions and other companies, and to give them interesting projects."

There has been criticism of Glaxo's spending on R & D facilities. Some accuse it of squandering the profits from Zantac – the blockbuster ulcer drug which was the foundation of its success, and which has annual sales of more than £1.6bn – on grandiose buildings with unnecessary frills.

Glaxo has also been good at managing its R & D. It is more ruthless than many of its competitors – weeding out compounds at an early stage if they do not look likely to succeed, but also committing large sums, early in the process, to promising compounds. "We are not interested in producing a drug for its own sake," said Dr Sykes. "There has to be a clear therapeutic benefit."

"It is a tremendous gamble, based on faith," said Dr Sykes. "But it is our business and we have to invest in it."

Source: Independent, 9 June 1992

At the end of the brainstorming session, all the ideas are considered and the best are selected to go forward to a more detailed examination. A report on all the ideas generated is sent to members of the meeting saying why they have been rejected, or stored, or taken a step further.

It is not true that brainstorming is a group activity only. A single person is capable of generating many ideas, though a group is perhaps one natural forum for developing ideas. Asking individuals for suggestions should also be part of the information gathering stage.

Research and Development

A strong argument in favour of large firms is that their substantial resources allow them to engage in researching new products and ideas. This is an important source of the new goods and services which continually enter the market.

Research and development (R & D) is concerned with discovering new products and bringing these to the marketplace, as well as making technical improvements to old ones. Although businesses in most industries spend money on R & D, the sums are much greater in technologically based industries such as pharmaceuticals and electronics. Businesses can have their own research and development departments and many large firms do. Alternatively, they may pay for others (universities, for example) to undertake the research on their behalf. This latter policy means that the business can avoid some of the heavy overhead costs associated with research. Once the idea has been generated and assessed, most development takes place within the company.

Research and development cannot be carried out in isolation from the rest of the business. Glaxo, who spend enormous sums on research and development (as highlighted in Figure 4.3, previous page), recognize the importance of carefully structured research teams as a means of motivation. It favours small work or 'discovery' groups to develop the human relationships essential for successful research. But it also encourages maximum interaction between staff so as to discourage isolation.

Links with the marketing department are essential to discover what it is that consumers want. Equally, the production department has to be kept informed. After all, once the product is designed it is they who will have to produce it. A change in product line requires a great deal of preparation.

Research and development budgets have grown in size over recent years as companies have recognized that failing to invest in new ideas and techniques can lead to competitors stealing a march. This has led to UK companies increasing their expenditure in this area. However, expenditure in R & D varies according to the type of company. For example, in 1991, ICI, the giant chemicals firm, spent 71 per cent of its profit on research and development whereas the conglomerate Hanson Group spent only 2.6 per cent of its profits. The Hanson Group operates in low-tech industries which require little research.

The R & D budget now attracts considerable attention from potential investors as one indicator of the business's future prosperity. It can be argued that a larger R & D budget is likely to result in more innovative goods and services and greater future profits. However, on occasions, the size of the R & D budget can become too large and threaten the company's immediate future. City analysts also look for evidence of this.

Look at Figure 4.4. Can you see any evidence within these figures to suggest that research and development is worthwhile? What extra information would you like to help you reach a decision on this?

Figure 4.4 – Top Ten Companies by R & D Expenditure for UK

	Current spend £000	% change	R & D per employee £000	Rank	Sales £m	% change	R & D % of sales %	Rank	Profit (loss) £m	R & D % of profit %	Rank
Imperial Chemical	596,000	1	4.64	20	12,488	–3	4.77	42	843	70.7	22
Glaxo	475,000	19	13.33	3	3,397	19	13.98	5	1,283	37.0	54
Shell Transport & Trading	472,000	–0	3.55	33	74,435	1	.63	184	5,440	8.7	149
General Electric	435,000	12	2.61	49	6,043	15	7.20	23	818	53.2	34
SmithKline Beecham	432,000	10	8.00	9	4,685	–2	9.22	10	1,002	43.1	44
Unilever	426,000	4	1.46	91	23,163	4	1.84	106	1,792	23.8	80
British Petroleum	308,000	–6	2.67	47	32,613	–1	.94	157	1,203	25.6	77
British Aerospace	263,000	11	2.14	61	10,562	0	2.49	83	(81)	n/a	n/a
British Telecom	243,000	7	1.02	119	13,154	7	1.85	105	3,075	7.9	155
Wellcome	229,700	4	12.28	4	1,606	9	14.30	4	403	57.0	31

Source: *Independent*, 9 June 1992

CASE STUDY

Product Development at Cadbury

Thinking up new products is creative stuff, but there is nothing magical about it. Creativity can be managed. It is above all a matter of knowing how to go about it and being prepared to put in the work. Cadbury's new product – Strollers – is a good example of the process.

Cadbury began by calling in Craton Lodge & Knight, the new-product development agency which is a master of the art. The key to its success has been the way it provides a team of people to work very closely with a client on new products ranging from confectionery to financial services.

Past Cadbury-CLK successes have been Biarritz and Whisper. Strollers – too early to declare a success, although take-up by the trade is reportedly excellent – is a bag of biscuit, caramel and raisins coated in chocolate. Launched in the South-East and London in January, Strollers was the result of strategic planning, market analysis and hard work.

The strategy began to form in 1987. It was based on changing consumer eating habits, which have been moving steadily away from proper meals towards 'grazing', and on noting an area of the confectionery market with growth potential where rival Mars was strong, but where Cadbury had no product at all. This is what Cadbury chocolate professionals call 'profusion lines' – bags of sweets to you and me.

You start with information. 'You wallow in it,' says Chris Wood, CLK managing director. 'That prepares a fertile mulch from which to grow ideas. You use it to create a blueprint, which describes the market, potential turnover, and distribution needs.'

Next, the team had an away day 'hothousing' with Cadbury. The point of this exercise, according to Sue Swalwell, research director at CLK, is to get away from the office environment, with its hierarchy and interruptions. People need to be able to argue and feel safe to come out with unfinished ideas. 'Humour and giggling is important,' she says, 'it means you can get around nervousness and worrying about what people will think which can kill ideas.'

The first step is producing a prototype. 'The product is the most important thing, but also there's the packaging and positioning, because people buy those first,' says Ms Swalwell. But it is only if they like the product that they will keep on buying.

Regular meetings and brainstorming sessions are backed by market research, trying out different products and packages. Researching the potential for a very chewy product, Ms Swalwell recalls a seven year old who said, rather unusually, that the product was for older children. (Children usually think the product is too young for them.) When asked why, he pointed out that he had wobbly teeth. Back to the drawing board.

Involving the client – Cadbury – was essential. 'You can't develop a new product in isolation,' says Ms Swalwell. 'You have to come up with a brand that the company likes and believes in. That way, when the brand goes on the market, they will support it in a way that will hopefully turn it into an established, viable brand.' In other words, the image has to fit.

In a speech on managing creativity, given at training company Video Arts' conference two weeks ago, John Cleese described this process neatly. He listed space, time to think and refine, confidence and some humour, as essential ingredients.

The techniques have changed little from those advocated in the 1960s, by writers such as Edward de Bono. But the re-emergence of creativity as a key ingredient in business has brought the issue back into the limelight.

Any company can apply them in its business. But Mr Cleese also listed the surest ways he knew of stamping out creativity. 'Allow your subordinates no humour . . . undermine your employees' confidence, and . . . demand that people should always be actively doing things,' he said. 'Demand urgency at all times, use lots of fighting talk, establish a permanent atmosphere of stress and crisis,' he added. That way you can be sure they will not come up with any bright ideas.

Source: Independent on Sunday, 3 February 1991

QUESTIONS

1 In what ways does Cadbury's style of ideas generation reflect the size and importance of the company?

2 What other methods of ideas generation might Cadbury engage in which are not mentioned in this article?

3 What type of leaders do you think would encourage creativity within their organizations? Why?

KEY POINTS 4.1

- A constant flow of new ideas is required in business
- It is essential to know what is happening in your business environment
- All ideas must be assessed and the originator must be informed
- Brainstorming and suggestion boxes encourage a lot of ideas and also an active involvement in the firm's future
- Research and development is expensive but makes companies more competitive and is essential in some industries

In spite of these changes, UK spending on R & D continues to lag behind that of competitor firms elsewhere in the world. Research carried out for the *Independent* newspaper showed that the UK's largest research and development spenders only just squeeze into the world's top 100 international spenders. The world's largest R & D spender, General Motors, had a budget five times as large as the UK's top spender, ICI. In view of this, it is interesting to note that in the six months following this huge expenditure on research and development, General Motors made a loss and halved the dividend it paid to its shareholders. This highlights the fact that R & D expenditure is a major drain on company resources and takes time to generate earnings.

Developing Ideas

In business, nobody can wait around for that 'good idea' to arise suddenly by chance. Idea generation must be planned, and opportunities for new business must be scanned frequently. If we regard idea generation as the 'seed corn', then the environment for growing it must also be planned and controlled. The new opportunity has to be developing into a profitable product or service.

Many ideas will fail during this development period for a variety of reasons. None the less, a large number of ideas need to be proposed for there to be a few winners. These successful products must also generate sufficient funds to cover the costs of all the unsuccessful ideas. Sometimes a firm is beaten to the market-place by a competitor; at other times a firm merely copies the idea of another and enjoys the benefits without all the research and development costs. It may be that the product is too expensive to produce in quantity; or that technological advances have made the product obsolete overnight.

New products which pass the various stages in product development also have to meet a number of safety and environmental standards as laid down by the UK government and the European Community. Such restrictions can slow down the rate of product development as well as impose additional development costs.

In order to avoid the risks in developing a new product or a new version of an existing product, it would be better to make something which already exists, and which has been thoroughly tested. This may be a foreign product which is as yet unavailable in this country for which you obtain a licence to make and/or sell. We shall discuss this idea fully in an international context in Chapter Seven. Alternatively, you may be given specific territorial rights to sell the product by means of an agency. A specific form of agency is a franchise.

Franchising

Every time you walk down the high street you are likely to pass businesses which operate on a franchise basis. Car manufacturers have franchises with car dealers to sell their vehicles, petrol companies have franchises with petrol station owners, and shoe manufacturers have franchises with shoe shops. You may be most familiar with fast food chains such as Burger King and McDonald's which are usually operated as franchises. In all these cases and others, the franchising agreement will relate to the product sold or the service given.

There will be certain constraints and advantages in the franchise agreement which operate in the interests of both parties. The supplier knows that the product is being sold in an acceptable manner. The franchise holder knows that he or she can sell the product without unfair local competition.

The British Franchise Association defines a franchise as a contractual licence granted by one person (the franchisor) to another (the franchisee) with the following terms and conditions:

- The franchisee is permitted to carry on a business under a specified name belonging to the franchisor (for example, 'Shell petrol station')
- The franchisor is entitled to monitor and control how the franchisee conducts the business
- The franchisor is obliged to assist the franchisee in carrying on the business
- The franchisee pays the franchisor money for the franchise, or for goods and services supplied, on a regular basis

Format Franchising

A special type of franchise is now becoming extremely popular in the UK. This is called Format Franchising. Unlike normal franchising, Format Franchising defines very clearly not only the product or service which is to be supplied, but also exactly how the business is to be operated.

Format Franchising is a very comprehensive and continuing relationship between the two parties, the franchisor and the franchisee. The franchisor would give assistance in choosing a suitable site, recruitment, selection, training of staff, marketing and sometimes in raising capital. It would certainly be easier for a small business to raise capital if it was planning to operate a franchise with a good track record.

In return, the franchisee would pay a licence fee at the start of business of £10 000 to £500 000 plus a payment dependent on time and volume of business. Sometimes, the franchisee would be required to purchase all materials from the franchisor. This is one way in which the franchisor can ensure uniformity of standards and product range.

To all intents, therefore, owners of a Format Franchise operate as if they were employed by the franchise holder, as managers of a local branch of the business.

But they are not employees; they are independent owners who agree to operate in a certain way for the right to deal exclusively with a potentially profitable product or service. Product development and centralized advertising will often be carried out by the franchisor at a level which would be impossible for independent owners. Centralized purchasing can also result in significant savings in the cost of materials. Well-known examples of Format Franchising are Body Shop and Kentucky Fried Chicken.

Advantages and Disadvantages of Franchising

In terms of opportunities for business, a franchise has the right to sell a product or give a service which is already established. There are advantages and disadvantages in using this method.

The main advantage to the franchisee is the minimizing of risk. The main disadvantage is the loss of full independence over the running of the business.

The main advantage to the franchisor is business expansion with minimum capital investment and release from day-to-day operational problems. The main disadvantage is dependence on franchisors who could create a bad image for the product if poorly selected and supervised.

Franchises bring together the advantages of big business (such as R & D, bulk purchasing and advertising) with the enthusiasm of owners of small businesses.

KEY POINTS 4.2

- Many new business opportunities arise from making and/or selling existing products under licence or by offering a service under licence
- Product development is a risky and costly activity, though the rewards can be great
- A Format Franchise is a special form of licence which controls not only the product or service details, but also the method of operation of the franchise holder

ACTIVITY 4.1

Your cousin has inherited a substantial sum of money and is considering setting up her own business. A friend has told her that buying a franchise is a less risky way of running a business than starting from scratch. She was told that operating a franchise 'combines all the advantages of a large scale business with that of a sole trader'.

Your cousin knows that you are studying business studies and asks for your help. Outline some advice for her on the risks of running this type of business in comparison to a sole trader, and try to explain the quotation set out above.

Protection of Ideas

If a business or an individual generates a new type of business activity, it is commonly agreed that there should be some method for preventing others copying the activity for a period of time. This will allow the innovator to recover his or her likely costs and to be rewarded for a good idea. Quite often, the idea does not result in a profitable activity, but at least the opportunity has been given. Unfortunately, in many cases, protection is sought merely to prevent a competitor from developing a design along similar lines and not to enable the innovator to gain a reward from a genuine desire to develop a profitable product. Obtaining protection is often very expensive and the legal costs involved in stopping imitators is even more expensive.

Protecting Designs

In this section we will examine methods for protecting workable ideas which are produced for commercial exploitation rather than works by artists or craftsmen, which are produced in very limited quantity. The idea could be a new invention, or a new way of designing an item in terms of shape. Authors of books, computer programs, music, etc fall into a different type of design protection, as do trade marks, brand names and company symbols.

The general principle regarding protection is that designers who have spent time in developing something which is new and valuable, and who have also taken significant risks, should be given protection from illegal copying for a reasonable time period. Laws have existed for many years in most industrialized or commercialized countries to give this protection. However, different countries have different ways of stating, interpreting and applying these laws which makes international protection extremely difficult and very costly.

The rapid rise of technology, especially in the area of computer technology, has resulted in designs which were not envisaged and taken into account when the laws were formulated. For example, the protection of computer programs is not clearly stated in many countries. As Figure 4.5 shows, the European Community members are working closely with each other to standardize protection systems, but even within this trading group significant differences exist.

Patent Protection

A patent may be granted to an inventor of a new idea which relates to a specified method of manufacture or a workable product. A patent does not relate to the appearance of the product, which can be protected by a Design Registration.

Let us assume that you have invented a new type of thin tubular plastic ladder which obtains its rigidity by being inflated using an ordinary bicycle pump. You feel that there is a commercial opportunity in this idea and after you have made a successful working model you want to make sure that you obtain the benefit of any eventual sales, either by making the product yourself, or by selling the 'rights' to an existing manufacturer. You want to prevent anyone else from exploiting the idea without your consent.

Initially you must apply to the Patent Office in London for a patent, before any details of the invention are made public. Normally, the services of a professional patent agent would be used to help prepare the design details and drawings for the patent application. The Patent Office carries out a preliminary search to see if the idea is indeed new and publishes details. This will allow interested people to see what it is you have invented, and to comment on the validity of the application if necessary. If there is no objection and you want to proceed further, you will then instruct the Patent Office to undertake a major examination. This will look at all the technical features of the application, and if this is successful, a patent will be granted. It could, however, take up to two years or more to reach this stage from the initial date of application.

The patent gives you a monopoly right to the design for a maximum period of twenty years, during which time no-one else may produce the design without your permission. The cost of reaching this stage could be anything between £3 000 and £30 000, the higher cost being for worldwide protection.

If your inflatable ladder turns out to be a commercial success, there is little doubt that others will try to copy your idea, by making something which is very near, but not identical, to your

*Figure 4.5 – **A European Patent System***

Pitted path to a pleasing patent

EFFORTS to introduce a European Community patent, guaranteeing holders minimum legal protection throughout the EC, may take a small but crucial step forward next week.

Portugal, the holder of the EC's six-month rotating presidency, will hold an inter-governmental conference in Lisbon to try to accelerate the application of a 1975 agreement establishing a Community patent before the single market deadline of 1 January 1993.

Progress on the sensitive question of patents has been blocked by a number of problems. Because the European Community Patent Convention, signed in Luxembourg in 1975, requires changes to the constitutions of Denmark and Ireland, the two countries need to hold national referendums before they can ratify it.

The Portuguese presidency will recommend next week that the EC Patent Convention should go ahead with only ten member states, until Dublin and Copenhagen can ratify it. Meanwhile, EC patents would apply throughout the Community, except in Ireland and Denmark.

'There would be no significant disruption to trade,' one official explained.

However, the issue is more complicated. Spain and Portugal signed up to the EC Convention just before they joined the Community in 1986. Despite being offered a temporary transition period until 1996, Madrid is still threatening to block agreement next week until all 12 member states can ratify it. Any decision to go ahead must be unanimous.

Spain is also believed to be stalling because of a separate row over where to locate a handful of new EC agencies. Madrid has applied to host the EC's planned Trademark Office and has implicitly linked this to the other intellectual property issue in an attempt to gain greater political leverage.

All the Community countries except Ireland (which is expected to join later this year) are already party to the European Patent Convention, along with Sweden, Switzerland, Liechtenstein, Monaco and Austria. The so-called Munich Convention, in operation since the 1970s, offers a European patent which is issued by the Munich-based European Patent Organisation, then registered separately in each of the 16 participating countries where the patent-holder wants cover, in line with national laws.

Source: adapted from the *European*, 30 April–3 May 1992

---

product. Your best course of action would be to try to reach some sort of commercial relationship with the imitator if it is a large, well-known organization. This is because the cost of defending your patent would be extremely expensive even if you were to win your legal action.

Registered Design

Let us assume that your inflatable ladder was not the great innovative idea you imagined. Say your patent application was turned down because someone produced evidence to show that an inflatable ladder similar to yours was exhibited at a trade exhibition in the early 1920s.

However, all is not lost. You realize that your ladder has a very distinctive shape, not dictated by the basic function of being a ladder. For example, your ladder has holes cut into a long, thin rectangular shape to provide foot and hand holds, rather than cross ties. You may well be able to apply for a Design Registration.

The procedure for registering a design follows basically the same procedure as a patent application, although you now apply to the Designs Registry in London. If the design is confirmed to be 'novel', a certificate is issued to protect your design from being copied for a period of up to fifteen years.

Copyright

Assume that your inflatable ladder needs quite a lot of advertising to help promote sales, and that you produce a video film to show how the ladder is transported, inflated and used. Your video, being an original 'work of art', is automatically copyright without any extra effort on your part. This also applies to any catalogue information, or any other product of your own creation, such as photographs of the ladder. There are no fees to pay or forms to fill in.

Copyright protection applies at once, whether you make one or many copies. Although copyright of literary works lasts for fifty years after the death of the author, as also do photographs, engineering drawings have a lower protection period with a minimum of fifteen years from the date of publication. The definition 'work of art' includes all items which are 'works of artistic craftsmanship'. Figure 4.6 (next page) highlights the controversy that can be associated with copyright.

Figure 4.6 – Copyright Law

Copyright law ruling angers movie makers

A MOVE to standardise copyright laws throughout Europe is causing a bitter row in the TV and film world.

An EC directive will establish new rights for performing artists and producers of records and cinema works. If passed in its current form, artists and directors could receive substantial 'windfall' back-payments while media companies such as CLT, Silvio Berlusconi's Fininvest and Carlton Communications may face large reductions in the value of their catalogues and audio-visual products.

The directive would particularly protect copyright owners from losing out in the video rental market.

Much of the controversy stems from the Commission's desire to extend the protection of copyright to four groups: authors, performing artists, record producers and producers of television and films. Copyright holders will have the right to authorise or prohibit the rental of their works. In some countries, such as the UK, producers will have to share copyright protection with performing artists and directors. In the UK the 1988 Copyright Act grants no such rights of ownership.

The directive also specifies that copyright holders have the right to an 'adequate return' from the exploitation of their works in secondary markets, over and above payments already made in their contracts of employment.

Bertrand Moullier, head of research at PACT, which represents British film and television producers, believes that despite the Commission's intention to create 'a level playing-field between producers, artists and performers, it simply meddles with industrial relations.'

The directive makes no attempt to define what is an 'adequate return'. Even worse, from the point of view of producers, is a clause which applies copyright 'retro-spectively' to all work protected by the copyright law of member states from 1 January 1993. At a stroke this could wipe out the potential value of programme and film libraries.

The Commission believes that the reform will benefit not only rights-owners themselves but also consumers, by making available a broad cultural supply. Producers and broadcasters fear it will have the opposite effect, raising the costs and risks in international co-productions.

Source: European, 9–12 April 1992

Trade Marks

We are all familiar with trade marks and company symbols, which are used to promote products and to inform customers of implied quality standards. Many of these names are protected and cannot be used by others to indicate that their product is in any way associated with the product owned by the trade mark holder.

A trade mark is a form of identification: it is a symbol used to distinguish the goods of one business from similar goods produced by a competitor.

The procedure for registering a trade mark is to contact the Trade Marks Registry at the Patent Office in London. It is often advisable to use the services of a trade mark agent who will guide you through the legal formalities. When a licence has been granted, no-one except the licensed user will be allowed to copy this mark in any form for renewable periods of fourteen years. Fees of approximately £500 would be needed to maintain a trade mark for twenty-five years or so.

ACTIVITY 4.2

Examine a number of old magazines which contain a reasonable number of advertisements by large companies and cut out and mount a selection of trade marks. An example of a trade mark is the name 'St Michael' which is registered worldwide by Marks & Spencer, or the parallel lines and arrows used by British Rail.

Since a trade mark is a means of identification, find out how good this is by numbering each mark and asking others to identify the company which owns the trade mark. It may be interesting to note which groups of people recognize which types of trade mark.

Summary of Protection

Patents, copyrights, registered designs and trade marks are all specifically covered by laws on which professional advice is required. Businesses are not allowed to imply that they have any protection when in fact they do not, and they must inform the public that they hold some form of protection by quoting the patent number and details on the product itself.

If you are awarded a patent for a very simple and much needed product, you own a very valuable 'thing'. The business term for this 'thing' is intellectual property. Elsewhere in this series you will see that a business has to list all its assets, all the property it owns. Intellectual property is becoming an important part of some businesses's assets, and is valued at the cost of obtaining the patent.

> ## CASE STUDY
>
> # The Harrods Case
>
> Harrods of Knightsbridge, the top people's store, has been enraged by a favourite nightspot for Britons on holiday on the Spanish Costa Blanca. Harrods of Benidorm has not only taken on the world-famous name of the exclusive London store where the Queen is a customer. It has also 'borrowed' the colours of the classic green and gold logo and the same lettering. The copycat sign flashes in bright yellow lights between the high-rise budget holiday hotels of Benidorm's seedy Bincon de Loix area. The district has none of the gentility of Knightsbridge. It is where boisterous tourists gather for cut price beer and all-night happy hours, fish and chips and bawdy toga parties in British style pubs.
>
> Harrods of London is not amused. The shopping emporium jealously guards its symbol. In the past the store has restrained various offenders, including a Harrods mail-order firm in Colchester, a Harrods furniture dealer in Clapham and even a Harrods restaurant 12 000 miles away in New Zealand. Michael Cole, a spokesman for Harrods, said: 'We are taking legal steps through our lawyers in Madrid to prevent this place infringing our copyright.' Pedro Jurado, Spanish manager of the Benidorm Harrods, is unconcerned. 'I've heard nothing about it,' he said, 'why should Harrods worry us? We are good publicity for them.'
>
> *Source: Times*, 29 July 1992, Rita Grosvenor.
> © Times Newspapers Limited 1989.91
>
> **QUESTIONS**
>
> 1 Why do you think that Harrods of Knightsbridge is particularly concerned to take legal action in this case?
>
> 2 What are the advantages and disadvantages for the Spanish disco in adopting the Harrods name?

> # KEY POINTS 4.3
>
> - A production process or a product detail which is new, workable and submitted according to strict rules can be patented, giving the patent holder a sole right to manufacture the design
>
> - The shape of a product can be a registered design
>
> - The drawings from which a product is produced can be a design copyright
>
> - The name of the product, or a symbol or other distinctive name, can be a trade mark for the producer of the product
>
> - All patents, registered designs, copyrights and trade marks are called intellectual property

The Competitive Structure of the Industry

A major external influence on businesses is the other firms that comprise their industry and are in direct competition with them. This might be the one-person business down the road or the enormous multinational which dominates the market for a particular good or service.

ACTIVITY 4.3

Look in your local copy of *Yellow Pages* at the section entitled 'Hairdressers, Ladies'. Count and make a record of the number of entries. Now go to your school, college or local library and use its reference section to find out the main firms in:

(a) the detergents industry
(b) the sugar refining industry

(c) the motor car industry

Note down your answers to the above questions. Why are there so many more firms in the hairdressing industry than in the others we identified? Which industry do you think is more competitive: that with many firms or that with few?

There is a system of classification for market structures, broadly according to the number of firms within the market, but also influenced by other factors.

The main classifications are:

- Perfect competition
- Oligopoly
- Monopoly

We shall briefly review these and consider the implications for the businesses which comprise that market or industry and how it affects the ways in which they compete.

Perfect Competition

This term is used to describe a market structure where competition is supposedly 'perfectly fair'. That is, no single firm has a competitive advantage.

Consider the case of vegetable producers. Ignoring the organic market, vegetables are pretty similar and prices tend to 'bunch' around a given level. For such competition to be fair, businesses would all have to be quite small and unable to dominate the market by setting a price which all other firms have to follow. In such circumstances, the interaction of supply and demand sets the price and all firms set their own prices approximately equal to this. We will look at the theory of supply and demand later in this chapter. Economists say that such firms are price takers. By this, they mean such firms are too small to be able to influence price.

Firms in perfectly competitive markets sell similar, if not identical, products and this further limits their freedom in setting prices. If their product is similar to that of their rivals, then a price rise is likely to result in a very high proportion of sales being lost. Indeed, in the extreme case where the products are identical, and the consumer has full knowledge of this, all sales could be lost following an independent price rise.

This type of market tends to have a large number of buyers of whom few, if any, purchase large quantities of the product. Most of the competing businesses are aware of one another's prices and products, which enables them to match their rivals's products and compete on an even basis.

In some situations, many small firms might compete but by selling significantly different products. This type of market is classified as being monopolistically competitive. This title is rather confusing. It has nothing to do with monopoly, which entails just one producer in a market, as we shall see later.

The monopolistically competitive market has most of the features of a competitive market, except that the product is differentiated which allows more freedom in setting prices. Examples of monopolistically competitive industries might be the fashion industry, with many small design firms producing differentiated products, and the provision of sports and leisure facilities through sports centres and clubs.

Competition in these types of market can be very fierce. Firms seek to build up a group of satisfied customers who they hope will continue to patronize their business. Word of mouth and reputation play a critical competitive role in these markets. Because of this, the quality of the good or service that they provide has to be consistently good. One poor product or piece of work can ruin years of quality provision.

In many cases, the firms are aiming at just a local market and their promotional work reflects that. A small promotional budget restricts their ability to advertise and the possibilities of gaining additional customers.

ACTIVITY 4.4

Look at a copy of your local newspaper and turn to the pages where local firms advertise. You will probably find adverts from estate agents, builders, solicitors, plumbers and others. How are their adverts worded? On what grounds are they trying to differentiate themselves from their competitors? Is it what you expected in the light of the discussion above?

Oligopoly

An oligopolistic market structure exists when there are few, relatively large suppliers within an industry. Indeed, the word 'oligopoly' derives from the Greek term 'oligoi', meaning 'a few'. In these circumstances, they are very conscious of one another and shape their actions towards the likely responses of their rivals. Thus, before an oligopolistic firm settles upon a price rise it will have considered carefully, amongst other factors, how its competitors may react. Will they also raise their prices or are they likely to hold their prices down and strongly advertise the price differential? This likely reaction will be an important factor shaping the final decision on the price rise.

This type of market structure is becoming increasingly common in developed economies as products and services become more technical and complex to research, design and produce, and require larger businesses to produce them and compete in the market-place. Figure 4.7 highlights the trend in UK markets towards an oligopolistic structure.

*Figure 4.7 – **Five Firm Concentration Ratios: Manufacturing Industries 1987.*** A five firm concentration ratio is simply the share of the market – in percentage terms – held by the largest five firms in the market. Hence, the largest five firms in the footwear industry together hold 42.2 per cent of market share.

Percentage of net output of the five largest firms in the industry	Number of industries
0-9	4
10-19	13
20-29	17
30-39	15
40-49	16
50-59	12
60-69	11
70-79	8
80-89	2
90-99	5

Source: Census of Production, Summary Tables, Business Monitor PA 1002

Concentration ratios by industry (%):
- Metal working machine tools 8.3
- Leather goods 10.4
- Printing and publishing 17.8
- Toys and sports good 22.5
- Motor vehicle parts 27.4
- Hoisery 31.2
- Footwear 42.2
- Pharmaceutical products 47.0
- Bread, biscuits & flour con. 49.8
- Basic industrial chemicals 50.3
- Soft drinks 60.2
- Motor vehicles and engines 79.2
- Cement, lime and plaster 89.8
- Man-made fibres 92.9
- Iron and steel industry 94.9
- Tobacco 99.0

Source: Census of Production, Summary Tables, Business Monitor PA 1002

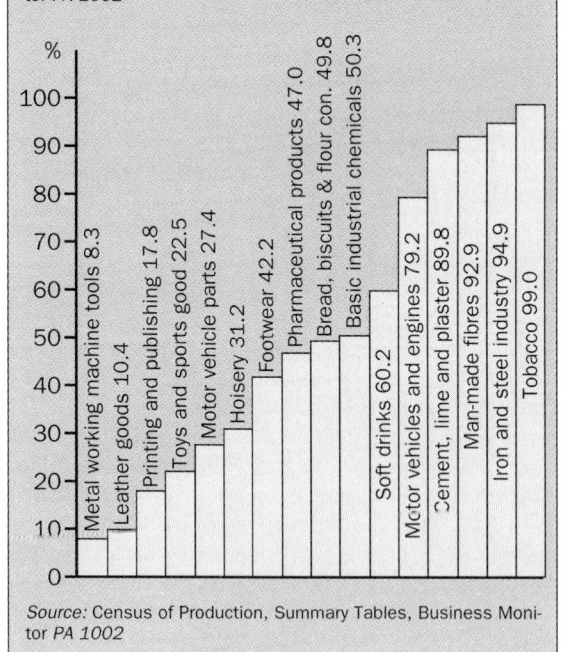

Markets with a few large producers can be highly competitive, but are not always so. The Holiday Price War Case Study (next page) refers to firms selling foreign holidays in what is a highly competitive oligopolistic market.

Such competitive oligopolistic markets are characterized by some or all of the following:

- Frequent price changes
- High levels of promotion
- Substantial investment in research and development, leading to a high rate of technical innovation of products

By looking at adverts in the media you should be able to see that industries such as tobacco, daily newspapers and household detergents fall into this category. What others can you find?

However, another type of oligopolistic market exists – one that is less competitive. Many oligopolistic firms fear a price war of the type highlighted in the Holiday Price War Case Study. Firms who engage in such wars cannot be sure that they will win. They do not know the exact resources that their rivals possess. Nor do they know the level of commitment of the opposing management team to winning such a war. Such uncertainty can kill competition in these markets. As a result, prices in some industries move together as competitors seek to avoid starting a price war. Prices tend to be stable with competition confined to quality and promotional issues. It is because of this that the petrol retail industry is frequently accused of lacking a competitive edge. Similar charges have, at times, been levied at the high street banks.

The trend towards oligopoly that we highlighted in Figure 4.7 has significant implications. It can lead to intense competition, which is in the consumer's interest since it promotes lower prices and encourages technical innovation. Such competitive firms may also succeed in international markets, offering employment and prosperity to the areas in which they are sited. However, not all firms will be successful and, inevitably, some firms in a competitive market will go to the wall. The Holiday Price War Case Study makes reference to ILG (the International Leisure Group) which did not survive in a highly competitive oligopolistic market. This highlights the risks firms take.

Alternatively, a less competitive oligopolistic market offers the consumer a less attractive deal since prices may be higher and products less advanced. However, the less competitive market may protect jobs and generally provide more certainty.

In Chapter Eight we will look in detail at the Single European Market which has been in operation since the end of 1992. This has created a more competitive market as other firms have

CASE STUDY

Holiday Price War

Thomson Holidays has stepped up the holiday price war with a declaration yesterday that it is prepared to sell Mediterranean packages from £99 throughout the peak summer period.

The continuing recession and an estimated over-capacity of one million package holidays has meant that holiday companies have all had to make large price cuts in order to maintain sales.

Charles Newbold, Thomson managing director, described it as 'an undignified scramble' for the late-booking holidaymaker.

Thomson, Britain's biggest operator, has been offering European packages from £99 and holidays to Florida from £199 rather than cut capacity. With a one-third share of the package holiday business, the company is anxious to maintain its lead over its rivals, Airtours and Owners Abroad.

The present over-capacity follows the collapse last year of ILG, which was the second-biggest operator. The major operators, including Thomson, increased the number of holidays they offered this year in the hope of picking up former ILG customers. To sell all the extra holidays made available, the package holiday market would this summer have to increase by 20 per cent on 1991. But at the moment it looks as if demand will remain the same as last year.

As a result tour operators are desperately cutting prices. Seat-only deals to Palma, Malaga and other Mediterranean destinations are widely available during May from Thomson and other operators from as little as £59.

Mr Newbold said that the battle for business this summer is certain to result in casualties: 'This is the folly of operators chasing market share. It is the return of the lemming syndrome.'

Source: Independent, 13 May 1992

QUESTIONS

1. Find out the meanings of the following terms: over-capacity, recession.

2. Why do you think that Mr Newbold considers 'chasing market share' to be 'folly'? Why might oligopolistic firms fear a price war?

---

entered the UK domestic market. Simultaneously, it has also accelerated the move towards oligopoly as firms have merged in order to be in a position to compete effectively in the larger European market.

Monopoly

Theoretically, a firm is a monopoly if it has no competition – that is, if it is the only firm in the industry. However, we shall see in Chapter Five that UK laws define a monopoly as a firm supplying in excess of a quarter of the market. In this section we shall concentrate on monopoly as the sole producer in an industry.

There are a few examples of monopolies in the UK. Some, like British Gas, are privately owned public limited companies following privatization. (We looked at privatization in detail in Chapter Two.) Others remain in the public sector – the Post Office is an example. The law gives it the sole right to deal with certain categories of mail.

Initially, it may appear that monopolies do not have to bother to compete since they are, in effect, the industry. However, this is not true. If we consider further the example of British Gas it has to compete against firms in other industries. Thus British Gas competes against electricity and coal in the domestic heating market. Interestingly, both of these industries are also monopolies! Consumers and producers can substitute either of these two fuels for gas and so British Gas must ensure that it remains competitive against such close rivals. Most goods and services have substitutes – these are products to which consumers switch when the price of the original product rises, its quality falls or some other similar factor reduces demand. British Gas advertises so as to attract customers away from other fuels. Imagine a builder about to construct an estate of one hundred houses. This would represent a significant market for, say, the local electricity board and oil suppliers as well as British Gas. It is the market made up of new houses, offices and factories that coal, electricity and oil provide the sharpest competition for British Gas. They all compete fiercely for this business. Existing users are unlikely to switch to new systems without major cause because of the high costs involved.

*Figure 4.8 – **British Gas Advertisements.*** This figure shows two of the company's advertisements. One is aimed at outcompeting its competitors – do you think it is successful? Which of British Gas's strengths are highlighted? What do you think is the purpose of the second advert?

Source: British Gas Plc

KEY POINTS 4.4

- **Competitors are a major external influence on business**

- **Industries can be broadly classified according to the number of firms competing in that industry**

- **Small firms often sell in local markets and rely heavily upon reputation**

- **There is a tendency towards oligopolistic market structures in many UK industries**

- **Monopolies can face competition from firms in other industries**

Technology and Competition

The pace of technological advance is ever more rapid. This has considerable implications for business. Those industries that produce technical goods, such as the motor vehicle and personal computer industries, compete heavily on the state of their technology. Firms competing in such industries cannot afford to fall behind in the technical race or they will lose sales. It is firms in these industries that have to invest heavily in research and development if they are to compete successfully.

ACTIVITY 4.5

Get hold of a number of newspapers and magazines and look at the advertisements. Concentrate on advertisements for technical products. What is the line taken by such advertisers? Do they highlight the technical sophistication of their products? Under what circumstances might they choose to lay emphasis on the price of their products?

Technical competition is not, of course, limited to what are generally recognized as high

*Figure 4.9 – **Nicotine Patches***

Smokeless Elan steams on

WHILE tobacco stocks continue to prosper as the smoking habit spreads through developing countries, a new class of stock is booming as health-conscious westerners turn to pharmaceutical aids in their battle to give up smoking.

One commentator suggested recently that a system to satisfy the physical craving for nicotine while the smoker fights the psychological addiction could become the fastest-growing pharmaceutical product ever.

Industry sources think the prediction is a little over the top, but it still suggests plenty of excitement ahead for Elan Corporation, a little-known Irish company which, with its nicotine patches, is one of the major players in the market.

Elan is much smaller than its rivals, which are giant US corporations. So its success could have a much greater impact on future profitability.

It was reported recently that the first company to sell an anti-smoking product in the United States, Ciba Geigy, had taken $67m between the November 1991 launch date and February with sales running at $5m a week. Product shortages have developed in many states, while estimates for the size of the market in the US have been hiked from earlier projections of $400m in 1995 to new targets of $800m to $1bn.

An unusual feature of the market is that three nicotine-delivery products have won approval and been launched in the US in close succession.

After Ciba Geigy came Marion Merrill Dow in December and then Elan in February.

It would be a mistake to imagine that Elan is a long-odds outsider, despite the power of the opposition.

Its distributor in the US is a company called Lederle, which is a subsidiary of a mighty US corporation called American Cyanamid.

Sales are already off to a flying start, with shipments to date of more than four million 24-hour patches in weekly packages of seven with a sales value of over $12m.

Like its rivals, Elan is also addressing the global market. The product has been doing great business in Ireland for 18 months and is now on sale in South Korea and Italy, where it is sold without prescription as an over-the-counter drug. Approval has recently been received for Germany, Denmark and Greece, with others expected shortly, though no date has yet been set for the UK.

Source: Independent on Sunday, 15 March 1992

---

*Figure 4.10 – **Anti Car-Theft Device***

Aspirin-sized bug gives car thieves a headache

THE James-Bond-style tracking device that distraught car-theft victims have always dreamed of can now finally be theirs. A computer chip available to French motorists for installation in their cars will alert police to its location anywhere in the country – should it ever have the misfortune of being driven away illegally.

The device is a revolution in the war against car crime, now at epidemic levels throughout Europe. From May, when the system goes live, an electronic tripwire will stretch the length and breadth of France, enabling monitors in a control centre to fix a 'hot' car's position as it crosses its beam. Eventually, say the system's backers there is no reason why the network should not extend across the continent.

All an owner has to do is secrete the transmitter, no bigger than an aspirin, somewhere about the vehicle: in the roof lining, under the carpet or in the bodywork. The chip carries encoded details of the car's identity, which are only activated once the owner reports the car stolen. Then it squawks like an airliner transponder, enabling the car's progress to be monitored.

Electronic beacons have been installed at secret strategic points along France's autoroutes, near frontier crossings, ports and airports. Some 270,000 cars were stolen in France last year – 20 per cent more than in 1990 – and 15,000 of those were 'exported'. The pattern is disturbingly similar in other countries.

The chip costs Ffr250 ($45) to install with a yearly Ffr530 ($96) premium to the firm which developed it.

Source: European, 6–12 February 1992

KEY POINTS 4.5

- The pace of technological change is ever increasing
- Technological competition is particularly important in high technology industries
- Technology is also a basis for competition in service industries
- Being technically ahead of the competition can earn firms substantial profits

technology industries. Figure 4.9 illustrates that this aspect of competition is important in less obvious industries. It shows how a small firm can compete with the giants so long as it has a technically advanced product and markets it successfully. Such successful small companies often become targets for a take-over bid by their larger rivals. Why might the 'shipments' figure referred to in the text be misleading as an indicator of sales?

Technology also plays an important part in competition in service industries. Your local banks, for example, make extensive use of technology for cash dispensing and use swipe cards behind the counter to identify accounts. Individual banks cannot afford to fall behind in the use of such technology either in terms of public image or keeping costs to a minimum.

Being ahead of the competition can earn businesses substantial profits and it is the prospect of these profits which fuel technical competition. This can involve enormous expenditure before the product reaches the market. Figure 4.10 features an invention in France to locate stolen cars. The firm behind this has incurred enormous costs before it has achieved any sales. What actions would you now expect this firm to take to maximize its earnings from its invention?

Markets and Price

We looked at market structures earlier in this chapter without formally defining what we meant by a market. A market is simply a place or an area where buyers and sellers of products contact one another and set prices. These may be international (for example, the oil market), national or local (for example, your local street market). Famous examples of markets include the Stock Exchange in London where stocks and shares are sold or Hatton Garden, also in London, which is the market for precious stones.

If a product is perishable or bulky, and therefore costly to transport, the market is likely to be a local one. Many markets, however, have no single location and much business is conducted worldwide, twenty-four hours a day, through telephone, fax and computers.

All sorts of goods and services are exchanged in these markets, where forces of supply and demand interact to establish their prices. We shall look at each of these factors in turn and shall develop the classical demand and supply model to explain pricing.

Demand for Goods and Services

The demand for a product is the amount that people are able and willing to buy in the market over a certain time period at the prevailing price. Any assessment of the demand for a good or service must:

- Refer to the effective demand – that is, the quantity which consumers can actually afford, not the quantity they would like to buy given the money
- Relate to a certain time period – a week, month or year are typical examples
- Relate to a certain price level per unit

A number of factors influence the quantity of a good or service which is demanded, the most notable of which is the price of the good or service in question. As the price of a good rises then the quantity of that good demanded in each time period will fall (assuming nothing else changes). You should be able to relate this to your own circumstances. How will your purchases of a certain brand of clothes alter as their price rises? Industry faces the same situation: a rise in wages makes labour more expensive within the organization and may result in less labour being employed. Perhaps firms may use more machinery in place of labour.

The Relationship Between Price and Quantity Demanded

An inverse relationship exists between the price of a good or service and the quantity of which it is demanded. This relationship can be set out as a demand curve similar to the one shown in Figure 4.11 for toasters.

The demand curve will show that, as the price of a product or service falls then the demand for it will rise. This is represented by a movement down the demand curve. However, if the price rises, then demand will fall and we move up the curve. Thus, if the price changes so will the quantity demanded in that time period. This relationship is of fundamental importance for business and is one to which we shall return a little later.

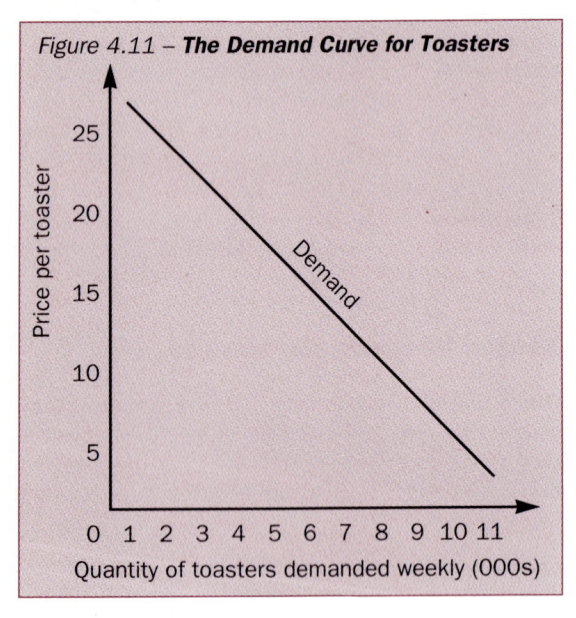

*Figure 4.11 – **The Demand Curve for Toasters***

ACTIVITY 4.5

Using Figure 4.11 as a guide to labelling the axes, plot the following data to create a demand curve. You should put price on the vertical (or y) axis and the quantity demanded on the horizontal (or x axis). The data refers to the demand for transistor radios in a certain town.

Price per radio (£)	Quantity of radios demanded weekly
60	130
50	375
40	565
30	890
20	1620
10	2500

You should produce a demand curve similar to the one in Figure 4.11. Now calculate the revenue that the electrical shop can earn from selling the radios at each of the six prices. Which is highest? Would it be sound advice to recommend that this is the correct price at which to sell? You need to explain your answer to the final part of this question.

The Conditions of Demand

Besides the price, a number of other factors also influence the demand for a product. Collectively these are known as the conditions of demand. These conditions include the following:

a Tastes and fashions

Choice is important in a free-market society. Taste will determine the choice of a consumer and this will, in turn, affect demand. However, our tastes tend to change over time as fashions begin to play a role. This is particularly true of certain products – for example, clothes and popular music. Our tastes are also influenced by advertising and the introduction of new products.

b Other prices

The amount of a good or service that is demanded depends upon the state of other goods and services. For instance, the increasing popularity of foreign holidays in recent years has led to rising demand for products associated with such holidays – for example, maps of other nations, sun tan lotion and foreign language tapes and phrase books. Goods and services which are purchased jointly in this way are called complementary goods.

ACTIVITY 4.6

In our earlier activity we constructed a demand curve for radios in a certain town. Now imagine that a new local radio station has commenced broadcasting in the area, which has led to a 10 per cent rise in demand for radios at all prices. Calculate the new levels of demand at each price and plot the new demand curve on the original diagram. Your new curve should be to the right of the original curve. Can you think of any factors that might cause the demand curve to move to the left?

However, another group of goods and services exist. These are in competitive demand (that is, one or another type of good is in demand, but not both). Over recent years the government has cut the subsidy it pays to British Rail, resulting in higher rail fares. Travellers have consequently switched to road and air transport. Thus, rail, road and air transport can be said to be substitutes for one another.

c **Real incomes**

Real income is income adjusted for inflation. The level of real income can also affect demand for goods and services – though some goods are more sensitive than others to changes in income. We mentioned above the rising popularity of overseas holidays. This partly reflects changing tastes and fashions. It is also a result of rising real incomes over time.

When people's income rise in real terms, they do not tend to spend their extra income on essential products; instead they look for new, and often more luxurious, goods and services to purchase. Many UK citizens have chosen to spend this 'extra' income on overseas holidays. This change has led to the demand curve for foreign holidays to shift to the right over time. At the same time, the demand curve for UK holidays has shifted to the left as they have declined in popularity.

d **Government policies**

We saw in Chapter Three that the government can have a huge impact upon business. Certainly, it can significantly influence the demand for goods and services. The government purchases huge amounts of goods and services. It equips schools and hospitals, provides social services and defence. A government decision to cut expenditure will cause a fall in demand for a wide range of goods and services. Further, as we discussed in Chapter Three, the government can influence households's demand by altering taxation, interest rates, pensions and unemployment benefit.

Sociologists would add other factors to this list. They would say that consumer purchases are determined to some extent by their cultural background and social changes. Education and upbringing will help decide what it is that consumers consider important to purchase. The Conservative governments of the 1980s and early 1990s encouraged a more self-reliant society. This change manifested itself in terms of more self-employed people and a dramatic increase in home ownership amongst other factors. Such changes can have very significant implications for producers.

Figure 4.12 highlights how important it is for firms to respond to changes in demand. It also illustrates how being responsive to changes in demand has implications for the organization and structure of the entire business.

We have seen so far that a change in price causes a rise or fall in demand and that this is represented only by a movement up or down the existing demand curve. As we saw, however, there are a number of other influences on the level of demand (known collectively as the conditions of demand) which can increase or decrease

---

Figure 4.12 – **Business and Changes in Demand**

Flexibility falls foul of fortress mentality

EUROPEAN manufacturers are in serious danger of being driven out of business by the Japanese, according to a survey from Insead, the international business school at Fontainebleau in France.

European factories are run like fortresses, taking no account of the customer, says Arnoud de Meyer, Insead's professor of technology management. He says that managers are to blame: "They want the easy life, set rules and a stable product."

Yet in the long run they cannot hope to compete that way. Customers demand new products, models, colours – and they want them yesterday.

The Japanese are responding to customer demand by using computers to give them manufacturing flexibility. Having spent six months in Japan studying manufacturing methods, Professor de Meyer is aware of how far ahead the Japanese are.

By comparison, European management's aims for the next two years, shown in Insead's survey of 224 large manufacturers, seem wildly off target. Their priorities are: quality, delivery and price. Flexibility comes last on the list.

Professor de Meyer and Professor Kasra Ferdows, the survey's co-author, reckon that only one in four European companies have any kind of integrated computer-aided design (CAD) and computer-aided manufacturing (CAM) equipment.

But they find that those European manufacturing companies which have invested in flexibility have been rewarded.

Among them is Benetton, the Italian clothing chain, noted for having upgraded its production plants at Veneto, near Venice, so it can change the colours and designs of its clothes in 10 days to respond to fashion demands.

ICI is another. Its speciality chemicals business in Manchester discovered a huge demand for small batches of particular chemicals. Using a new process, it can now switch rapidly from one to another.

The professors emphasise that in order to succeed, European companies must adopt a new attitude towards manufacturing if they are to sweep away barriers that insulate their factories from the market. This includes integrating functions which currently operate separately from production, such as inventories, forecasting systems, distribution, purchasing and marketing. "Most of them protect manufacturing, to make it easier to manage . . . but now we need a different model," the professors argue.

Source: Independent on Sunday, 3 February 1991

76   The Business Environment

> # KEY POINTS 4.6
>
> - A market is a meeting place for buyers and sellers, though it may not be a single location
> - An inverse relationship exists between price and quantity demanded
> - Only a price change can cause a movement along a demand curve
> - Other factors such as fashions and real income can change and cause the demand curve to shift
> - Cultural and sociological factors also influence our choice of goods and services

demand, but these cause the demand curve to shift to the right or left. Changes in price alone cannot do this. This is an important distinction as we shall see later.

Supply of Goods and Services

Supply is derived from the word 'sellers' and is the quantity that sellers make available for purchase in the market over a given period at any prevailing price. A direct relationship exists between supply and price: if price rises so will supply; if it falls then supply does also.

Supply increases along with price because the greater return is sufficient to attract additional producers into the market who believe that they can earn a profit. Equally, a fall in price may dissuade some existing suppliers from continuing to produce and the quantity reaching the market will decline.

The supply curve shown in Figure 4.13 is typical in its shape. The upward slope from left to right illustrates the direct relationship between supply and price.

The Conditions of Supply

As with demand, supply is subject to other factors apart from price. These factors are termed the conditions of supply and cause the supply curve to shift to the left or right depending upon the circumstances. Decisions on whether or not to supply goods or services depend upon the judgement of entrepreneurs or groups of entrepreneurs. Clearly, what is considered to be appropriate conditions to increase output by one group may be deemed unsuitable by another. The conditions of supply include:

a   The cost of inputs
Changes in the cost of labour, raw materials and

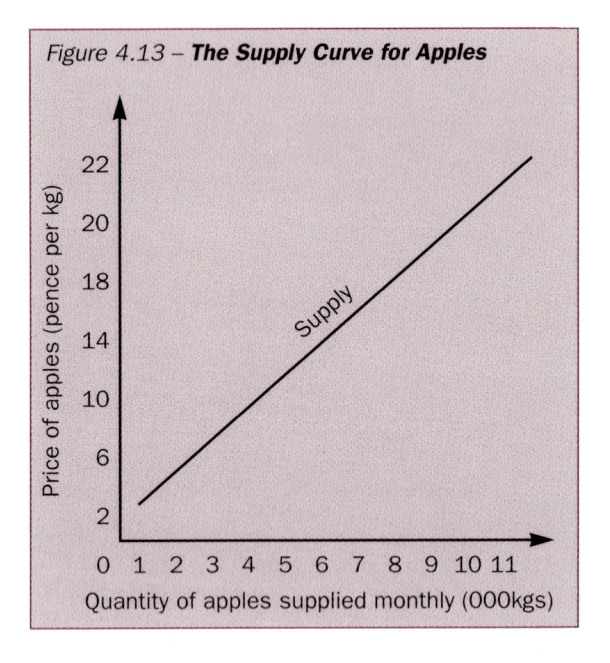

*Figure 4.13 – **The Supply Curve for Apples***

so on will alter production costs. This will cause the supply curve to shift to a new position. For example, rises in the rate of interest will increase the cost to businesses of capital. This might mean that some firms would not be able to continue to produce and will cease trading. As a result the supply curve will shift to the left.

b   Natural influences
Industries such as building and agriculture are particularly susceptible to changes in weather conditions. For example, the death of many bees in the summer of 1991 shifted the supply curve for honey to the left. Alternatively, if a late frost destroyed much apple blossom, then the supply curve for apples drawn in Figure 4.13 may shift to the left.

c   Techniques of production
New inventions tend to lower costs of production and shift the supply curve for goods and services

to the right. Many new newspapers have appeared since the introduction of new technology into the industry.

d Joint supply

Some goods are in joint supply. For instance, a decision to slaughter cattle to supply beef will inevitably create a supply of hides to the leather industry. Similarly, growing barley for, say, the beer industry, entails the supply of large quantities of straw. Indeed, in recent years disposing of surplus quantities of straw has posed problems for many farmers.

Supply and Demand Together

Neither supply nor demand operate in isolation. Both respond to the level and changes in the other which are signalled by price changes.

In Figure 4.14, we can see that the market price is determined at the price and quantity at which supply of, and demand for, chocolate bars are equal. The equilibrium price is 17½ pence per bar and the quantity that will be bought and sold each week at that price is 6 000 bars.

A higher price would mean that more of the product would be supplied than consumers were willing to purchase at that price. If, for example, the price was set at 25 pence per bar then a surplus of chocolate bars would accumulate. Suppliers would be bound to lower their price to clear this surplus. Equally, at a price below the equilibrium, demand would exceed supply and consumers would be seeking supplies of chocolate bars which are not available. Profit-seeking suppliers would then take the opportunity to raise prices.

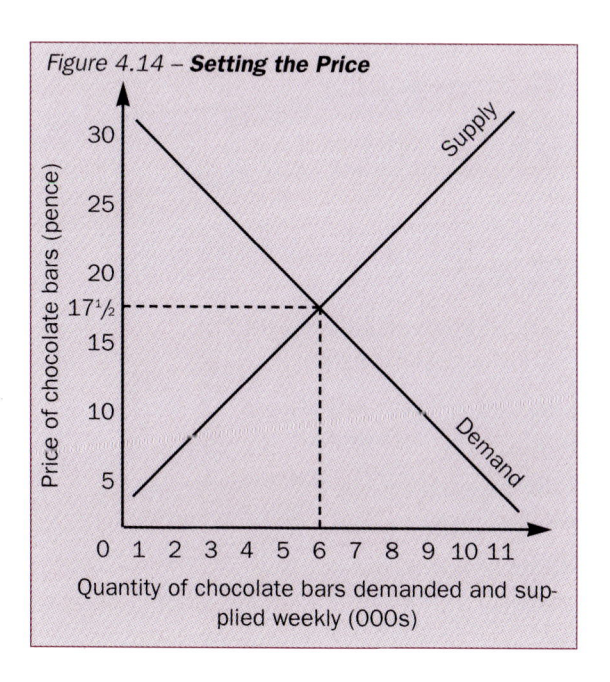

The market for chocolate bars as shown in Figure 4.14 is in equilibrium since the price has settled at a level which equates supply and demand. Indeed, one of the strengths of this market system is that this level is found automatically. No government intervention is required.

SHIFT IN THE DEMAND CURVE

Changes in a number of factors can upset this equilibrium. A change in any of the conditions of demand can cause the demand curve to shift, creating a new equilibrium in terms of price and quantity. In Figure 4.15, the demand curve for chocolate bars has shifted to the right. This may have been caused by the fact that eating chocolate bars has become more affordable following a rise in consumer income.

You can see in Figure 4.15 that the demand curve for chocolate bars has shifted to the right (Demand 2) causing a rise in price to 20 pence per bar. This in turn has led to suppliers being willing to increase their supply, sensing higher profits. The new equilibrium is, therefore, represented by a higher price and a greater quantity traded on the market. You should be able to think of changes in demand factors that would cause the demand curve to shift to the left, lowering price and supply.

*Figure 4.14 – **Setting the Price***

*Figure 4.15 – **A Change in Demand***

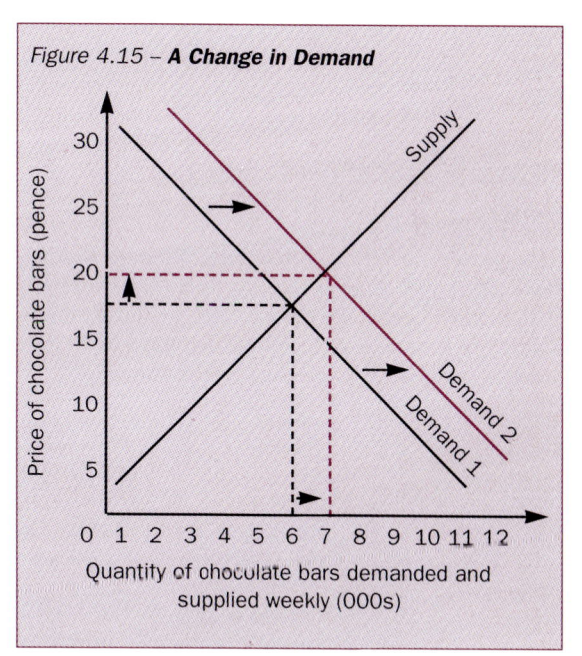

SHIFT IN THE SUPPLY CURVE

Figure 4.16 shows a change in supply and the changes which follow this. If a new, more efficient method of producing chocolate bars were introduced then, assuming no other changes, the

78 The Business Environment

result would be a rise in the supply of chocolate bars on to the market. This is shown by the shift of the supply curve to Supply 2. The result is a lower selling price that creates additional demand. A new equilibrium is, therefore, established at a lower price (15 pence) and a larger quantity (7000). Changes in other conditions of supply (for example, bad weather and a poor harvest of cocoa beans) can cause the supply curve to shift in the opposite direction.

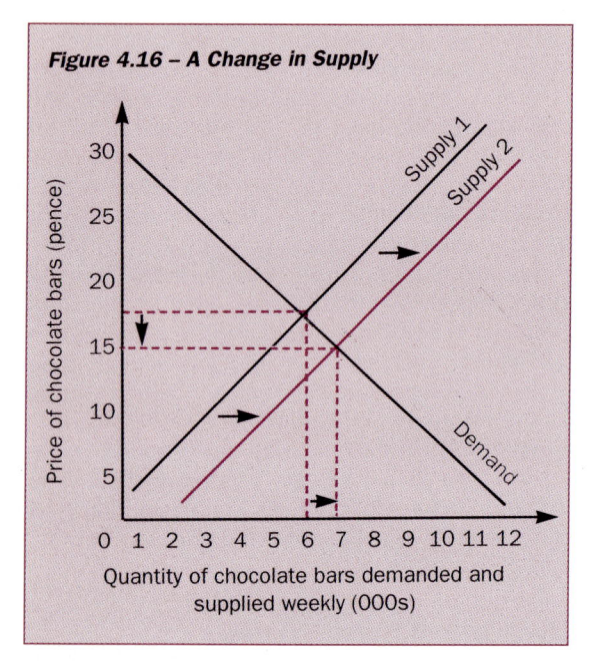

Figure 4.16 – A Change in Supply

An Assessment of the Supply and Demand Model

The classical model of price determination that we have discussed here is highly theoretical and the real world doesn't always operate in this manner. There are a number of factors which have to be considered as a part of any assessment of the model.

Firstly, the model of supply and demand attributes a central role to price in the marketing mix and gives scant attention to the other elements of the mix. Although the demand aspect of the model reflects factors such as tastes and fashions, it fails to allow for the firm's promotional activities. Advertising and other promotional work have a major influence on both demand and the pricing strategy that the firm may elect to follow.

The theory fails to acknowledge that other non-price elements play a critical role in determining demand. Certainly, a marketing manager would stress the importance of factors such as design, product range, delivery dates, after-sales services and, crucially, quality. Many firms emphasize quality rather than price when advertising; clearly they believe that consumers consider this to be important.

The theory assumes that consumers have a perfect knowledge of the current market price for a good or service and, hence, will not purchase more expensive items. This is unlikely in spite of the efforts of various consumer magazines to increase consumers's knowledge in this area. Furthermore, the model assumes a single product – or at least little or no variation in quality – and so a unique price for each good or service. In reality, a range of prices exist for each good or service according to their attributes and qualities.

In spite of these criticisms, the model has an important role in the theory of pricing. It provides a broad framework within which managers can assess the likely implications of a variety of changes. For example, it is likely that increasing supply will depress prices.

ACTIVITY 4.7

Using the supply and demand model we have so far developed, sketch a diagram to analyse what will happen to price and the quantity traded in the market in the following circumstances:

KEY POINTS 4.7

- Supply is the quantity that sellers make available on to the market over a given time and at a certain price

- Factors such as the cost of inputs and natural influences cause the supply curve to shift when they change

- Market price is established at the price at which the demand for the product is just equal to the supply of it

- This classical model of price determination gives little or no role to factors such as advertising and quality

(a) The market for luxury cars, after a rise in real incomes.
(b) The oil market, after a minor civil war breaks out in one of the supplying nations.
(c) The market for season tickets at a certain football club, following its relegation to a lower division.
(d) The market for salmon, as salmon farming becomes a more practical proposition and more common.
(e) The market for running shoes, as the health and fitness craze catches on.

The Effect of Price Changes

We have seen that both demand and supply are dependent to some degree upon price. However, although they respond to price changes, they do so to differing extents. This degree of responsiveness to price changes is termed elasticity and has considerable implications for business. Elasticity exists in a number of forms.

Price Elasticity of Demand

The price elasticity of demand measures the responsiveness of demand for a good or service to a change in price.

Demand for some goods and services is not responsive to price changes – petrol and alcohol fall into this category. This means that if the price of these goods rise then demand will change by a relatively small amount. Goods and services of this type are termed inelastic goods. The Demand Curve A in Figure 4.17 illustrates this type of demand for an imaginary good. You can see that the price fall from £8 per unit to £6 per unit provokes a relatively small increase in the quantity that is demanded.

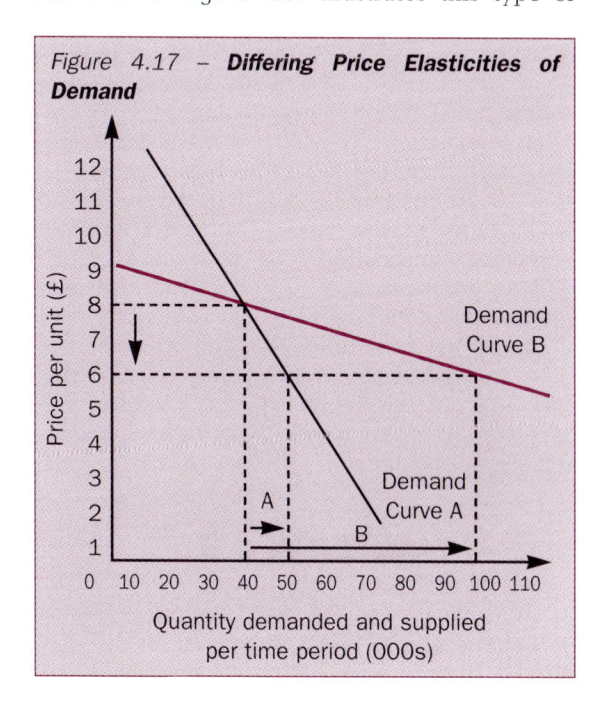

By comparison, some goods and services are highly sensitive to price changes. Thus, if retailers of a particular brand of cigarettes increase their prices, then they can expect to lose a substantial number of sales to rival products. Similarly, a reduction in price might lead to a significant increase in demand for the cigarettes. The demand for this type of product is highly sensitive or responsive to changes in price. Goods and services of this type are termed elastic goods and are illustrated by Demand Curve B in Figure 4.17. We can see that the same price reduction as for our inelastic product now provokes a much larger rise in quantity demanded.

FACTORS THAT AFFECT PRICE ELASTICITY

A number of factors affect the price elasticity of demand to which goods and services are subject:

a Availability of substitutes at a similar price
As the price of a good or service falls, it becomes cheaper relative to substitutes. Consumers are induced to buy the now cheaper alternative. The extent to which this substitution occurs depends upon whether the good or service in question has many close substitutes. Hence, goods with few or no close substitutes, such as water, have inelastic demand – that is, they are not particularly responsive to price changes. Firms with many competitors (and many substitutes for their products) face elastic demand.

b The proportion of income spent on the good or service
When only a small proportion of a consumer's income is spent on a product (for example, matches or salt) no great effort is made to seek a substitute when the price rises. Equally, it is unlikely that a price reduction will attract many extra sales. Demand for such goods is inelastic.

c Whether the good is a necessity or a luxury
Essential items such as food or clothing tend to be in inelastic demand because consumers have to purchase them to survive. Other less essential items, such as video recorders or compact disc players, may not be purchased by many potential consumers if prices rise. A price fall might bring them within the reach of a large number of purchasers. Thus, such goods are in elastic demand. However, over time, what were once thought of as luxuries become to be regarded as necessities. Refrigerators and cars may fall into this category.

Figure 4.17 – Differing Price Elasticities of Demand

d The period of time

Since it takes time to find substitutes or change spending habits, demand for goods and services tends to become more elastic as time passes.

ACTIVITY 4.8

(a) Look at the advertisements for ten goods or services on television, in newspapers or magazines. Decide which are in elastic demand and which are subject to inelastic demand. Which category of good emphasizes price heavily as a part of its promotion?

(b) Why do you think that the Chancellor of the Exchequer imposes taxes upon petrol, alcohol and tobacco?

(c) What do you think is the difference in terms of price elasticity of demand between alcohol as a group of products and a single brand of lager? Why does this difference exist?

(d) What does price inelastic demand mean to a business when it comes to set its price?

Price Elasticity of Demand and Total Revenue

It is a great advantage if the managers of businesses have some knowledge of the price elasticity of demand for the goods and services that they sell. Price elasticity of demand tells them what will happen to sales, and hence the total revenue generated from those sales, following a change in price. A rise in total revenue (TR) does not necessarily mean a rise in profits since we do not know what effect increasing output will have upon costs. A rise in price will increase total revenue if demand is inelastic. To increase total revenue when demand is elastic, a price fall will be required.

Figure 4.18 – Price, Elasticity and Total Revenue

	Price rise	Price fall
Elastic demand	TR falls	TR rises
Inelastic demand	TR rises	TR falls

Calculating Price Elasticity of Demand

Price elasticity of demand is calculated by dividing the percentage change in the quantity demanded by the percentage change in price.

Thus:

$$\text{Price elasticity of demand} = \frac{\text{Percentage change in quantity demanded}}{\text{Percentage change in price}}$$

This formula becomes more manageable if it is rearranged as follows:

$$\frac{\text{Change in quantity demanded/Original quantity demanded}}{\text{Change in price/Original price}}$$

An example should make this easier to follow. If an engineering firm raises the price of its 2cm-diameter steel rod from £1.50 a metre to £1.65 a metre and this results in a fall in weekly demand from 10 000 metres to 8 000 metres, then the calculation will be as follows:

$$\frac{2\,000/10\,000}{15/150} = \frac{1/5}{1/10}$$

$$= 2$$

The figure which results from calculations such as this is known as the coefficient of elasticity. A figure in excess of one denotes the good as being in elastic demand. The higher the figure the more elastic – or responsive – is demand. On the other hand, a coefficient with a value of less than one indicates that demand is inelastic. A figure of zero shows that the quantity of a good or service that is demanded is completely unresponsive to price changes.

To illustrate further the impact of how price elasticity of demand affects total revenue following a price change, consider the following case.

Maple & Son Ltd sell a certain product at a price of £10 per unit. It currently sells 1 000 units. Hence, its current total revenue from selling this product is £10 000. It knows that the price elasticity of demand for this product is 0.5 and is therefore price inelastic. If it now raises its selling price by 10 per cent to £11, then we know that the change (in this case a fall since price is increasing) in quantity will be half as much because elasticity is 0.5 or $1/2$. Thus, the new quantity demanded will be 5 per cent lower (half of the 10 per cent price change), which is 920 units. Hence, the new total revenue will be 920 × £11 = £10 120. We should expect this to be higher since we raised the price of a product which was in inelastic demand.

ACTIVITY 4.9

(a) With reference to Figure 4.17 above, calculate the value of price elasticity of demand for the price fall from £8 to £6 for the products whose demand is shown by Demand Curves A and B.

(b) By multiplying the price and quantity demanded for each of the two products at each of the two prices, show which benefits from a rise in total revenue as a result of the price cut.

(c) With reference to the example of Maple & Son Ltd above, calculate what would happen to its total sales revenue if it decided to lower the original price for 1 000 units by 10 per cent.

The theory of price elasticity of demand is valuable in that it helps businesses to predict the likely financial consequences of altering the prices of their goods and services. In practice, however, firms often lack sufficient data to make use of the theory. They rarely have enough knowledge of their markets to allow them to construct demand curves. This means that it is nearly impossible to calculate accurately price elasticity of demand in any market. In any case, price elasticity may vary over time or between market segments. An essential item to one group of consumers may be a luxury to another, different group.

Other Types of Elasticity

Three other types of elasticity have relevance to businesses:

- Price elasticity of supply
- Advertising elasticity
- Income elasticity of demand

PRICE ELASTICITY OF SUPPLY

Price elasticity of supply measures the responsiveness of supply to changes in price. As with price elasticity of demand, goods and services are categorized as having elastic supply or having inelastic supply.

Price inelastic supply exists when the output of goods or services is not responsive to price changes. Thus, an increase in the price of natural rubber may not provoke an increase in supply as it takes a considerable time to grow extra rubber trees. This example highlights the fact that over time a product may become more responsive to price changes. In general, the greater the time period in question the more elastic is supply. Stocks of unsold goods also help to make supply more elastic.

Goods and services which have elastic supply are those which can respond significantly and quickly to price changes. Thus, a rise in price of a product may lead to a substantial and rapid increase in supply. Manufactured products which do not require a long process are often regarded as price elastic in supply. For example, if the demand for, and price of, an item of fashion clothing rises, then suppliers can react quickly to supply the market and earn profits.

Price elasticity of supply is calculated in a similar manner to price elasticity of demand using the following formula:

$$\text{Price elasticity of supply} = \frac{\text{Percentage change in quantity supplied}}{\text{Percentage change in price}}$$

ADVERTISING ELASTICITY

Through the use of this concept, marketing managers can assess the impact on sales of an increase in expenditure on advertising or other sales promotion. The formula necessary to calculate this is:

$$\text{Advertising elasticity} = \frac{\text{Percentage change in quantity demanded}}{\text{Percentage change in expenditure on advertising/promotion}}$$

The higher the figure which results from this calculation the more effective (in terms of increasing sales) is the expenditure on advertising or sales promotion.

INCOME ELASTICITY OF DEMAND

Income elasticity of demand measures the responsiveness of demand to changes in income. Changes in the incomes of consumers will lead to changes in demand for most goods and services. However, the change in demand from any given alteration in income is likely to vary according to the nature of the good or service. Thus, we might expect that the demand for food would remain relatively unchanged when incomes alter, whereas the demand for foreign holidays or leisure activities are more sensitive to changes in incomes.

The following formula is used to measure income elasticity of demand:

$$\text{Income elasticity of demand} = \frac{\text{Percentage change in quantity demanded}}{\text{Percentage change in income}}$$

For example, if incomes rose by 10 per cent and, as a consequence, the demand for cars increased by 20 per cent, then income elasticity would be:

$$\frac{20}{10} = 2$$

The higher the value of income elasticity, the more sensitive demand for the good or service is to changes in income. Income elasticity of demand for most goods and services is positive as we demand more of them as we become richer.

However, demand for some goods and services may fall as incomes rise. Public transport and black and white televisions come into this category of inferior goods and they have a negative income elasticity figure. Thus, a rise in income provokes a fall in demand for such goods.

CASE STUDY

The North Norfolk Brewery

The North Norfolk Brewery has a long history, having been established in 1876 by Josiah Burrell. His family had gained wealth through farming their estates, which were scattered across the county of Norfolk. Josiah showed little interest in farming and used a small proportion of the family's wealth to set up his brewery in Stalham, a few miles north of Norwich. The Norfolk Broads were used as a means of transporting the necessary raw materials as well as the finished product.

For most of the first ninety years of its existence, the Brewery made reasonable profits based on its success in local markets. Its most famous beer was, and remains, 'Wherry Bitter' which enjoys an enviable reputation locally and amongst connoisseurs in a wider geographical area. Its major local competitors are Greene King Brewery in Bury St Edmunds and Adnams Ales of Southwold. The Burrell family had retained control throughout this time and held the majority of shares in what had become a private limited company. They were content with a relatively low return on capital and did not look to innovate either in relation to production processes or the product range. Indeed, the company had developed steady sales in Norfolk based on the quality of their beers and the traditional brewing process.

Competition emerges

The competitive position for the North Norfolk Brewery began to change substantially in the mid 1970s. Three major factors caused their market to change. Firstly, many mergers had taken place within the brewing industry with the result that much of the beer sold in the UK was produced by large brewers. Secondly, the nature of the beer market had changed. In spite of the efforts of the pressure group CAMRA, the fashion amongst beer drinkers had switched away from heavier bitters and towards lighter beers and especially lagers. Finally, increasing numbers of beer drinkers were choosing to drink at home and hence sales of beer in cans and bottles were rising rapidly.

The North Norfolk Brewery had suffered on two fronts from these changes. Increasingly, they found it difficult to match the prices of the bigger and more cost-effective brewers who were increasing output and forcing smaller, local brewers out of business. At the same time, sales declined because their products were regarded as less fashionable, and were not packaged in the right way.

The North Norfolk Brewery's sales decline

The company's attempts to respond to the position in which they found themselves were initially unsuccessful. For too long they did nothing, as the then Managing Director, Tony Burrell, refused to recognise the long-term nature of the change in their market. As a consequence, the company's sales in the bitter beer market steadily declined over a number of years.

An index of sales of bitter beer by the North Norfolk Brewery

Year	Index of Sales Volume
1976	100
1977	101
1978	102
1979	94
1980	92
1981	85
1982	72
1983	71
1984	69
1985	73
1986	77
1987	76
1988	75
1989	80
1990	83
1991	88
1992	90
1993	94

Eventually, in 1987, declining sales and profits and a number of redundancies at the Stalham brewery led to major changes in the composition of the board of directors. The new board was committed to a far more responsive approach to the changes in the market. They intended to prepare the company to compete fully in the modern beer market.

Report commissioned under new management

The new Managing Director, Sarah Burrell, commissioned a major report by a management consultancy group to look at the position of the company and the market in which it operated.

The group's report was wide-ranging and detailed and was in some senses surprising. The first point they made was that the firm had developed and penetrated a worthwhile niche market in Norfolk and north Suffolk for its traditional quality ales. Market research suggested that most of those consumers who had heard of the North Norfolk Brewery's products held them in high esteem. However, the company's narrow range of outlets and lack of advertising meant that too few potential consumers were hearing of the company and its products.

Recommendations of the management consultancy group's report

The report recommended that the company widen its geographical market by seeking to increase sales, especially in London and the South East. The management consultants advised that the company concentrate on a quality image and emphasise the history of the business. They felt that this would allow a premium price to be charged for the products, and that the relatively prosperous South East of England would be the obvious target market.

They recommended that the company produce a range of their products in small glass bottles as opposed to cans. They felt that bottles better reflected the quality image the company should project. They also advised that the company should open negotiations with retailers with a reputation of quality, such as Marks & Spencer. They argued that the distribution must enhance the quality image.

A considerable section of the report was devoted to the possibility of producing lager beers. After some considerable analysis the management consultants rejected the idea on the grounds that it would prove expensive and perhaps detract from the image the company was attempting to create.

Their final major recommendation was that the company substantially increase its advertising expenditure. The report argued that it was essential for the company to raise its profile amongst those who might buy their products. This should then be supplemented by extensive brand advertising. They offered a number of suggestions as to how brand and company awareness might be raised.

The presentation of the findings of the management consultants to the Board of Directors of the North Norfolk Brewery was successful and their recommendations were well received. Over the following three years many of their recommendations were implemented and the company's market and financial position steadily improved.

QUESTIONS

1. Research the meaning of the following terms: return on capital, niche market, pressure groups, management consultancy group.

2. Draw a demand and supply diagram to illustrate the changes in demand for, and supply of, bitter beer in the late 1970s and early 1980s.

3. For what reasons do you think that the series of mergers which took place in the brewing industry put pressure on small independent brewers such as the North Norfolk Brewery?

4. What does the case study suggest about the price elasticity of demand for the beers produced by the North Norfolk Brewery? You should explain your answer.

5. Assume that you are the marketing manager for the North Norfolk Brewery. How would you raise the profile of the company and its products? You will need to think carefully about ways to bring the company's name to the attention of the general public, as well as how to target your advertising successfully.

KEY POINTS 4.8

- Price elasticity of demand measures the responsiveness of quality demanded to a change in price
- Availability of substitutes and the proportion of income spent upon the good are important determinants of price elasticity of demand
- Price elasticity of demand determines the effect upon quantity demanded and total revenue when price is changed
- In reality, a lack of data means that few firms are able to calculate accurately price elasticity of demand for their products
- Price elasticity of supply measures the responsiveness of supply to changes in price
- Advertising elasticity measures the effect on sales of a change in expenditure on advertising and promotion
- Income elasticity can be negative or positive depending upon whether more or less of the product is demanded as incomes rise

EXAM PREPARATION

SHORT QUESTIONS

1. A business decided to increase the price of its product from £1.00 to £1.40. As a result, sales fell from 1 200 a week to 900 a week. Calculate the price elasticity of demand for the product.

2. What action should a business selling in a market in which demand is elastic take if it wishes to increase its sales or total revenue?

3. Demand for a particular product is price inelastic. What is the significance of this for a firm considering a change in the price of this product?

4. A business decides to reduce the price of its product from £3.00 to £2.80. As a result, sales rise from 2 500 to 3 000 units. Calculate the price elasticity of demand for the product.

DATA RESPONSE QUESTIONS

1. Fine Fastenings Ltd produces pre-packaged nails and screws for the DIY market. The prices of its five most popular lines are shown below:

   Product A £0.25

   Product B £0.40

   Product C £1.00

   Product D £1.50

   Product E £2.00

   The quantities sold are respectively 100 000, 70 000, 20 000, 150 000 and 50 000. The price elasticities of demand are estimated at 0.1, 0.5, 0.4, 1.2 and 0.3 respectively.

   (a) Calculate the total sales revenue of Fine Fastenings Ltd.

(b) What effect would a 10 per cent increase on the price of all the products listed above have on the total sales revenue of the company?

(c) Fine Fastenings Ltd wishes to increase its total sales revenue by £100 000 in order to cover an increase in costs and maintain its existing profit margins. Which products should bear the brunt of its price increases? Explain your answer.

2 Study the information and answer the questions that follow.

The Universe of Franchising

The franchising business has mushroomed during the past decade. Not only have numbers of franchisors multiplied, the number of franchisees per franchise has also increased.

A clear indication of the health of franchising compared to the generality of small businesses appears in a survey undertaken for the *Financial Times* in 1986. Within a five-year period, 80 per cent of all new small businesses had ceased trading, for one reason or another. By contrast, well over 80 per cent of franchised businesses were still trading after a five-year period. However, the more recent Power Report also notes an increase in the failure rate of both franchised systems and of individual franchised outlets, although these come out at a modest 14 per cent and 10 per cent respectively. Problems, it observes, stem not only from the franchises themselves, but from failures of other kinds, in selling and basic business and marketing skills.

Scale and growth potential of franchising

Year	Annual sales from franchise units £bn	Numbers of units operated	Jobs attributable to franchising
1984	1.0	8 300	71 000
1986	2.2	12 500	149 000
1987	3.1	15 000	169 000
1992 (projected)	7.7		

(a) Explain the term franchising. *(4 marks)*

(b) (i) Calculate the percentage change between 1986 and 1987 of each of sales from franchised units, units operated and jobs attributable to franchising. *(4 marks)*

(ii) What do your figures suggest about developments in franchising between 1986 and 1987? *(5 marks)*

(c) (i) Explain the advantages to a business of selling franchises. *(6 marks)*

(ii) Explain the advantages of starting a business by buying a franchise.
(6 marks)
(AEB November 1990)

ESSAY

1 Explain why the real price of computers has fallen so rapidly in recent years. (AEB November 1990)

CHAPTER 5

Business, Government and the Law

> ▷ ▷ **QUESTIONS FOR PREVIEW** ▷ ▷
>
> 1. How does the government affect business activity through the legal system?
> 2. How can government initiatives help to stimulate business activity?
> 3. In what ways will businesses be affected by the shift towards less state intervention in the business world?

THE GOVERNMENT has a major influence upon business activity in a number of ways and is a very important factor in shaping the environment in which businesses operate. In this chapter we will look at a range of such influences and gain an overview of the government's role. In doing this, we shall bring out the ways in which government activity can enhance and constrain businesses and their operations. We shall also identify the role of the government as an instigator of change. This chapter does not, however, discuss all aspects of the law as it affects business. In this series we have tried to integrate the legal aspects of business studies with the other elements which make up the subject. Thus, for example, we look at consumer protection as part of our section on marketing, and employment protection is dealt with as part of the personnel function of the business.

The government is responsible for establishing, updating and operating the legal framework within which businesses operate. Indeed, the law determines the structure, powers and responsibilities of the business organization itself.

Although recent Conservative governments have reduced the role of the state in the business world, it still offers substantial support to industry and particularly small businesses. We discussed the government's wider policies in respect of the economy (known as macroeconomic policy) in Chapters Two and Three.

The Legal Structure

The law affects us all throughout our lives. Similarly, it affects businesses large and small. Our society has created a complicated set of rules to control the behaviour and activities of its members: this includes businesses as well as individual citizens.

Laws affect us when we travel to school, to college or to work. They influence us during our working day and they influence our behaviour during our leisure hours outside work. A typical worker may be affected by Road Traffic Acts during his or her drive to work; during work time the employee is likely to be subject to the Health and Safety at Work Act. Finally, his or her leisure time may be affected by laws which limit the opening hours of pubs or by laws designed to control gambling.

Equally, almost all areas of business activity are affected by the law. Marketing, production, financial activities, the employment of people, the establishment of the business itself are examples of the areas of business activity influenced by the law.

The bodies of law which govern our behaviour can be categorized in a number of ways. The most useful classification system for our purpose is that which distinguishes between civil and criminal law. Civil law concerns disputes between individuals or groups of individuals such as businesses. The criminal law covers actions such as murder or misleading advertisements which are deemed to be actions against the state, and any prosecution is undertaken by the state.

Business, Government and the Law

Figure 5.1 – Types of Law

CIVIL LAW	CRIMINAL LAW
Relationship between citizens and individuals	Relationship between citizens/organizations and the state
This concerns disputes between individuals and/or organizations	This comprises offences against the state
Individuals and organizations sue one another.	Individuals/businesses are prosecuted by the state
Punishments include damages and injunctions to restrain people's actions	Punishments include prison sentences, fines, probation, etc
Businesses may be sued for negligence (say resulting in injury), breach of contract, etc	Businesses may offend against the Sex Discrimination Act, Data Protection Act and many others

The two extracts in Figure 5.2 illustrate the distinction between the two categories of law and provide further examples.

Sources of Law

So, from where does the law come? A number of sources exist:

a Acts of Parliament

While in office, each government passes a series of Acts through Parliament; these generally reflect the policies expressed in its manifesto. Laws arising from such a source are termed statute law. Once approved by the House of Commons, the House of Lords and signed by the Queen, these Acts become law. In recent years, a number of laws which affect business

Figure 5.2 – Business Law In Action

Eurotunnel set to sue

EUROTUNNEL IS suing the British and French governments for up to £200 million for breach of contract under the concession granted to the Anglo-French consortium in 1987 to build and operate the Channel Tunnel.

Lawyers for Eurotunnel have begun drawing up a writ alleging that the two governments have failed to honour a commitment to provide adequate rail infrastructure at either end of the link, and that they have increased the costs of the project by imposing excessive safety requirements.

The writ, likely to be served in the next few months, will claim damages on both these counts. It is also possible that Eurotunnel will widen the legal action by suing the two governments for allegedly granting rival ferry companies unfair competitive advantages in the shape of duty-free concessions.

No figure for a damages claim has yet been decided but senior Eurotunnel executives said it would be at least £100 million and possibly as much as £200 million.

Source: Independent on Sunday, 26 April 1992

Olivetti boss faces six years in jail

CARLO DE BENEDETTI, the Chairman of Italian computer group Olivetti, is one of thirty defendants facing prison sentences at the Milan trial for the collapse of the Banco Ambrosiano.

Prosecutor Pierre Luigo dell'Osso is seeking a six-year sentence for De Benedetti who he claims contributed to the Bank's collapse by accepting a hefty pay-off after serving as deputy Chairman for just sixty-five days up until January 1982. Dell'Osso claimed that the Olivetti Chairman extorted the golden handshake by threatening to reveal all he knew about the Bank's disastrous financial position. Italy's largest private bank went broke ten years ago with debts of Ecu1billion.

Source: European, 19–22 March 1992

have been created in this way – for example, a series of acts designed to control the actions of trade unions.

ACTIVITY 5.1

The press frequently carries articles concerning the creation and impact of laws relating to business. During your course you should maintain a file of press cuttings covering the major happenings in the field of business law. These cuttings should be grouped according to the type of legislation. You may choose, for example to collect cuttings in the following areas: consumer legislation, employer legislation, the law of contract.

b   Delegated legislation

The workload of Parliament is ever-increasing and, at the same time, it has to deal with many detailed and specialized matters. Because of this, Parliament cannot deal in detail with each piece of legislation. Hence, some laws are termed 'enabling acts' as they simply state the framework of the law concerned. Authority is then delegated to some other body to draw up detailed regulations. Such authority may be delegated to government departments or the secretaries of state in charge of them, to local authorities or to the boards of nationalized industries. Under this system local authorities can produce by-laws and government departments can establish rules and regulations which are termed 'statutory instruments'. An example of a statutory instrument is Section Two of the Health and Safety Act 1974, which concerns the appointment of safety representatives from amongst employees and their role in consultations with employers. The regulations relating to this area were drafted by a government minister and have been in force since 1977.

c   Common Law (Judicial Precedent)

In spite of the large number of acts passed by Parliament, much of the law faced by businesses is based upon the decisions of judges. This has been the case for such Common Law since the eleventh century. Common Law may involve the interpretation of a new statute law or alternatively a decision given when a new circumstance arises. Common Law impacts heavily upon the operation of businesses, notably in the area of contracts.

Common Law sets a precedent for other judges and courts to follow, particularly if a case is being tried in a lower court. The more powerful the court that sets the precedent the more binding it is upon lesser courts and the greater its authority. This process helps to ensure the fair application of existing law as well as the creation of new law.

The chart in Figure 5.3 summarizes the hierarchy of courts in England and Wales. (Note: Scotland's and Northern Ireland's legal systems differ from that in operation in the rest of the UK.)

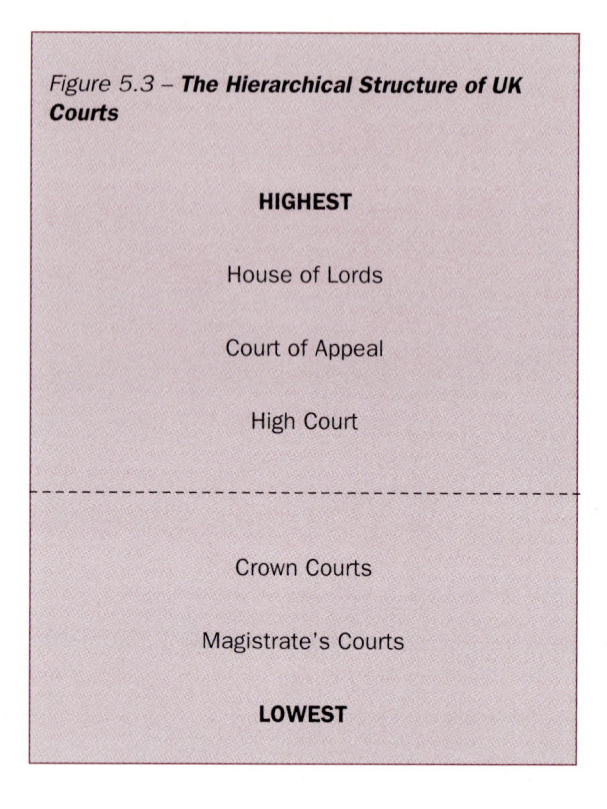

Figure 5.3 – **The Hierarchical Structure of UK Courts**

HIGHEST

House of Lords

Court of Appeal

High Court

- -

Crown Courts

Magistrate's Courts

LOWEST

The courts above the line have the authority to set Judicial Precedent, whilst those lesser courts below the line cannot set, but must follow, Judicial Precedent. However, a new and powerful force is now influencing our legal system – that of European Community law.

d   European Community law

As we shall see in Chapter Eight, since joining the EC on 1 January 1973 the UK has been subject to the Treaty of Rome. This law is of particular importance to businesses as many of the EC's objectives are economic. The EC has laws covering free competition between firms, free flow of capital and labour, total output of coal and steel, the price farmers receive for their produce and many others. Much EC law is derived from the treaties which established the Community. Additionally, the Commission and Council of the EC can make new law. The Court of European Justice is further empowered to make binding judgements on EC law.

The laws that originate from this source are applicable throughout the EC, do not have to be ratified by national parliaments and overrule any national laws which may contradict them.

*Figure 5.4 – **The EC's New Competition Law***

The Commission's new kingdom

The European Community's new competition law came into force on September 21st.

WITH the arrival of the EC's new competition law, the European Commission has exclusive rights to police big mergers and takeovers. The new regime offers businesses a 'one-stop shop'. Firms had worried that some mergers needed the approval of both the commission and the national authorities; over the past few years the commission had, with increasing frequency, started to use the vague powers that the Treaty of Rome gave it to examine mergers after they had been cleared by national authorities.

A task force of 50 officials will man the one-stop shop. The task force forms part of the competition directorate and demands that firms complete a detailed 'application' form within a week of announcing a bid, acquisition or takeover. Any firm supplying false information (or implementing a deal without gaining prior clearance) is liable to be fined up to 10 per cent of its annual sales.

Any investigation will centre upon the share of the market, both national and EC-controlled, by the newly formed organisation, its impact upon related markets and most crucially the effect on free competition.

Source: adapted from *The Economist*, London, 22 September 1990

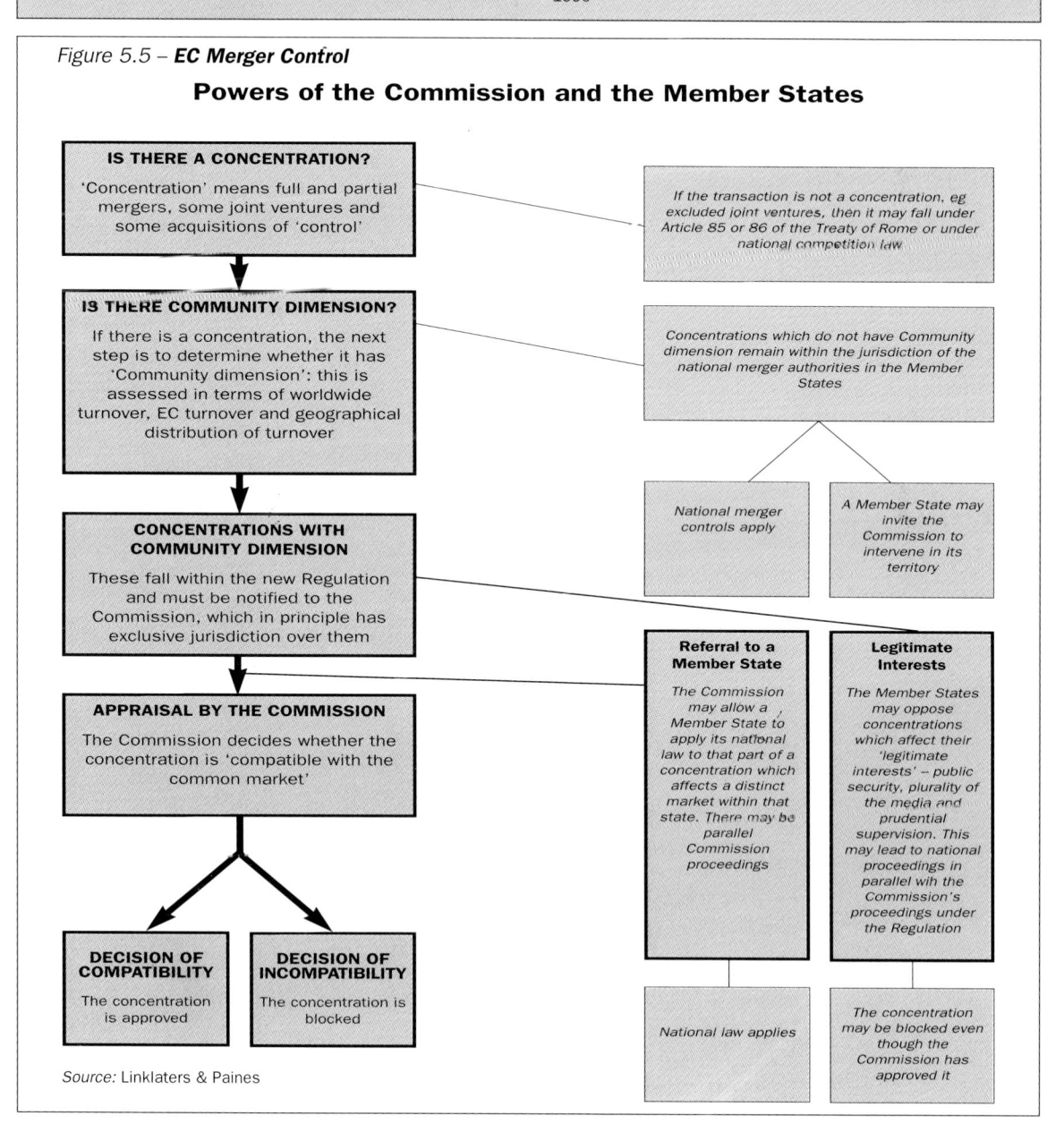

---

*Figure 5.5 – **EC Merger Control***

Powers of the Commission and the Member States

IS THERE A CONCENTRATION?
'Concentration' means full and partial mergers, some joint ventures and some acquisitions of 'control'

→ *If the transaction is not a concentration, eg excluded joint ventures, then it may fall under Article 85 or 86 of the Treaty of Rome or under national competition law*

↓

IS THERE COMMUNITY DIMENSION?
If there is a concentration, the next step is to determine whether it has 'Community dimension': this is assessed in terms of worldwide turnover, EC turnover and geographical distribution of turnover

→ *Concentrations which do not have Community dimension remain within the jurisdiction of the national merger authorities in the Member States*

  - National merger controls apply
  - A Member State may invite the Commission to intervene in its territory

↓

CONCENTRATIONS WITH COMMUNITY DIMENSION
These fall within the new Regulation and must be notified to the Commission, which in principle has exclusive jurisdiction over them

↓

APPRAISAL BY THE COMMISSION
The Commission decides whether the concentration is 'compatible with the common market'

↙ ↘

DECISION OF COMPATIBILITY — The concentration is approved

DECISION OF INCOMPATIBILITY — The concentration is blocked

Referral to a Member State
The Commission may allow a Member State to apply its national law to that part of a concentration which affects a distinct market within that state. There may be parallel Commission proceedings
→ National law applies

Legitimate Interests
The Member States may oppose concentrations which affect their 'legitimate interests' – public security, plurality of the media and prudential supervision. This may lead to national proceedings in parallel wih the Commission's proceedings under the Regulation
→ The concentration may be blocked even though the Commission has approved it

Source: Linklaters & Paines

> ## CASE STUDY
>
> # Baby Poster 'Banned' by Advertising Watchdog
>
> The Advertising Standards Authority yesterday asked Benetton, the fashion retailer, to withdraw a poster which shows a new-born baby smeared in blood.
>
> The authority also asked publishers and poster contractors to back the move and said the poster was 'effectively banned'. Its announcement was coupled with a sharply-worded attack on the clothes company – rare for the authority which operates a code of practice through widespread consent in the industry.
>
> The watchdog report said it was reacting to more than 800 complaints about the posters, showing a baby with the umbilical cord still attached.
>
> Caroline Crawford, authority spokeswoman, said the strong language used in its statement was a reaction to Benetton's decision to ignore its advice not to use the poster. 'In practice what we have announced amounts to a ban on the poster,' she said. 'We don't have legal powers to prohibit it, but our aim is clearly to have the advertisement withdrawn.' The authority had every confidence that the poster would be withdrawn.
>
> *Source:* adapted from the *Independent*, 4 September 1991
>
> **QUESTIONS**
>
> 1. For what reasons might Benetton have decided to ignore the original warning from the Advertising Standards Authority?
> 2. What advantages does a voluntary code of practice offer in respect of advertising as opposed to legislation?
> 3. For what reasons do governments use voluntary codes of practice rather than passing legislation?

e   Voluntary codes of practice

These codes are not really law and are not enforceable in the courts. They are established freely and used to supplement legislation and may be replaced by legislation if they are ignored. They are commonly found in the area of consumer protection (for example, advertising). Such codes establish a standard of business practice which all businesses in that industry are expected to follow. Recent governments have favoured such an approach as they have sought to reduce the role of the state in the operation of business affairs.

ACTIVITY 5.2

Use your school, college or local library to find out the role and activities of the Advertising Standards Authority. In particular, discover what voluntary codes of practice it operates and why it is generally regarded as performing its role successfully.

> # KEY POINTS 5.1
>
> - The law affects most aspects of business activity
> - A major distinction is between criminal and civil law
> - Several sources of law exist of which that created by EC institutions is becoming increasingly important
> - EC law takes precedent over the national laws of EC member states
> - Increasingly, businesses are being asked to conform to voluntary codes of practice

Competition Policy

We saw earlier in this chapter that the EC's new laws are designed to run alongside any national legislation, even though the former prevails in the event of a dispute.

A number of Acts have been passed since 1948 in the UK to try to ensure free and fair competition in domestic markets. The original Act (Monopolies and Restrictive Practices Act 1948) established the Monopolies and Restrictive Practices Commission, now renamed the Monopolies and Mergers Commission (MMC). This Commission was empowered to investigate circumstances

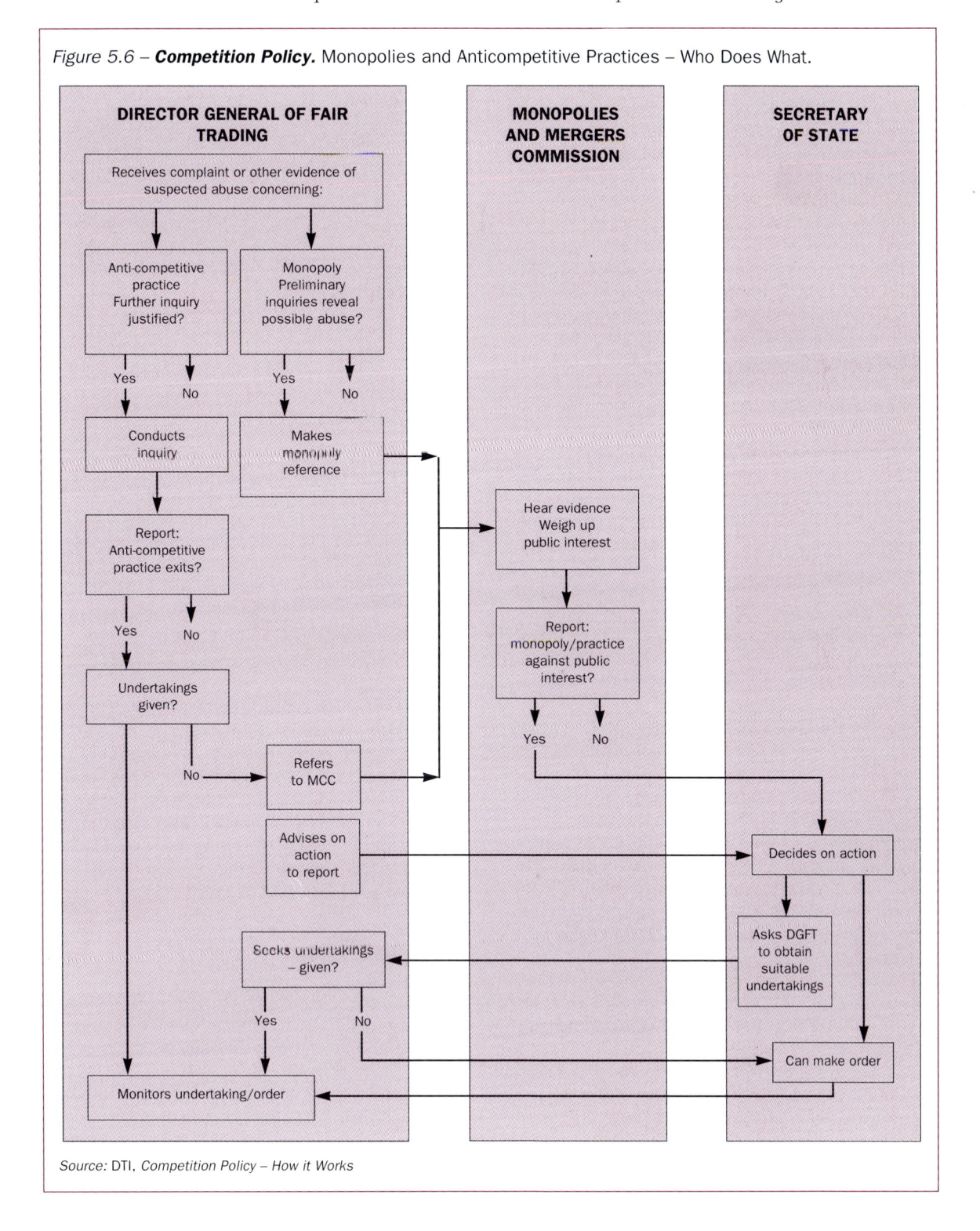

Figure 5.6 – **Competition Policy.** Monopolies and Anticompetitive Practices – Who Does What.

Source: DTI, Competition Policy – How it Works

where single firms (through merging with other firms or otherwise) dominated a particular market. If the firm was found to be acting against 'the public interest', then the Commission could act against it.

Later, in 1956, the Restrictive Practices Court was established to rule, not on monopolies, but on restrictive practices, such as firms agreeing collectively to fix prices or control selling conditions. Any agreement that might limit competition between two or more firms has to be registered with the Court. The Court is required to assume that each agreement is against the public interest unless a good case can be made to prove otherwise. This is the reverse of the usual English legal principle which states that someone should be presumed innocent unless or until proved guilty.

The central UK Act relating to competition policy is the Fair Trading Act of 1973. The Act defines a monopoly as existing when a firm or group of firms hold more than 25 per cent of a market. An anti-competitive practice is deemed to be any behaviour which distorts the operation of the market. This Act brings together the bodies responsible for competition policy and consumer protection. It established the Office of Fair Trading run by the powerful Director General of Fair Trading (DGFT). The competition aspect of the DGFT's job is to investigate anti-competitive practices, and if firms will not cease such practices the DGFT can refer them to the MMC. He is also able to refer monopolies to the MMC if he thinks it necessary. The Secretary of State for Trade and Industry is empowered to take action against offending firms if they refuse to heed the recommendations of the MMC following an inquiry.

The DGFT also looks into proposed mergers and advises the Secretary of State, who in turn may refer the merger to the MMC for investigation as to whether it is against the public interest. Mergers can only be referred to the MMC if the assets involved exceed £30 million or if a market share in excess of 25 per cent is created. The MMC can block mergers which are deemed to be against the public's interest or can impose conditions on the parties involved to protect the public's interest.

The DGFT also registers restrictive agreements and refers them to the Restrictive Practices Court to judge whether or not they are against the public's interest.

The Competition Act 1980 allowed the DGFT and the MMC to investigate a wider range of anti-competitive practices. A principal change was that public sector enterprises, such as the railways, were brought within the scope of the legislation. The DGFT can investigate nearly any business practice which distorts free and fair competition – even if the 25 per cent market-share threshold is not reached.

The underlying philosophy of the UK's competition legislation is entirely pragmatic. Each case is investigated on its merits and appropriate action – if any – is taken. Thus, it is not assumed that monopoly is undesirable – each situation is individually assessed on its merits.

---

*Figure 5.7 – **MMC Allows Merger***

MMC go-ahead for William Cook

COMPETITION from imported steel castings will prevent William Cook, the UK's largest steel castings manufacturer, abusing its dominant position, the Monopolies and Mergers Commission said yesterday as it cleared three acquisitions which take the company's share of the market to 55 per cent.

The MMC found that the acquisitions of the Paramount Foundry, Lloyds (Burton) and assets from the Armadale Steel Works would increase William Cook's share of UK production by 11 per cent, equal to a market share of 46 per cent.

The next largest UK manufacturer has only 3 per cent of the UK production but imports, which account for between a fifth and a third of the market, provide an alternative source of supply.

Some of the customers who gave evidence to the MMC said the acquisitions would restrict their choice and force them to consider foreign suppliers. Some also complained about recent price rises by William Cook.

The majority of its competitors, however, welcomed further rationalization, saying the UK would benefit from having a manufacturer large enough to compete with international suppliers.

Source: adapted from the Independent, *31 August 1990*

Contract Law

This is a very significant part of English law and one with considerable implications for businesses and their selling, buying and employment activities.

A contract is quite simply a legally binding agreement between two or more parties. It is enforceable by courts, but can be in written or oral form. Indeed, many of the contracts that businesses take out will be in this latter form –

frequently purchases take the form of an oral contract.

Although such contracts are legal, they can be difficult to prove if a dispute arises. Most businesses, therefore, prefer to record such agreements in a written form. Then, if one party defaults on the contract the other party would be more able to seek compensation in the courts. This is a civil action which may seek damages or perhaps an injunction to prevent the other party undertaking some action contrary to the agreement in the contract.

A valid contract, in whatever form, should have a number of essential elements, including:

- An agreement, where one party makes some kind of offer which is accepted by the second party

- An element of exchange, where the second party agrees to pay a specified sum of money as 'consideration' for the product to be supplied by the first party

- Both parties are legally bound to honour their agreement

If a contract does not fulfil these conditions it may be deemed invalid.

As an example of this type of legislation, employers are legally obliged to give their employees a written contract of employment within thirteen weeks of commencing work. A further example occurs when a company decides to raise capital by selling shares, it issues a prospectus and anticipates receiving applications from investors. Once agreement has been reached a contract exists.

An earlier press cutting (Figure 5.2) concerning

Figure 5.8 – **Contract of Employment**

II Terms and conditions of employment

1. HOURS
The contractual working hours are 35 hours per week. Normal daily hours of work are from 9.15am to 5.30pm on Monday to Thursday inclusive and from 9.15am to 4.15pm on Friday each week.

One hour is allowed for lunch on each working day.

2. SALARY
Salaries are paid by equal monthly instalments, in arrears, by credit transfer to your bank account, normally on the third last working day of each month.

Salaries are normally reviewed on the 1st January each year.

3. OVERTIME
Generally, overtime is not paid other than in exceptional circumstances and then only with the approval of the Head of Department.

For overtime worked the Company will normally allow time off in lieu.

4. EXPENSES
Expenses are rarely incurred by office-based staff. Therefore, any expenses incurred must be approved by the Head of Department beforehand.

Staff incurring regular expenses, e.g. sales representatives, should complete a monthly return, supported by receipts, which should be forwarded to their Head of Department for approval.

5. HOLIDAYS
The holiday year runs from 1st January to 31st December. For the first part-year in service, holiday entitlement is calculated on a pro-rata basis. Subsequent full years in employment carry a holiday entitlement of 23 days.

An additional 3 days annual holiday is traditionally tied-in to the Christmas and New Year statutory holidays to enable the London Publishing offices to close over this period.

Inclusive of the Christmas and New Year statutory days, employees normally receive 8 fully paid statutory holidays each year.

Full holiday entitlement (annual plus statutory days) therefore amounts to 34 days per year.

Non-designated holidays may be arranged at any time with the previous consent of the Head of Department by completing the Holiday Request form. Only in exceptional circumstances approved by the Head of Department, can more than two weeks holiday be taken consecutively. Holidays may not be carried forward to the next year.

Sources: HarperCollins Publishers

Figure 5.9 – **Domino Amjet Limited and the Impact of EC Legislation**

Domino is the market leader in the application of ink jet systems and other printing technologies serving a wide range of industries throughout the world. These machines can be used to label all sorts of products at high speeds so as not to interrupt the flow of the production line. The machines incorporate computers which can automatically calculate data such as the 'best by' date and label accordingly. The ink jet systems are used in a wide range of industries, from labelling shirt collars to putting 'use by' dates on milk cartons to putting numbers on each copy of a newspaper.

The company was established in 1978 by Graeme Minto with a licence to manufacture and market ink jet printers.

An important breakthrough for Domino came in 1980 with the EC directive to label perishable goods with a 'sell by' date. The market for Domino ink jet printers expanded rapidly from food and dairy, beer and beverage applications to cosmetics and pharmaceuticals, electronics, automotive, household and many more industries and products.

This, along with subsequent labelling legislation from the EC, has created a new market for machinery to undertake the labelling. Domino has produced a high technology response to the changing environment and has enjoyed rising sales and profits.

Source: adapted from Domino's *Customer Newsletter,* Autumn 1991

---

legal action being taken by Eurotunnel highlights how important a role contract law plays in the business world.

Other Legislation

Businesses are subject to legal constraints in a number of other areas. The law requires that they have insurance to cover possible injury to employees (known as 'employer's liability insurance') and members of the public ('public liability'). You may have seen certificates confirming such insurances on display during a visit to a firm. Businesses are also required to insure motor vehicles and it is prudent to insure against fire and theft.

Businesses must conform to local planning regulations. Thus, they are unable to build factories or offices wherever they wish, nor can they freely change the use of an existing business. The Data Protection Act 1984 regulates organizations in their use of data which is held and processed electronically. We saw in Chapter Four that businesses are subject to laws relating to patents and copyrights.

The Impact of Legislation

It is easy to think that the legislation we have discussed in this and other chapters may offer some benefits to consumers and employees but merely constrain the activities of businesses. Indeed, some would argue that strict legal controls on businesses can impose intolerable costs, particularly on small firms, and may reduce competitiveness in international markets. There is some truth in this assertion in that Acts, such as the Health and Safety at Work Act 1974, complicate production and force up costs since the consumer must ultimately bear the cost of employee protection. It can be argued that fewer controls are in the consumer's interest in terms of lower prices. Similarly, forcing firms to produce environmentally friendly products and services limits efficiency and adds to costs.

Legal controls can also increase the proportion of non-productive personnel (such as health and safety personnel) as full and correct implementation must be ensured and overseen. Competition legislation, such as that we discussed earlier, can serve to keep UK firms small and reduce the efficiency of those domestic firms on the international market. At the same time, competitor nations may not discourage their own monopolies which puts domestic firms at a disadvantage. Legislation which forces companies to disclose details of their trading position and accounts can offer advantages to competitors who operate under less strict regimes.

In the light of the above arguments, it may seem surprising that governments enact legislation in these areas. However, there are strong arguments in favour of strict legal controls to constrain business activity, particularly if less powerful members of society are to be protected. A workforce which is well looked after and protected may prove to be more productive and responsive to new ideas and techniques since their security needs have been met. As we shall see in Chapter Seven, much of the UK's trade is with other developed nations (notably members of the EC) who operate similar rules, which means UK firms are not placed at a disadvantage. Indeed the move to the Single European Market since December 1992 resulted in uniform legal controls. Pressure groups, such as Greenpeace, increasingly cross national frontiers and assist in imposing common standards even on non-EC countries.

Legislation to protect the consumer also protects foreign consumers and so helps maintain a reputation for quality. High standards of production and high quality output help to earn nations's reputations for quality products, which should lead to high levels of foreign sales. The products of several German car producers may fall into this category. Remember, consumers take other factors into account than merely price. Finally, the retention of a large domestic monopoly is not necessarily in the public's interest since it is unlikely to be highly efficient in its operations.

Changes in legislation can also offer opportunities to businesses to develop new products and to explore new markets (see Figure 5.9, previous page).

Legislation also impacts upon large firms since legislation such as that which encourages competition is more specifically directed at them. Large firms often strive to establish a good reputation and have much to lose by infringing consumer or environmental legislation.

The legislative framework, therefore, assists and enhances businesses as well as constraining their activities. Any assessment should consider the benefits and costs to society of such controls. We shall examine in more detail the relationships between business and society in Chapter Six.

KEY POINTS 5.2

- The Monopolies and Mergers Commission exists to prevent the abuse of monopoly power
- The Fair Trading Act created the post of the Director General of Fair Trading who plays a central role in competition policy and consumer protection
- Businesses employ written contracts for important matters because they are easier to enforce in the event of a dispute
- Legislation both constrains and enhances the activity of businesses

The State's Role in Business

In Chapter Eight, we will discuss the changes taking place in Eastern Europe as these economies emerge from many years of communist rule and the centrally planned system that this form of government entailed. All of these economies are moving towards a market economy. Most Western nations, including the UK, have mirrored – albeit to a lesser extent – this shift towards a more market-orientated system.

In spite of this shift, the government still offers a wide range of services to businesses and, in particular, small businesses which are perceived as the so-called 'seed-bed' of invention. They are also viewed favourably by ministers because they are not usually capital intensive and so employ large numbers of people. They are significant employers because they are often in the service sector which relies heavily upon people as a resource. Also those small firms which are involved in manufacturing frequently cannot afford expensive machinery since their output levels do not justify it and so hire labour instead. Finally, small businesses do offer competition to large firms and increase consumer choice.

ENTERPRISE INITIATIVE

On behalf of the government, the Department of Trade and Industry operates the Enterprise Initiative. The DTI describes this as 'a comprehensive package of DTI services to help enterprises of all kinds to build for the future'. The DTI claims it is 'a self-help package of advice, guidance and practical help for business'.

The Enterprise Initiative, which is aimed mainly at small businesses, comprises a number of elements:

a Consultancy help

This is available to all independent manufacturing and service businesses with less than five hundred employees. Firms are granted a free initial meeting with consultants to discuss their needs. Beyond this, the DTI will pay between half and two-thirds of the cost of up to two weeks of consultancy. The DTI also offers advice on consultants who may be appropriate to an individual firm's circumstances.

Consultancy is available in a range of fields. Subsidized experts are available to assist firms with long-term planning. This can allow firms to develop a business plan for immediate use as well as facilitating regular reviews of business objectives. Consultancy is also available to help improve product and packaging design, meet consumers's expectations in terms of quality and on successful marketing. Other aspects of business activity in which consultancy help is available include financial advice and information systems. Many thousands of businesses have received consultancy support under this DTI scheme, but it is difficult to assess objectively the impact of such a scheme.

b Managing into the 90s

This programme offers firms advice and support on how to integrate the various facets of management (perhaps gleaned from consultancy support) in order to improve the overall quality of business management.

c The Export Initiative

The initiative, supported by the British Overseas Trade Board, offers a range of services to exporters. This is discussed more fully in Chapter Seven.

d Other assistance

Under the Enterprise Initiative, the DTI offers support with research and technology, principally in the form of collaborative research between industrial and commercial firms and universities or government research laboratories. Advice is also offered to businesses on environmental matters to help firms meet rising consumer demand for environmentally friendly goods and services. Finally, as we will note in Chapter Eight on business in Europe, the DTI offers much advice on preparation for the Single European Market which was completed at the end of 1992.

LOAN GUARANTEE SCHEME

The government can assist small firms to obtain finance through the Loan Guarantee Scheme. Under the Scheme, the government offers a guarantee to the bank or other financial institution lending the funds. This guarantee can cover up to 85 per cent of the value of the loan and is intended to help firms who would otherwise be unable to offer collateral or do not have a suitable financial history.

SMALL FIRMS SERVICE

The Department of Employment operates the 'Small Firms Service'. The aim of this service is to provide small firms with information on a wide range of subjects, from sources of supply to government legislation. It is particularly aimed at people who intend to start their own business.

TRAINING AND ENTERPRISE COUNCILS

A significant part of the government's assistance to industry is in the support it gives to the training of employees. Until recently the Training Agency was the government-sponsored body charged with this duty. However, the authorities felt that this national body was unable to respond to local training needs and was unable to play an effective part in planning local training. Hence, in 1988, the government announced in a White Paper, *Employment for the 1990s*, the creation of new bodies to take responsibility for local training as well as promoting enterprise within the locality. The intention was to place responsibility for training in the hands of those responsible for recruiting and training locally. The aim of the new bodies is to 'improve the overall skill level of all the people in the community'.

In England and Wales eighty-two Training and Enterprise Councils (known as TECs) have been established, whilst in Scotland equivalent organizations called Local Enterprise Companies were set up with the same brief.

TECs are expected to acquire information about current training and enterprise activities in their area; to research the needs of industry and commerce; and to provide a vision of the future.

ACTIVITY 5.4

Find out the address of your local TEC and contact them to ask for a leaflet, or leaflets, describing their current activities. Look for examples of their promotion of:

(a) Training activities
(b) Enterprise activities

What evidence is there in the materials to show that your TEC's activities relate to the industries and problems of your area?

TECs support training both through subsidies and through providing courses themselves as well as overseeing the Youth Training programme. They particularly favour courses and training schemes which result in the award of a qualification recognized by the National Council for Vocational Qualifications – these are universally known as NVQs. Additionally, TECs have been given responsibility for operating the Enterprise Allowance Scheme. This offers weekly financial support for unemployed people who set up their own businesses. This allowance is available for up to sixty-six weeks in appropriate circumstances. Furthermore, students who pay for their own training within much of the NVQ system can receive tax relief on the fees they pay.

TECs face a difficult task. They were created at a time when the economy was moving into recession and employers were cutting their training budgets. With the economy in this state, stimulating entrepreneurial activity in the community becomes a more challenging proposition. Furthermore, TECs have to overcome a traditional reluctance amongst UK employers to train their employees to the degree their foreign competitors do. Comparisons with Germany and Japan show that the UK lags significantly behind in the training league.

REGIONAL POLICY

As we saw in Chapter Three, the government operates a regional policy with the object of stimulating business activity in regions which suffer relatively high rates of unemployment and enjoy low levels of prosperity.

Recent Government Policy

Over the last decade or so the government's role in business activity has lessened as a deliberate matter of policy. It has expressed that one of its aims is to 'roll back the frontiers of the state'. This reflects a belief that the uninterrupted operation of market forces is likely to result in a highly successful business sector. We noted in Chapter Two that the government had sold many previously state-owned businesses as part of its privatization programme. By so doing, it has increased the role of the private sector in the economy. At the same time the government, with a few exceptions, has refused to support so-called 'lame duck' firms, believing that support for new, young and growing enterprises represents a more sensible industrial policy.

The belief in the effectiveness of the market system is well illustrated by the government's transport policy. The role of government in the public railway network has declined and government financial support has withered. It is likely that a slimmed down rail network will eventually be privatized. The government has continued to invest heavily in the road system, but has recently espoused the case for private or toll roads.

The lessening of the government's role has considerable implications for business. Most obviously firms are more liable to failure if government support in times of trouble is unlikely to be forthcoming. This has, however, promoted greater competitiveness within UK firms; indeed, the government's objective was to create a more self-reliant business philosophy and to reduce the burden of taxation. Business has been affected financially by the reduction in state intervention. Tax cuts, most notably the tax on profits (corporation tax), have been most welcome, though offset to some degree by rises in Value Added Tax. At the same time, firms have found that benefits offered by the government have diminished as cutbacks have taken place. For example, public expenditure on research and development has been reduced, thus limiting the commercial opportunities which arise from undertaking such

CASE STUDY

Toll Road Complex Planned

The private venture selected to build a £450million tolled motorway around Birmingham is studying plans for retail and commercial developments alongside the road. These could eventually involve the building of a giant shopping complex.

Midland Expressway, the Trafalgar House-Italstat consortium chosen last week to build and operate Britain's first new toll road in 200 years, will have exclusive control over access to the road and land developments next to it. The 30 mile three-lane dual carriageway motorway, to be known as the Birmingham Northern Relief Road is due to open in 1997. The Consortium, which plans to charge an initial toll of £1.50 (at 1990 prices) for cars and £3 for lorries, believes the road will start making a return within two years.

Source: adapted from the *Independent on Sunday*, 18 August 1991

QUESTIONS

1 What benefits will (a) the government and (b) the Consortium gain from building this toll road?

2 How do you think the Consortium assessed the costs and likely returns involved in this project?

3 Imagine you are a critic of such a scheme. What arguments could you put forward against it?

---

work and developing the results of it.

The impact on orders has been similarly mixed. The construction industry has been hit by tight government controls on local authority expenditure. Local authorities have built far fewer houses in recent years, but at the same time a number of government initiatives have encouraged private house purchase which has provided opportunities for the construction industry as well as linked industries (for example, DIY retailers).

The construction industry does not face a unique situation: circumstances have changed but opportunities remain for adaptable and flexible organizations.

KEY POINTS 5.3

- Many nations have increasingly favoured the market system of organizing their economies in recent years
- The UK government supports small firms in a variety of ways
- Training and Enterprise Councils have been established to provide a local focus to training and enterprise initiatives
- The government has, in spite of its assistance to small businesses, reduced its support for industry and commerce

EXAM PREPARATION

SHORT QUESTIONS

1. List four aspects of business activity affected by the law.
2. Distinguish between criminal and civil law.
3. Explain the term 'delegated legislation'.
4. What is a voluntary code of practice?
5. Give one example of EC law which affects UK businesses.
6. State two functions of the Director General of Fair Trading.
7. What is a contract?
8. Give three types of insurance cover needed by a company.
9. How might a change of government policy in the UK affect UK firms?
10. Give two examples of government help offered under the Enterprise Initiative.

DATA RESPONSE QUESTIONS

1 Licensing crisis for casino group

The City is braced for potentially dramatic losses on the £125 million management buyout of London Clubs International, the casinos group, after action by the Gaming Board to oppose licences for all six of its London casinos.

The Gaming Board lodged objections with Westminster licensing magistrates late last week, claiming the company was not fit and proper to run any of its casinos, some of the most prestigious and lucrative in London. The Gaming Board's move is its most wide-ranging since it successfully stripped the Ladbroke Group of its casino licences in the 1970s.

If the company, which made pre-tax losses of £12.3 million last year, loses its licences it would almost certainly be worthless and the City would lose most, if not all, of the £125 million put up two years ago to finance the company's buyout from Grand Metropolitan.

Source: Independent on Sunday, 15 March 1992

Questions

(a) Research the meaning and advantages of 'management buyouts'.

(b) For what reasons does the law closely regulate the activities of casinos? Do you think these reasons are sufficient to justify this power?

(c) What advantages and disadvantages does the legal control of businesses offer to those businesses?

2. Read the following extract and answer the questions below.

The Bolton Committee (1971) suggested that the three main characteristics of a small firm were that it had a relatively small share of the market; that it was managed in a personalized way by its owners who took all the principal decisions and exercised the principal management functions; and that it was independent in the sense that it did not form part of a larger enterprise.

These characteristics provide an economic definition of a small firm, but in censuses and surveys, firm size is determined by means of statistical measures such as employment or sales, and in terms of employment, for example, the largest size of firm which will typically conform to the Bolton characteristics varies with industry. In some manufacturing industries, firms with 500 employees will often conform, whilst in retailing a firm with 200 employees will be relatively large, and in the world of finance firms with fewer than 50 employees will typically not conform. Since similar remarks also apply to any other statistical measure of size, considerable care needs to be taken when using such measures to define a small firm. However, provided account is taken of industry, they do give at least a rough guide. In the manufacturing industry, for example, nearly all firms with less than 200 employees will also be small according to the economic definition.

Source: Allard, R, 'The importance and position of small firms', *The Economic Review*, Vol 1, No 2, November 1983

Questions

(a) State **three** methods of comparing the size of firms in the same industry other than by 'number of employees'. (3 marks)

(b) Explain why 'number of employees' on its own might be a misleading indication of size of firms. (2 marks)

(c) Give **two** reasons why small firms tend to be less capital intensive than large ones. (6 marks)

(d) Explain **four** different methods governments have employed in an attempt to encourage the small firms sector. (8 marks)

(e) Outline **two** reasons why the small firms sector is considered to be important to the UK economy. (4 marks)

(AEB June 1988)

BTEC ASSIGNMENT

In this assignment you should put yourself in the role of a factory inspector.

As a group, arrange a visit to a nearby manufacturing firm. Prior to your visit, research the Health and Safety at Work Act 1974, so that the group are familiar with its provisions. Whilst in the factory, look for evidence of the operation of this Act: for example, guards, safety clothing and notices.

Arrange an interview with the factory's safety officer or other person knowledgeable about health and safety matters. Ask him or her how the Act affects the operation of the factory to support the evidence you have gained on your tour.

On your return, write a report outlining the operation of the Health and Safety at Work Act within that factory and the **implications** for the business concerned of this piece of legislation. You should also record examples which you consider to be infringements of the Act.

ESSAYS

1 'Legislation such as that concerned with employee and consumer protection and the regulation of potential monopolies causes the loss of international competitiveness. This is too high a price to pay.' To what extent do you agree? (AEB June 1989)

2 'Government legislation mostly affects firms which can least afford to pay for it, namely the small and the vulnerable. Large powerful firms are in a position to ignore, avoid or pass on the consequences to the consumer.' Put the case for and against this statement. (AEB November 1990)

CHAPTER 6

Business and Society

> ▷ ▷ **QUESTIONS FOR PREVIEW** ▷ ▷
>
> 1. How might anticipated changes in the population size and structure affect businesses in the UK and how should they respond?
> 2. What factors have led to demands for a shorter working week and what are the implications for businesses?
> 3. What are the costs and benefits to businesses of being socially responsible?
> 4. What types of industrial pollution exist and how are they controlled?
> 5. What impact has the environmental lobby had on business practice in the UK?
> 6. What are business ethics?

SOCIETY IS comprised of individuals and groups, organizations and institutions. Business cannot be separated from society as a whole – it is an integral part of it. Many relationships exist between business and society. It is not simply a matter of businesses responding to social changes; they also cause social change. In this chapter we shall look at a number of social changes and how they affect business – for example, the decline in the birth rate causing a shortage of entrants to the labour force (the so-called 'demographic time bomb') and the increased demand for leisure time and activities. We shall also look at instances where business decisions and actions have influenced society – for example, with respect to the environment. We shall consider the role of ethics in modern business and whether businesses have a responsibility to society beyond that set out by the law.

The Demographic Time Bomb

The 1990s will see a considerable change in the structure of the UK's population. Because of a decline in the number of births, as well as a fall in the death rate (the number of deaths per thousand of the population), the UK's population is ageing (i.e. its average age is rising).

The fall in the birth rate (the number of live births per thousand of the population) has been caused by a number of factors. Some couples are delaying having children because they want a high standard of living and do not wish to lose one of the partner's salaries – even temporarily. Also, many women wish to pursue a career and either are reluctant to have children or delaying having them until late in life, thus reducing the number they are likely to have. A key factor has undoubtedly been the increased use and reliability of modern methods of contraception. As with many social changes it is difficult to establish a single or most important cause.

A study by the National Economic Development Office (NEDO), *Defusing the Demographic Timebomb* (1989), identified a number of critical factors inherent in these changes:

- During the first half of the 1990s the number of school-leavers will decline dramatically. The number of sixteen year olds in the population will decline by nearly 30 per cent from its peak in the mid-1980s. The number will rise again in the latter part of the 1990s, but will remain below the mid-1980s figure. The graphs in Figure 6.1 (next page) illustrate the number of sixteen to nineteen year olds in the population as well as those of pensionable age.
- During the 1990s the age of the working population is set to rise. In 1988, 40 per cent of the

*Figure 6.1 – **Changes in the Make-Up of the UK's Population***

(a) Population aged 16 - 19

(b) Population of pensionable age[1]

1 1989 based projections.

1. Men aged 65 and over, women aged 60 and over.
2. 1989 based projections

Source: Social Trends 1991

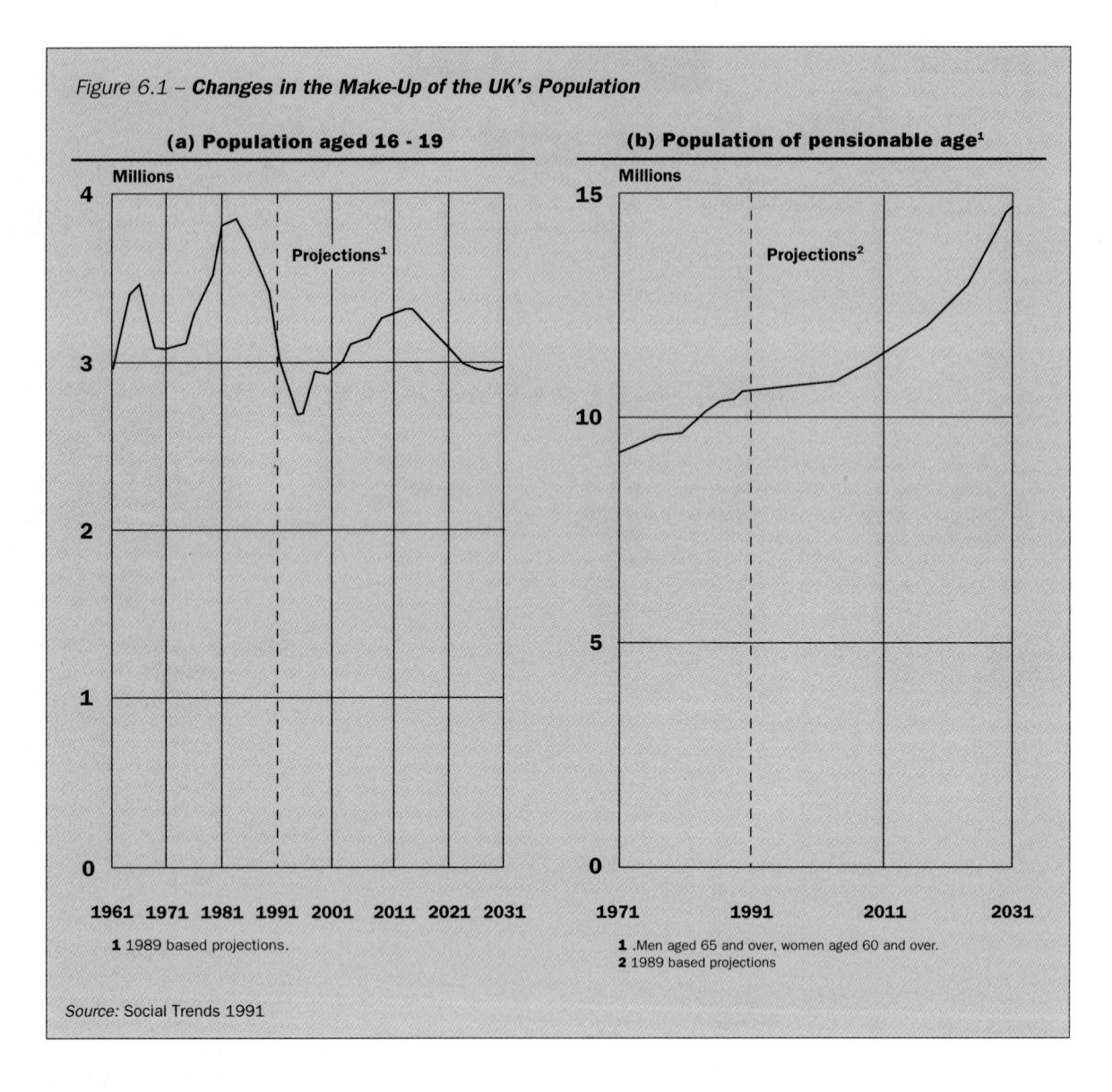

workforce was in the 35–54 age group – this is expected to rise by 46 per cent by the year 2000. At the same time a substantial fall in workers aged under twenty-four will occur

- Women are likely to replace the missing youngsters from the workforce. By 1995, women will represent nearly one half of the labour force available for work and will take four out of every five new jobs

A survey by the Institute of Manpower Studies conducted in 1989 showed that the decline in school-leavers is not spread evenly throughout the UK. The South East is expected to be least affected whilst the major cities (including those in the South) are anticipated to be worst affected. Those areas facing the largest fall in school-leavers are those with the greatest numbers of unemployed.

Most Western European nations are experiencing similar demographic changes and, therefore, are unlikely to provide the missing workers.

The report by NEDO showed that most employers were aware of the falling numbers of school-leavers and, indeed, a significant number had already experienced difficulty in recruiting young people. The report also revealed that although some were considering policy changes within their organizations, most were concentrating their efforts on trying to recruit from a dwindling pool of young people.

ALTERNATIVE SOURCES OF LABOUR

A number of possible solutions exist to this problem. Businesses can look to alternative sources of labour. Indeed, the Confederation of British Industry (CBI) emphasized this approach in its report, *Workforce 2000*. The group set to fill the gap and who have received the most attention are

> **CASE STUDY**
>
> ## Working Wives 'Will be the Key to Family Wealth in the 1990s'
>
> Families will be the key consumer group of the decade, with the working wife as the the key to household wealth, according to *British Lifestyles 1990*, a report by the market analysts Mintel.
>
> By 2001, there will be 2.7 million fewer people aged 15 to 29, but 2.9 million more aged 30 to 59, the report estimates. The number of children under 14 will rise by 1.1 million.
>
> The population shift towards the 30 to 59 age group will hit the clothing industry hardest, the report warns. The childrens' wear market will remain buoyant as the birth rate rises, but the decline in the 15 to 29 age group, traditionally the heaviest spenders on fashion, spells gloom for most clothing retailers and manufacturers. Average household spending on clothing is expected to decline in real terms by 7 per cent between 1989 and 1994.
>
> Families will spend more on savings, insurance and pensions, medicines, drinks and housing. Spending on pensions and life insurance is expected to increase by 12 per cent to £13.66 billion in 1994, with spending on medicines rising by 7 per cent to £1.37 billion.
>
> Household wealth has also been increased by the growing numbers of working wives. More than half the households with an income above £14 300 include a working wife, and nearly 7 out of 10 where income exceeds £29 000. Mintel predicts a surge in demand for nannies, but with the traditional nanny age-group declining, they will be hard to find.
>
> Source: *Independent*, 7 February 1990
>
> **QUESTION**
>
> 1 Assume you work for a clothing manufacturer. Your boss has seen the report by Mintel and is worried by it. She has asked you to write a brief report for a forthcoming board meeting to outline the implications of these population changes and the responses that a clothing manufacturer could take.

women re-entrants to the labour force – the so-called 'women returners'. The major barrier (as identified by the CBI's report) to large numbers of women returners entering the labour force is the need to look after pre-school age children.

Several surveys, including that of Mintel, have suggested that the offer of improved child-care facilities is the best way to increase the flow of women into the workforce. Many women returners also consider the provision of training – or retraining – as critical. Employers will also need to remove discriminatory age ceilings and place greater emphasis on job sharing, school-term contracts and breaks for having families. Such policies will involve firms in substantial expenditure, but this will be essential to attract large numbers of women into unfamiliar industrial sectors such as engineering. To attract women returners firms will not only need to provide physical facilities such as creches, but also alter company policy to allow training (remembering that women returners' training needs are likely to be different) and career development while recognizing women's responsibilities to their families.

ACTIVITY 6.1

Ask your female friends and relatives who have recently returned to work after a period at home the following questions:

(a) Why didn't they return to work earlier?
(b) For what reasons did they choose to work for the organization they joined?
(c) What could their employer do to make it easier and more enjoyable for them to pursue their career?

Their answers to these and any other questions you might ask should help you to gain an insight into the employer's need for staff, attitudes to women returners and the state of company policy in this area. Different friends and relatives are likely to give different responses.

Other groups exist which could help to overcome the demographic downturn. Businesses could increase the number of older workers on their payroll and recent redundancies mean that there is a plentiful supply of such workers. Alternatively, they may review their retirement age and policy. However, a change in employer attitudes is necessary if this source of labour is to be fully utilized. Many employers believe older workers have greater problems with change, are relatively difficult to retrain and are reluctant to take on increased responsibility. Such attitudes are reflected in ageist adverts which appear in the jobs sections of the press.

Employment patterns show that older workers often fill low-level, low-skill and low-pay positions. There is a tendency amongst employers to continue this pattern by putting older workers – irrespective of ability and commitment – into the sort of positions they already hold.

Other groups, such as the disabled, which have recently suffered high rates of unemployment may benefit from the demographic downturn by enjoying enhanced employment prospects.

OTHER STRATEGIES TO OVERCOME LABOUR SHORTAGES

Other strategies are available to businesses to overcome the problems inherent in the demographic downturn. Many firms are looking to strengthen their links with schools and colleges in order to encourage more applications from leavers. Firms may invest in institutions to gain a higher profile with students or may sponsor a student to ensure that he or she joins the firm on completion of studies. It may be that firms improve and extend their training to re-equip existing workers as well as to attract new employees into the organization.

It could be that firms will seek to maintain their current workforce and attract new entrants by enriching the jobs. This involves rearranging jobs to give workers greater responsibility and enjoyment. Such a strategy is not always appropriate and, indeed, enhancing some employees's jobs can have a detrimental effect on those of other employees.

As technology advances at an ever-increasing rate it becomes possible to replace labour with technology. The introduction of information technology into the newspaper industry caused enormous changes, including massive job losses and the relocation of much of the industry to more modern offices outside Fleet Street. The incentive for employers to follow this route will become greater as young labour becomes scarcer and – if the laws of supply and demand operate – more expensive.

Some firms, particularly those who are not tied to the UK, may seek to locate abroad. However, the creation of the Single European Market in 1992 means that barriers will exist for many goods imported from outside the EC. This may mean that firms have to stay within the EC, at a time when most members are facing similar population trends. Therefore, such a solution may be applicable to only a small number of firms.

Finally, as indicated earlier, a short-term solution could be simply to offer higher wages in order to attract the required number of appropriately skilled young people.

In the long term, businesses will have to develop a strategy which is suitable for them. The options discussed above cannot be ranked in order of preference since circumstances differ. For example, a manufacturing firm might be able to use technology to replace people, but this may not be an option for some firms in the service sector.

Although the changes in the population structure pose problems for businesses in terms of their labour supply, they also offer opportunities. The UK's ageing population means that more products and services associated with old age will be required. Thus there will be an increasing demand for old people's and nursing homes, for mobility aids and sheltered housing. As we saw in the last Case Study, firms that produce fashion items or other products mainly demanded by the young may well have to adapt their product to meet changing demand patterns.

KEY POINTS 6.1

- **Business influences society just as society influences business**
- **The number of school-leavers entering the UK workforce will decline until the mid-1990s and remain low**
- **Firms will need to consider other groups of workers to replace these 'lost' employees**
- **Much of the growth in the labour force will come from 'women returners'**
- **The ageing of the population will provide business opportunities for some firms**

The Length of the Working Week

Many people in the UK expect increased amounts of leisure time. This is a pattern which has firmly established itself over many decades. In Victorian times the standard working week was in excess of sixty hours.

*Figure 6.2 – **Weekly Hours Worked (UK Full-Time Manual Employees).*** This graph shows the steady decline in both actual hours worked and the length of the basic week since 1961. Why do you think that occasionally the actual hours worked figure rises?

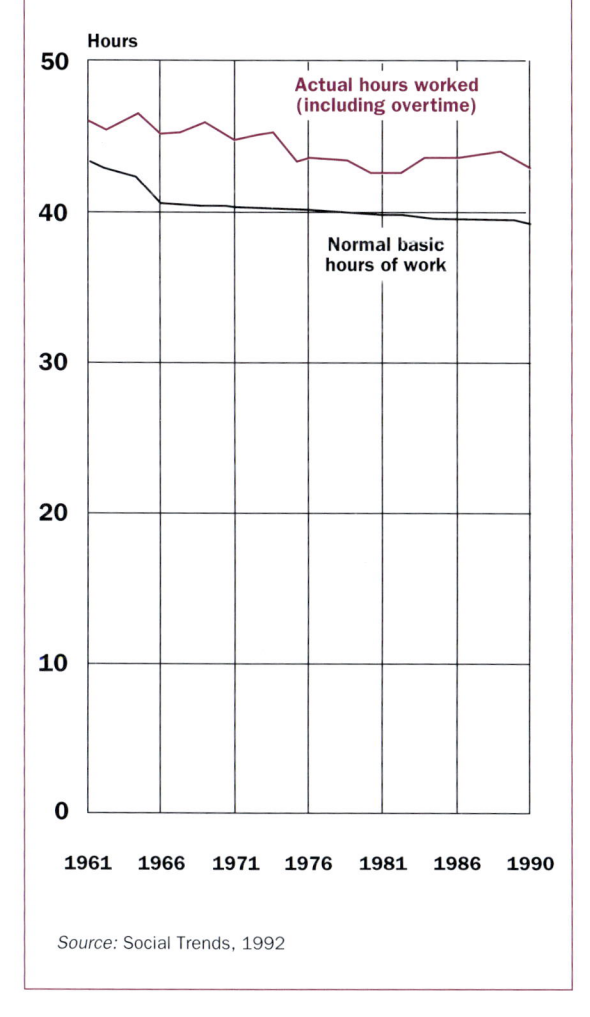

Source: Social Trends, 1992

Other nations in Europe have experienced similar expectations of reduced working weeks. Businesses have contributed towards these desires by adopting more efficient methods of output which allow production to be maintained during a shorter working week. They have also increased wages over the past few decades, giving people sufficient spending power to enjoy their increased leisure time, but at the same time leading them to demand more leisure time. The latest demands for a shorter working week have put pressures upon businesses because unless they can increase productivity to match the drop in hours, their costs of production will rise.

ACTIVITY 6.2

To establish the changes in the working week, ask some of your older relatives or friends what their working hours were when they first entered the labour force. You might also care to ask whether they were obliged to work at weekends and how they spent their leisure time. Now compare how they used their leisure time with people of today and think about the implications for business.

Such pressures can encourage employers to adopt new techniques of production which are more dependent upon technology and result in

*Figure 6.3 – **Battles Over Working Week***

Firms brace for battles over the 35-hour week

LEADERS of Britain's two million engineering workers are publicly committed to winning their members a 35-hour working week – the shortest in the industrial world. But they are still not sure how much cash and shopfloor muscle they can mobilize in pursuit of this prize.

After six months of skirmishing, the employers are increasingly convinced the union bosses will not, in the end, muster sufficient support. But if they do the directors and managers of the country's core manufacturing companies are determined to fight them every step of the way.

The average number of hours people work in a week has been dropping steadily everywhere since the nineteenth century, and is now typically around 40 or less (apart from Japan, where the figure is 46 to 48). But although 35 hours has been a widely quoted target for many years, and about 7 per cent of UK firms (mostly in finance and distribution) actually apply it, it has never been accepted nationwide in any country.

Source: adapted from the *Sunday Times*, 10 September 1989, Peter Wilsher. © Times Newspapers Limited 1989.91

job losses. It has been calculated that a four-hour cut in the average working week (from the current thirty-nine hours to thirty-five) with no improvement in productivity would lead to a 7.5 per cent rise in wage costs. Obviously some of this rise in costs would be passed on to the consumer in the form of higher prices. This would probably lead to less sales both at home and overseas. Overall it is estimated that the loss in jobs from a four-hour reduction in the working week would exceed a quarter of a million.

As Figure 6.3 (previous page) illustrates, there has been a steady trend towards a shorter working week for the majority of employees. This has not been achieved smoothly. Progress has been more rapid during periods of prosperity, with employers less willing to concede shorter hours during periods of recession. The recession experienced by the UK, and other countries, during the early 1990s certainly served to limit, and to a great extent halt, the move towards a reduced working week. Many employers are happier to grant large pay rises rather than cutting the working week since the former can be eroded by inflation whereas the latter is a once-and-for-all change.

*Figure 6.4 – **Britons Take More Holidays**. The graph shows that UK citizens have steadily taken more holidays since 1971. As with many of the issues discussed in this chapter, this has implications for businesses in terms of their workforce as well as their sales.*

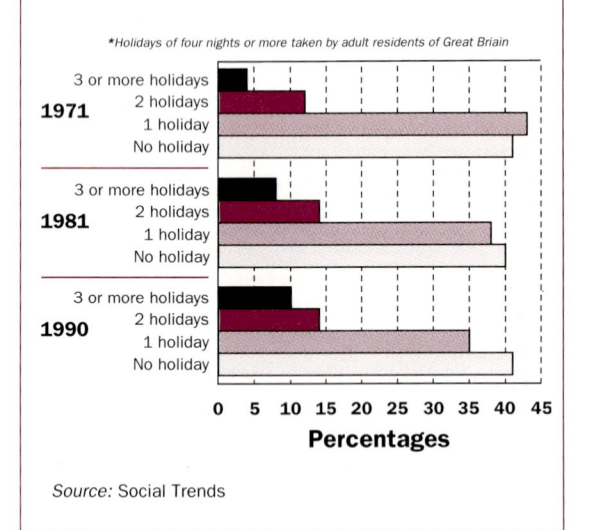

Source: Social Trends

---

*Figure 6.5 – **Household Expenditure 1988–89**. These figures relate to the percentage of total household expenditure on each item.*

United Kingdom — Percentages and £ per week

Average weekly household expenditure as a percentage of total (1988–89)

	Housing	Fuel, light and power	Food	Alcohol and tobacco	Clothing and footwear	Household goods and services	Motoring and fares	Leisure goods and services	Miscellaneous and personal goods and services	Average expenditure per household (£ per week)
United Kingdom	17.2	4.9	18.5	6.5	6.9	13.2	15.3	13.4	4.2	216.05
North	15.7	5.4	19.5	7.7	7.0	12.7	15.9	12.4	3.6	191.68
Yorkshire and Humberside	15.0	5.5	19.5	7.4	7.7	12.5	15.8	12.5	4.3	188.80
East Midlands	17.2	5.2	18.8	6.8	6.2	12.7	16.1	12.6	4.5	199.39
East Anglia	17.6	4.7	18.2	5.4	6.2	13.0	15.1	15.6	4.2	219.30
South East	18.6	4.1	17.7	5.5	6.8	13.8	14.8	14.3	4.5	250.98
South West	17.0	4.9	18.1	5.9	6.0	13.9	15.8	14.5	3.9	220.11
West Midlands	17.9	5.1	19.1	6.6	6.8	13.0	16.2	11.4	4.0	200.72
North West	16.8	5.1	18.3	7.7	6.7	12.2	14.6	14.2	4.4	205.26
England	17.5	4.7	18.3	6.3	6.7	13.2	15.3	13.6	4.3	219.57
Wales	15.4	5.7	19.2	7.0	7.6	13.1	15.8	11.8	4.2	197.10
Scotland	16.3	5.4	19.6	7.9	8.1	12.4	14.2	12.1	4.0	196.27
Northern Ireland	11.9	7.4	21.0	5.7	9.2	13.9	17.6	9.7	3.7	200.99

Source: Family Expenditure Survey, Central Statistical Office

> **KEY POINTS 6.2**
>
> - Society has expected and achieved increases in leisure time since the turn of the century
> - Rising real incomes have provoked a greater desire for, and ability to enjoy, increased leisure time
> - Conceding to demands for a shorter working week could significantly raise businesses's costs and possibly lead to job losses
> - Increases in leisure time also create opportunities for businesses

The pressure for such a change in working practices comes from a society in which expectations are continually rising. Leisure is becoming more important and people demand the time to enjoy it. This is also reflected in the holiday entitlement of the UK's workforce. Social Trends tells us that in the UK, 91 per cent of full-time manual employees were entitled to more than four weeks' paid holiday in 1989. Back in 1961, 97 per cent of employees were entitled to only two weeks. Judging by experience, however, the trend towards a shorter week is inevitable.

We have seen that society impacts on business through its demands for less time at work. This is partly fuelled by the continual rise in real wages enjoyed by employees which has allowed them to use their increased leisure time enjoyably. At the same time, the increased demand for leisure has provided a number of business opportunities. This is evidence of the close interaction between business and the remainder of society.

The whole sports industry, for example, has benefited from increased demand over recent years. Golf clubs have been opened, sports centres built and sales of associated products have increased. Expenditure on holidays at home and overseas has risen as has spending on admissions to a wide range of entertainments. Many firms have been quick to exploit these growing markets; a look at a colour magazine will confirm that marketing is often directed towards such new demand patterns.

Business and Social Responsibility

WHAT IS SOCIAL RESPONSIBILITY?

Various explanations of the term 'social responsibility' have been put forward, with many stating that it means being responsible to groups such as customers beyond the requirements of the law. However, Morgan in the *National Westminster Bank Review* in 1977 produced a wide ranging and useful definition which encompassed both internal and external aspects of the term. He defined it as:

> the extent to which individual firms serve social needs other than those of the owners and managers even if this conflicts with the maximization of profits.

Morgan's definition identifies a number of groups to whom a firm should be socially responsible. In relation to these groups firms should ask themselves: 'Do we obey the letter of the law or do we go beyond it in a number of areas?' For example, employees form a group which is part of the business. During a recession, a socially responsible firm may seek to maintain employment within the local community even at the expense of lowering profits.

However, this expresses only one view. Milton Friedman, the famous free-market economist whom we profiled in Chapter Three argues that a business can best meet its social responsibilities by making the largest possible profit and then by using its resources efficiently. A complex economic argument leads to the view that, to pursue any other policy would lead to a loss of competitiveness and ultimately to lower living standards and social welfare. However, this view tends to ignore the social costs of production (those that are borne by others), such as pollution, when measuring profitability.

HOW FIRMS MEET SOCIAL RESPONSIBILITIES

As we noted earlier, businesses have social responsibilities to a number of groups. For example, a firm

ANITA RODDICK
b. 1942

Anita Roddick and her husband Gordon are the two people who have masterminded the rise of the hugely successful Body Shop chain. The first shop was opened during the summer of 1976. The business commenced with a loan and prospered despite being sited next to a funeral parlour.

The Body Shop was instantly different from its competitors because it insisted on the use of natural ingredients and was strident in its encouragement of recycling materials, including the use of refillable containers.

It was Gordon Roddick who came up with the idea of franchising the business package in order to achieve rapid growth. (If you are unsure about franchises, re-read the appropriate section in Chapter Four). Franchising was a great success. By 1992 the Body Shop organization operated over 750 shops in forty-one countries using nineteen different languages. Somebody buys something from a Body Shop outlet somewhere every 0.57 seconds! In 1991, the business was worth £608 million with profits of £25.5 million. In April 1984 the business was floated on the Stock Market. During the first day its share price rose from £1.42 to £1.65.

Despite drops in its share price during the second half of 1992, Body Shop has continued to do well and fared much better than many other retailers over the course of the late 1980s and early 1990s recession, when consumer spending declined.

Another distinguishing feature is its concern for the environment. In May 1992 the Body Shop became the first UK company to issue an environmental statement (the Green Book) based on a full audit of its operations at its head office site. The business refilled nearly 560 000 bottles during 1991–92 and recycles a large amount of the packaging that it uses. Body Shop is now entering into an understanding with National Power, National Wind Power and Taylor Woodrow to identify a suitable site for a wind farm by the end of 1992. The intention is to hold a stake that is equivalent to the amount of electricity the business consumes. Unsurprisingly, Body Shop has won a number of environmental awards.

Body Shop also meets its social responsibilities in a number of ways. The company has organized the sending of relief supplies to Eastern Europe, runs nearly 750 community projects and operates schemes to raise awareness about endangered species.

The success of the Body Shop organization has led to Anita Roddick becoming arguably the UK's best-known female entrepreneur. Her involvement in environmental and social issues has meant she has a high media profile. The Body Shop organization shows no sign of resting on its laurels. It is looking to open retail outlets in the newly democratized Eastern European states and to encourage its employees to play greater roles in the management of the business.

(*Photo:* The Hulton Deutsch Collection)

---

may meet social responsibilities by building new factories on derelict land rather than on 'greenfield' sites. A firm can also have such responsibilities to customers to produce, for example, products or services which more than meet the minimum safety standards.

An increasing number of firms are analysing the social impact of the policies through studying such areas as health and safety, advertising, safety of products and environmentally sound products and processes. Social responsibilities can extend to providing local amenities such as sports centres and children's play areas. Alternatively, they may involve the provision of cultural facilities. For example, the supermarket chain Sainsbury's has endowed the city of Norwich with an art gallery (The Sainsbury Centre for Visual Arts) sited at the University of East Anglia.

Activity 6.3

Look at the area in which you live. Make a list of any examples you can find of firms exhibiting social responsibility. This section gives you examples of what you should be looking for. What are the differences between social responsibilty as displayed by big and small firms, by manufacturing and service industries?

Social responsibilities also include the training of employees (even though they might leave the firm once employed). Finally, such responsibilities could also be said to include using local suppliers in order to promote prosperity in the local community.

This does, however, pose difficulties since, given the limited resources available to most businesses, trade-offs exist. For example, a firm might be able to adopt ecologically sound production techniques only by installing new machinery which involves job losses. Moreover, businesses can suffer a competitive disadvantage by paying more than lip service to social responsibility – in extreme cases this could result in business failure. Such an argument is especially valid in respect of businesses engaged in international trade who may be competing with less responsible international competitors.

Social responsibility can increase costs in a number of ways. Training local unemployed workers rather than importing skilled employees from elsewhere can prove an expensive option, especially when the detrimental impact on productivity is taken into account. Such a choice can also prove costly when the alternative was to use modern, highly efficient technology.

Locating on a derelict site as opposed to a greenfield one is likely to be more expensive because of costs involved in clearing the site. Furthermore, the communication links may be better for a greenfield site rather than for a congested inner city location. The provision of social amenities to the local community can be costly even if they do help in obtaining planning permission from local councils.

WHY MEET SOCIAL RESPONSIBILITIES?

So why, you might ask, do some firms go to all this trouble and expense? They are not, after all, legally obliged to do so and by so doing may come into conflict with their shareholders who are likely to be seeking the highest possible profits.

Some firms do it because of the social conscience of the owners: they believe it is essential to meet responsibilities to the local community. Others engage in at least some socially responsible activities because it assists in improving their public image. Building a children's play area is a good piece of public relations. Certainly they wish to avoid the damaging publicity which may result from any form of environmental pollution. They believe socially responsible actions will improve their sales and profitability in the long term. It may also be that such actions enhance industrial relations with consequent commercial benefits. Undoubtedly such an approach improves communications with the local community and so confers benefits on both parties.

Increasingly firms use their caring social policies as a basis for their publicity. Nowadays many businesses produce publicity materials relating to, for example, their caring environmental policy. Obviously they believe that consumers are influenced by this aspect of business behaviour and respond accordingly. In other cases this kind of promotional literature and policy can be a reaction to past adverse publicity or a response to pressure from environmental groups or consumers. In recent years environmental protection has become an increasingly important aspect of business management.

Business and the Environment

Managing businesses so as to minimize the adverse impact on the environment now attracts an enormous amount of media and public attention. Society has come to expect higher standards of environmental performance. Opinion surveys conducted by the Department of the Environment

---

KEY POINTS 6.3

- Social responsibility means meeting the demands of society beyond the requirements of the law

- Businesses have social responsibilities to a number of groups such as local residents, local suppliers, customers and employees

- Meeting its social responsibilities can raise the costs of operating a business

- Businesses can derive positive publicity from fulfilling their social responsibilities

110 The Business Environment

Figure 6.6 – **Seeking Out Talent.** This poster is designed to show the general public that British Gas is not an uncaring monopoly! If you read the text you will see that it sets out some of the socially responsible activities in which British Gas is involved. In which publications would you place this advert if you were British Gas's publicity director?

British Gas is building new platforms for gas, oil and natural talent.

As you might expect, discovering new energy sources is one of British Gas' major goals.

Slightly less expected maybe, is our determination to help discover new sources of natural talent in the community.

To this end, we give substantial support every year to all areas of music and the arts, and direct this support to the places where it is most needed and most useful.

Without the British Gas funded Ballet Central, many inner city youngsters would never get to see, or try, ballet.

Our sponsorship of Cathedral Classics gives local choirs the chance to perform alongside the London Festival Orchestra.

We also sponsor the National Youth Jazz Orchestra, British Youth Opera, The English National Opera's Baylis programme and the National Youth Theatre. While our support of the Youth and Music Stage Pass Scheme gives young people the chance to enjoy performing arts at reduced prices.

Recently, we have also assisted the Royal National Theatre with sign language interpreted performances for the deaf.

But sponsorship of the arts is just a small part of our commitment to the community. By putting our energy into supporting projects that form part of the everyday necessities of life – from education to the environment – we believe we can help improve the quality of life for everyone.

British Gas

*Figure 6.7 – **The Public's Concern for the Environment***

People's interest is fickle but rising

OPINION polls suggest that most people's concern for the environment is a little fickle and strongly influenced by media coverage.

When times are good and the economy is growing, people worry about the fate of the planet and future generations. When recession looms or an international crisis blows up, green worries are shoved aside by more immediate concerns about personal security.

But polling suggests that something more fundamental happened in the late 1980s. A substantial proportion of the population – about a fifth – have had their environmental consciousness raised permanently and have changed their lives.

The changes made by these 'green activists' may not appear profound. They may have joined a pressure group, begun recycling bottles, cans and newspapers, switched to lead-free petrol. But they are starting to take the environment into account in everyday decisions. Green issues will affect what they will buy, where they holiday, and how they vote – even if it is not for the Green Party. The activists tend to be younger, better educated and more affluent than average.

Source: *Independent*, 10 September 1991

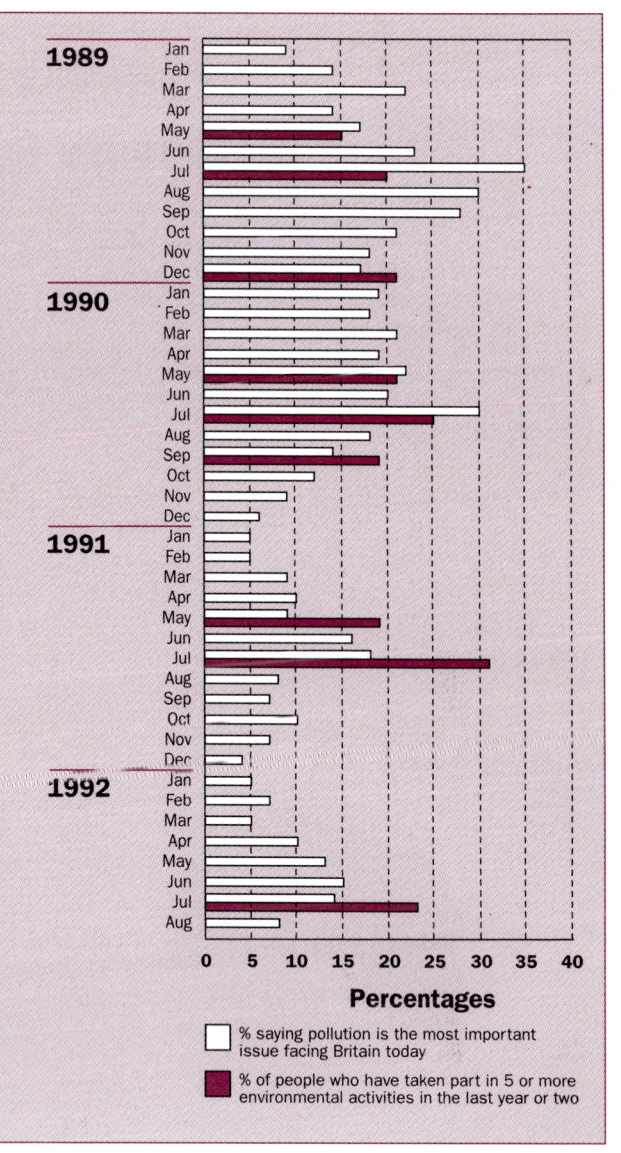

□ % saying pollution is the most important issue facing Britain today
■ % of people who have taken part in 5 or more environmental activities in the last year or two

showed that in 1990 about a third of those responding considered environmental matters as one of the most serious issues facing the government compared with a figure of only 8 per cent in 1986. The media attention given to the environment has both been stimulated by and a response to public interest in this topic. As a result, it has elicited a significant response from businesses. Firms have become aware of the importance of being seen as environmentally responsible and reacting to the growth of 'green consumerism'. Demand from consumers for 'greener' products is also creating opportunities for businesses.

Pollution and its Causes

A number of causes of damage to the environment have emerged over recent years. This is an enormous and complex area of study, but we shall briefly review a few of these and consider the role of businesses in causing environmental damage and their response to it.

a   Global warming

An insulating layer around the earth has been formed over many years by a concoction of gases, mainly carbon dioxide and chlorofluorocarbons (known for obvious reasons as CFCs!). This layer admits the sun's rays but prevents heat generated on the earth from escaping. As these gases develop in the atmosphere so the temperature on the planet's surface rises. These gases operate like the glass in a greenhouse to retain heat, giving rise to the name 'greenhouse effect'.

The Business Environment

CASE STUDY

Greenhouse Carbons Fear

Environmental groups hope Western European nations may be able to prevent President Bush from using this week's White House conference on global warming to slow moves to cut carbon dioxide emissions.

The President's senior advisors have attempted to pour cold water on scientists' growing beliefs that industrial nations must cut emissions of carbon dioxide, methane, nitrous oxide and chlorofluorocarbons (CFCs) if the earth's atmosphere is not to heat up – the 'greenhouse effect'.

Source: Sunday Telegraph, 15 April 1990

QUESTIONS

1. Why do you think the President's senior advisors 'have attempted to pour cold water' on the plans to cut emissions of allegedly dangerous gases?

2. What business activities cause the emission of methane into the atmosphere?

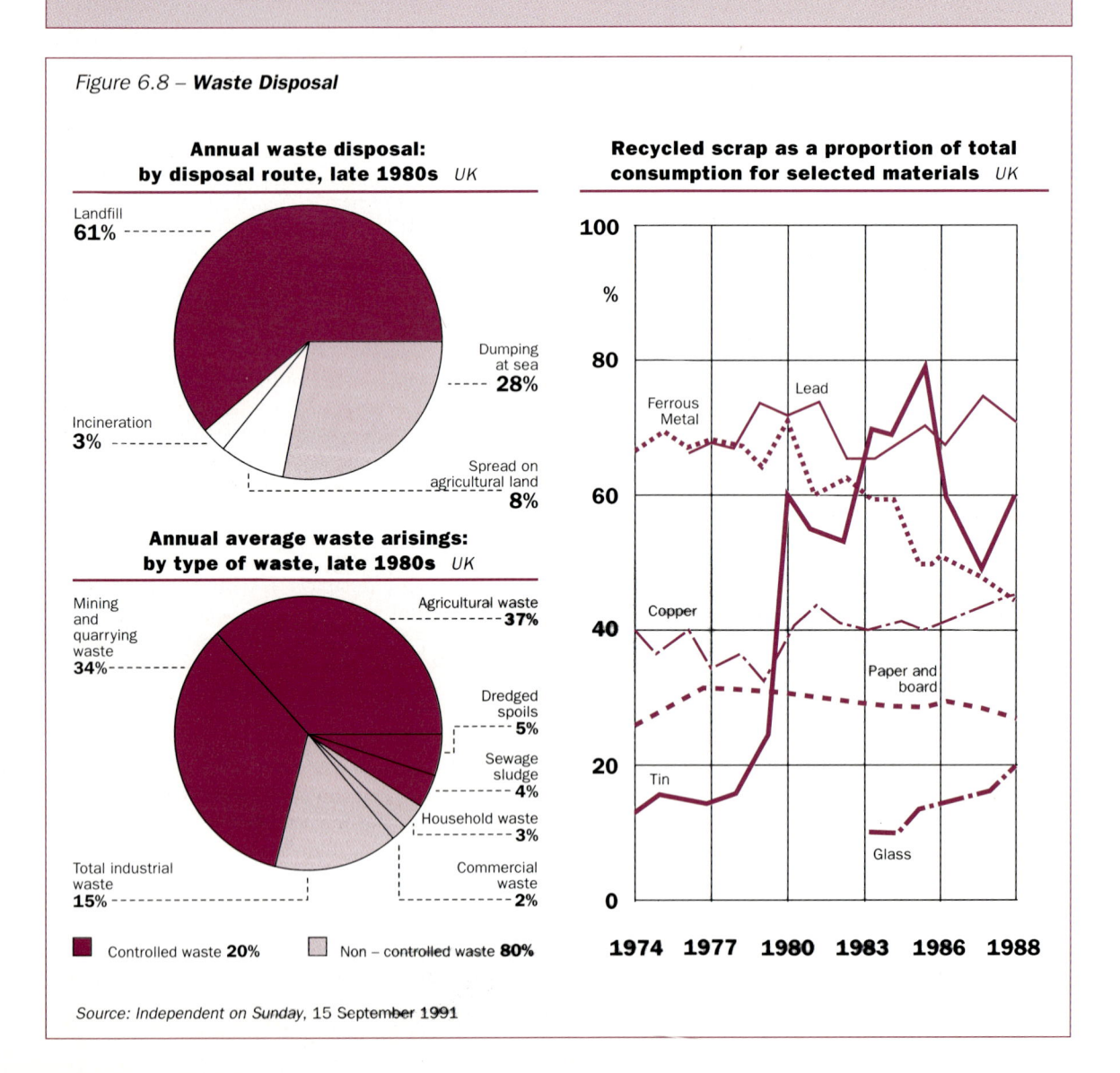

---

*Figure 6.8 – **Waste Disposal***

Annual waste disposal: by disposal route, late 1980s UK

- Landfill **61%**
- Incineration **3%**
- Dumping at sea **28%**
- Spread on agricultural land **8%**

Annual average waste arisings: by type of waste, late 1980s UK

- Mining and quarrying waste **34%**
- Agricultural waste **37%**
- Dredged spoils **5%**
- Sewage sludge **4%**
- Household waste **3%**
- Commercial waste **2%**
- Total industrial waste **15%**

■ Controlled waste **20%**   ☐ Non–controlled waste **80%**

Recycled scrap as a proportion of total consumption for selected materials UK

(Line chart showing %, 0–100, years 1974, 1977, 1980, 1983, 1986, 1988 for: Ferrous Metal, Lead, Copper, Paper and board, Tin, Glass)

Source: Independent on Sunday, 15 September 1991

b Acid rain

This is the result of acid substances and hydrocarbons entering the atmosphere and falling as rain. These substances can travel huge distances and fall as rain far from the source of pollution. For example, the Scandinavian countries have suffered acid rainfall as a result of emissions of sulphur dioxide from power stations in the UK. Acid rain causes damage to trees and animal life as well as buildings. It is also believed to have adverse long-term effects on water supplies. Businesses and society in general contribute to this type of pollution in a number of ways. By generating electricity using fossil fuels without the use of special filters, pollutants are emitted into the atmosphere. The results of this industrial process are exacerbated by society's profligate use of energy. Emissions from motor vehicles – which include hydrocarbons – also contribute to acid rain, yet society remains firmly reliant upon this form of transport.

c Depletion of the ozone layer

CFCs along with Halons (found in fire extinguishers and many other products) contribute to the depletion of the ozone layer. This is a thin layer about twenty-five kilometres above the planet's surface which filters out harmful ultraviolet rays from the sun. Scientists believe that the rays are a particular risk at the poles. If the amount of ultraviolet rays reaching the earth's surface increases substantially, then the result is likely to include an increase in the incidence of skin cancers and stunted plant growth. CFCs are found in aerosols, refrigerators and air conditioning systems as well as being employed in production processes required to produce foam – for example, packaging. As we saw earlier the use of CFCs in the EC has not diminished in spite of the adverse publicity surrounding their use.

d Waste

Almost every business activity produces waste of one kind or another. It is estimated that the UK generates between 500 and 700 million tonnes of waste annually. Figure 6.8 gives details of the UK's waste generation and disposal. This vast quantity of waste is disposed of in a variety of ways, the main one being the use of landfill sites and dumping at sea. Landfill sites can result in the build-up of harmful gases under the soil, whilst the pollution of the sea resulting from dumping is a highly controversial matter. UK industry produces waste which is categorized as 'non-toxic' as well as 'toxic'. The former is termed 'controlled waste' and contains substances harmful to life. The chemical industry produces large quantities of toxic waste whilst agriculture produces a large quantity of the non-toxic variety.

These are the major types of pollution and some of their causes. Scientists readily admit that they do not know all the causes or consequences of pollution. It is an area that continues to be researched by industry and governmental bodies.

---

*Figure 6.9 – **Effects of Pollution Not Fully Understood***

Pollutants damaging marine life

SCIENTISTS may have underestimated the damage to marine life caused by a group of pollutants released into the North Sea.

Researchers believe that organic compounds, such as pesticides and polychlorinated biphenyls, could be killing fish and other marine creatures in lower concentrations than previously thought. This reassessment is the result of new methods of detecting the presence of organic compounds in fish.

Source: adapted from the *Independent*, 30 August 1991

Private and Social Costs

Environmental pressure groups have caused many businesses to re-evaluate their costs of production. Businesses have been long aware of private costs – that is, the costs borne directly by the producer. These include rent and rates, labour, material and transport costs. They are relatively easy to calculate and are employed in the calculation of profits. However, the environmental lobby has increasingly felt that the true cost of production should include also those costs borne by third parties – the social costs of production.

Costs that businesses impose upon society include noise and congestion as well as air and water pollution; all of these can affect other local businesses and residents. If the polluting business either had to pay compensation to the third parties affected or adopt new (and presumably more expensive) production techniques, then the costs of production would be higher. As a result, the output and sales of polluting products would fall or the new techniques would eliminate or reduce pollution.

Measures to Protect the Environment

As protecting the environment has achieved a higher priority amongst societies throughout the world, so the pressures upon businesses to adopt environmentally friendly processes and products

*Figure 6.10 – **Lynx: Opposing the Use of Fur in Clothing***

"It takes up to 40 dumb animals to make a fur coat. But only one to wear it."

If this card seems offensive, it's because we find fur coats offensive.
Did you know that up to 40 animals had been gassed, electrocuted, strangled or lethally injected, just to make you feel <u>good</u>?
Or that many skins are torn from animals caught in traps long banned in this country due to their extreme barbarity?
We believe that anyone who knows what animals have to go through to make a fur coat, won't wear it.
We hope you won't. If you still do, you're even more dumb than we thought.

LYNX
PO Box 509 Dunmow, Essex.

Source: Lynx, PO Box 300, Nottingham NG1 5HN

internationally have grown. These pressures emanate from a variety of sources:

a Pressure groups

In Chapter One we looked at the activities of pressure groups. The environment is probably the main focus of pressure group action. Groups such as Greenpeace and Friends of the Earth are well known – indeed, attracting publicity to their causes is an important strategy pursued by most

*Figure 6.11 – **Green Audits***

Plan for 'green' audits

BRITISH AIRWAYS and Norsk Hydro, the Norwegian manufacturing group, are to conduct annual environmental audits to assess the ecological impact of their business activities.

Norsk Hydro's plans, amongst the first announced in the UK, involve adding an environmental statement to the annual accounts of its UK subsidiary, starting from the current financial year.

British Airways is drafting the first of what it hopes will become an annual environmental report to accompany the annual accounts, which will be published this summer. It will contain a numerical assessment of the business under six headings: noise, emissions, congestion, waste, tourism and staff involvement in the community.

Source: Financial Times, 18 March 1992

pressure groups. More specialized pressure groups exist – for example, Lynx which campaigns against the trade in animal furs (see Figure 6.10).

Businesses tend to make some response to the actions of pressure groups if only to avoid adverse publicity (see Figure 6.11, for example). Consumers are becoming more sophisticated in deciding what to buy and demand less environmentally damaging goods and services. Businesses which fail to respond to these changes will be at a significant competitive disadvantage. Later we shall look in detail at how businesses have responded to such pressures.

The development of the Green Party in many European states has reflected people's growing awareness of environmental issues. This has been further reflected by the adoption of environmental protection policies by more established political parties.

b The government
The UK is developing a range of legislation to cover most aspects of environmental pollution. This is a response to the demands of the electorate and also the European Community. The centrepiece of the control system is currently the Environmental Protection Act passed by Parliament in 1991. This introduced the notion of Integrated Pollution Control which recognizes that to control just one aspect of pollution is inadequate since the environment is an integrated system – damage to one part means damage to the whole. This Act therefore requires businesses to minimize pollution as a whole rather than simply concentrate on one aspect (such as water borne pollution).

The principle that 'the polluter pays' was enshrined by the passage of the Environmental Protection Act. The Act strengthens the environmental controls on industry. It sets higher standards for industrial emissions, effluents, waste disposal and resource management and provides the instruments for tougher enforcement.

The Department of Trade and Industry launched an environmental programme in May 1989 (see Figure 6.12 on next page). To oversee its work in this area the DTI has created an Environmental Unit. The DTI also operates an environmental hotline to provide businesses with a full range of information and advice relating to environmental issues.

The government's policy was clarified in September 1990 when it published its White Paper, *The Common Inheritance*. This set out the government's commitment in terms of minimizing energy use (and consequent pollution), ensuring labelling so that consumers can identify environmentally friendly products, reducing emissions from motor vehicles and cleaning up untreated discharges into the sea. So, for example, the disposal of sewage sludge into the sea is to be banned from 1997.

c The European Community
The EC has passed more than 200 regulations and directives relating to all aspects of environmental pollution. Directives cover the disposal of waste, control of air pollution, emissions from motor vehicles and freedom of access to environmental information. As an example, under a regulation introduced in March 1991 the production of all CFCs must be phased out by mid-1997 and halogens by the year 2000.

d International agreements
UK businesses are also affected by international agreements aimed at dealing with environmental problems. Indeed, some people argue that the only realistic response to protecting the environment is on a global scale. The consequences of the 1986 nuclear disaster at Chernobyl in the Soviet Union were felt throughout the world and highlight the need for international agreements on protective measures. As an example of an international agreement, the UK signed the Montreal Protocol of 1987 (revised in 1990 to include CFCs) which seeks to control the production of ozone-depleting chemicals throughout the world.

The Implications of Environmental Control for Business

The necessity of altering business practice and policy to take account of environmental protection has implications for most aspects of business behaviour.

There is pressure on businesses to redesign products so as to eliminate those that are most damaging to the environment. Thus, a new generation of environmentally friendly products are being developed. Some firms have invested huge sums in order to achieve this. Imperial Chemical Industries (ICI), for example, has developed a substitute chemical for CFCs for use in domestic fridges and freezers as well as air conditioning systems in cars. The programme to develop this new material entailed investing in new plants at Runcorn and Louisiana in the United States. However, ICI acknowledges that production costs for the substitute are 'at least five times as much . . . even after production economies of scale come into play'. This has obvious implications for the consumer in terms of higher prices.

Businesses are also seeking new sources of supply – either from sources whose supplies are renewable or result from recycling. You will have noticed the rapid increase in collection points for cans, glass and newspapers. That the public are prepared to use such facilities reflects the importance attached by society to the environmental

Figure 6.12 – The DTI's Environmental Programme

SELF HELP: A CHECKLIST

Business needs to plan now to improve its environmental performance and to meet the challenge of greater regulation and growing customer demand for goods and services which have a minimal impact on the environment. The best firms already include environmental considerations in their operations. Can you afford to be left behind?

The following questions may help you in your planning:

- What environmental risks do your firm's activities pose?
- Do your processes and materials pose any danger?
- What impact do your products (including their disposal) and services have on the environment?
- Do you know what quantity and type of waste you produce?
- Do you know how it is disposed of and what the cost is?
- Is your firm operating the most cost effective method of controlling or eliminating pollution risk?
- Are there hidden benefits (for example greater production efficiency) – or even straight business opportunities (for example commercial utilization of waste) – from adopting alternative methods of controlling or eliminating the risk of pollution?
- Can you meet the consumer demand for environmentally improved products?
- Are you aware of existing environmental standards and legislation in the UK and overseas?
- What arrangements do you have for monitoring your compliance with environmental regulations?
- Is senior management actively involved in ensuring that proper weight is given to environmental considerations throughout the firm?
- Could you improve your environmental image to the public and your employees by providing better information on environmental issues?
- Are you highlighting your environmental performance to private investors, financial institutions and shareholders?

Information contained in this booklet will help you in your consideration of the issues involved and provides sources of independent advice to help you plan for your business.

Setting environmental objectives

All environmental issues affecting your firm need to be addressed in your business plan. A good environmental plan would start with a statement which:

- commits the business to considering the environment as an integral part of its strategy, and ensuring that any threats of pollution from its activities are identified and either eliminated or effectively controlled;
- is endorsed by the head of the firm and committed to, where appropriate, at Board level;
- is brought to the attention of all employees;
- is available to the authorities and to the public.

And they carry through this commitment by:

- actively involving senior management and the workforce in ensuring that proper weight is given to environmental considerations throughout the firm;
- making all employees aware of their individual responsibilities for acting in accordance with the firm's policy, with clear lines of accountability back to senior management.

More than ever before, good environmental management makes good business sense.

Source: DTI, *The Environment – A Challenge for Business*

*Figure 6.13 – **British Airways Environmental Review.*** The aim of the Review is to assist British Airways in operating with minimal harm to the environment. To help achieve this aim, the company has established an Environmental Management Team.

Examples of the actions in hand, including some arising from the Technical review, are given below. The list is not comprehensive and forms only part of the environmental programme developed by the airline as part of its commitment to the environmental goal:

✔ **Commit at Board level to a corporate goal:** To be a good neighbour concerned for the community and the environment.

✔ **Prepare an inventory of aircraft emissions, including CO_2, CO, NOx, and UHC.**

✔ **Reduce and eliminate the use of CFCs in our operations:**

1) reductions of 20 per cent already achieved in cleaning of electronic parts,
2) substitute methods identified and being introduced for aerosol applications;
3) investigation of regulatory constraints that require use of CFCs;
4) release of CFCs in mandatory fire training

✔ **Convert the majority of the road transport fleet, where relevant, to lead-free petrol.**

✔ **Reduce the numbers of Chapter 2 aircraft in advance of regulatory requirements.**

✔ **Order, US$5,731 million worth of new technology aircraft and Rolls-Royce engines.**

✔ **Initiate an annual environmental report which will act as a measurement of the airline's performance.**

✔ **Survey our waste generation and disposal at Heathrow.**

✔ **Establish the quantity and quality of our aqueous effluents.**

✔ **Extend Energy Management schemes which have already achieved savings in energy consumption of value £6 million.**

✔ **Establish cross-functional working groups to address a range of topics, including waste, recycling and aqueous effluents.**

✔ **Increase staff awareness on environmental issues.**

✔ **Initiate 'Greenwaves', an environmental suggestion scheme, and 'Greenseal', an award for excellence for staff contributing to environmental conservation.**

✔ **Continue the conservation of species at risk through our 'Assisting Nature Conservation Scheme' programme, which has already aided the survival of more than 50 species worldwide.**

✔ **Continue a long-term programme of re-using, selling on and recycling many items that may have otherwise gone to waste.**

✔ **Establish at Director level an Environmental Council to review Environmental issues.**

Source: British Airways

---

question. Such new sources can be of lower quality and involve more processing at extra cost.

Possibly the most significant implication of the environmental question for businesses applies to production processes. These are often major sources of air, water and noise pollution and frequently result in large amounts of waste products, some of which are toxic in nature. Businesses are now being increasingly forced to invest in new factories and equipment by legislation as well as by the need to maintain a 'clean' public image.

For example, Shell UK has invested substantial sums to reduce the pollutant effects of its oil refineries and chemical plants. It invested £4 million in an energy recovery plant which burns waste materials from oil and chemical production and then returns the heat generated in the form of steam to the main plant. This process also segregates dangerous toxic waste for safe disposal. Similarly, ICI is investing millions of pounds in a new complex at its Billingham factory to, in its own words, 'completely eliminate the need for disposing in the Tees and at sea the acidic ammonium sulphate waste arising from its manufacture of perspex'.

New processes and products affect the human side of the organization as well. Change can sometimes be difficult to introduce, though many workers welcome changes intended to help protect the environment. New processes can result in redundancies as some jobs and skills become obsolete. It can, however, lead to the recruitment of people with new skills or to the retraining of existing workers in new techniques. A major area of training is that of environmental management. This entails ensuring that managers are aware of current environmental legislation, developing processes to meet the new legislative requirements and monitoring the changes implemented. Figure 6.13

illustrates British Airways's response to greater environmental awareness. Studies on behalf of the government suggest that even the largest firms are deficient in this respect and that further training is necessary.

Marketing is an area of business activity which has been greatly affected by the growing emphasis on protection of the environment. A brief look at the labelling of products in your local shops will indicate the changes that have taken place. Many aerosols are advertised as environmentally friendly, meaning that they contain no CFCs. Washing powders are promoted as containing less chemicals such as phosphates which can pollute the water supply. A number of firms have advertised on television and other media to assure potential customers of their concern for the environment and to inform them of the actions they are taking to protect it. Finally, most large businesses produce a variety of booklets and leaflets describing their activities, particularly in relation to the environment.

ACTIVITY 7.4

Write to the public relations department of a large company of your choice. Ask for details of their policies in respect of the environment. This material will give you a detailed insight into their operations as well as providing necessary and valuable examples for essays and coursework.

The implications of environmental protection for businesses are profound, especially for those in the 'polluting' sector such as chemicals and oil refining. They require a corporate response which affects all aspects of business behaviour. The exact nature of the response will depend upon the nature of the firm and its products. However, as with many changes in the business world, the environmental issue provides commercial opportunities. Firms who can be seen to meet society's need for a cleaner environment will gain a competitive advantage. Furthermore, a new market is developing for those who provide environmentally friendly technology or testing equipment to monitor waste products.

Business and Ethics

Ethics is defined as a code of behaviour considered morally correct, especially that relating to a particular group, profession or individual. This code of conduct is generally considered to be correct by most members of that society. Ethics relate to much business behaviour and they suggest what a business should and should not do in certain circumstances. Our individual ethics are shaped by a number of factors: the values and norms of our parents or guardians, those of our religion and those of the society in which we are raised.

Ethics in business raises a number of questions to which answers are usually unsatisfactory. To decide whether something is morally right or wrong depends upon your own moral code – only you can apply that. This section is intended to raise a number of issues but to leave you to draw your own conclusions about the rights and wrongs of each case.

Ethics in business is receiving a great deal of media attention at the moment giving rise to the question of whether tighter controls on business activities should exist. Ethical issues crop up in a variety of business activities.

In some cases, business behaviour borders on the criminal and on a relatively few occasions has been seen to cross that boundary. You may have seen or read about cases in which companies have been involved in what many people regard as highly unethical behaviour, such as selling weapons to irresponsible governments or groups.

KEY POINTS 6.4

- Society has come to expect higher standards of environmental performance from businesses
- Global warming, acid rain and the depletion of the ozone layer are believed to be major indicators of industrial pollution
- Businesses are encouraged to take account of the costs they impose on others by their activities
- Pressure groups, the UK government and the EC all seek to improve the environmental performance of UK businesses
- Protection of the environment requires a corporate response that will affect all areas of a firm's activities

CASE STUDY

BCCI Fraud

Deposits worth billions of pounds were frozen yesterday when the Bank of Credit and Commerce International, one of the biggest privately-owned financial companies in the world, was closed down after the discovery of widespread fraud.

The Bank of England set up a special unit to co-ordinate action against the Luxembourg-based bank in 69 countries, and papers have been sent to the Serious Fraud Office. Robin Leigh-Pemberton, the Governor of the Bank of England, said he had moved after an accountants' report disclosed 'widespread fraud at a very high level'.

The bank has 25 branches in Britain, most of them in London. It is a leading banker for the Asian business community and about 120 000 accounts are held by Britons whose deposits total £250 million. Commercial banks around the world may lose billions on inter-bank trading in the collapse.

Last year the bank admitted laundering drug money for the former Panamanian leader General Manuel Noriega and was fined $15 million by a Florida court.

Source: adapted from the *Times*, 6 July 1991, Neil Bennett and Stewart Tendler. © Times Newspapers Limited 1989.91

QUESTIONS

1. What groups will suffer as a result of the Bank's fraudulent activities?

2. Could any benefits have resulted from the Bank's 'support' for the South American drug trade?

Another major ethical issue relates to the activities of the tobacco companies. Is it ethical to promote a product which most of the medical profession believes to be a major cause of premature deaths? Although disputed by the tobacco companies, critics offer much evidence to support the claim that tobacco endangers life. Furthermore, opponents of tobacco companies now argue that they are targeting the less sophisticated consumers of the Third World with their products (see Case Study on next page).

Advertising is an area of business activity that has been closely scrutinized on ethical grounds in industries other than tobacco. For example, is it ethical to advertise children's products during intervals on children's television programmes and so, in some cases, create expectations that cannot reasonably be fulfilled? Other cases have appeared where it was felt by some that the advertising was misleading or unfair.

Advertising has been criticized on ethical grounds, for creating desires for goods and services which may not have existed otherwise. If consumers cannot afford these goods they may end up in debt and experience dissatisfaction at being unable to fulfil their desires. Vast amounts of money are spent on advertising: in the UK it is between 1 and 2 per cent of the nation's national income. Critics argue that this only adds to the cost of goods and services. Moreover, as the Sugar Controversy Case Study shows (on page 121), advertisements can be used to encourage people to consume goods which are addictive and harmful to health.

Businesses defend their advertising policies by saying that it is an important part of communication between the business and the consumers. How, they argue, would customers get to know about new goods and services otherwise? They also contend that it is an important part of healthy competition and encourages research and the development of new products. Furthermore, it encourages competitive pricing which helps the consumer. Finally, some firms express the view that much advertising is informative and thus helps the community – for example, advertising that explains the dangers of AIDS and the precautions that should be taken.

There is a sense in which these arguments differ. Critics tend to attack advertising on ethical grounds whilst the defence tends to be more commercial. Does the fact that advertising leads to economies of scale and cheaper, more modern goods comprise an answer to an accusation of a moral wrong?

Recently, supermarkets have attracted considerable criticism for their pricing policies. Opponents of their policies have argued that by maintaining artificially high prices for essential purchases they are exploiting consumers. Verdict: a retail industry analyst has produced figures showing that the gross margin on fresh foods

CASE STUDY

Tobacco Companies Target New Markets

Cigarette sales are declining in the health conscious West, so tobacco giants are turning to the Third World, where poverty and ignorance provide a market that is easy prey to modern marketing. The British company BAT is heading the drive and believes it is doing nothing wrong.

Standing outside his corrugated iron home in the uplands of central Kenya, Francis Kabui draws deeply upon a Sportsman cigarette. He has already lost part of one lung to cancer and is waiting for the results of tests on the other, which has developed an ominous shadow. Francis Kabui started smoking because everyone in the adverts wore shoes. Today he is dying.

Kabui, 46, a farmer on the arid plateau between Nairobi and Mount Kilimambogo, has been smoking for 32 years and is resigned to his rapidly deteriorating condition. As his young family put their arms around him last week, he said softly: 'If I had known tobacco was going to kill me, I would have banned anybody from growing it. Now I don't have the strength. If I'm to die, what difference does it make anyway?'

Four years ago when he had his lobectomy at Kenyatta National Hospital in Nairobi, Kabui did not understand the word. Lung cancer was very rare in his country.

Kabui is, in part, a victim of an aggressive international marketing strategy practised by the world's biggest tobacco companies over many years.

Today, faced with a decline in the traditional markets in the West, where health warnings and advertising regulations have pushed down sales, the tobacco giants are stepping up their drive into the growing markets of the developing world.

Leading the campaign is BAT, Britain's fifth largest company and joint biggest tobacco company in the world. Last year, 20% of the 3 000 billion cigarettes consumed in the free world were produced by BAT.

An investigation by the Insight team into BAT's marketing strategy has revealed that it is operating a double standard – one for the West and another for the Third World.

It is taking advantage of loosely enforced or non-existent government health restrictions to target millions of poor and ignorant people in what is becoming tobacco's final frontier. Its strategy entails:

- Marketing brands of cheap addictive cigarettes
- Making misleading claims to governments in developing countries that smoking is not harmful and that health warnings are counter-productive
- Using political and economic leverage to support its market dominance
- Designing advertising to play on the desire in developing countries to mirror Western sophistication

Source: adapted from the *Sunday Times*, 13 May 1990.
© Times Newspapers Limited 1989.91

QUESTIONS

1. Do you think the article is purely factual and unbiased?

2. Do you think BAT is behaving unethically? In about 100–200 words write down your conclusions.

3. Write to the Tobacco Advisory Group (the trade association of companies manufacturing tobacco in the UK) and ask for a copy of its materials relating to the smoking debate. Read critically the materials you receive and review your answers to the first two questions.

---

in UK supermarkets has risen from 21 per cent in 1986 to 28 per cent in 1990 (see Figure 6.14). Suggestions have, however, been made that a lack of competition between UK supermarkets has accounted for a part of the rising profit margins enjoyed over recent years.

Ethics have taken a higher profile in the business world in recent years. Businesses want to be seen to act ethically, partly because a 'good' image helps boost sales and to attract investment.

In the past, some individuals and organizations

CASE STUDY

Sugar Controversy

A glossy teaching pack sent by the sugar industry to all primary schools was 'misleading and inaccurate', according to a group of health experts.

Action and Information on Sugars, a group of doctors, dentists and nutritionists, said information it contained contradicted the Department of Health's dietary targets.

The group said the 75-page teaching pack presented by the British Sugar Corporation and Tate & Lyle as educational material was scientifically inaccurate and nothing more than marketing which encouraged excessive consumption of sugars.

The Department of Health's dietary targets effectively recommend that children cut sugar intake considerably. The maximum recommended for seven to ten year olds is on average 10 teaspoons a day from all sources, yet one Coca-Cola contains seven and a Mars Bar five.

Source: *Independent*, 9 September 1991

QUESTIONS

1. What type of organization is 'Action and Information on Sugars'?

2. To what extent do you think this extract is a clear indicator that unethical business has been practised?

Figure 6.14 **High Retail Profits.** The UK's supermarkets enjoy high profits in comparison to their European rivals. When profits are expressed as a percentage of the value of capital employed in the business, the returns of UK supermarkets can be seen to be more than twice as high.

The great divide
Food retailers 1989–90

Britain	Net profits as % of: assets	sales
Kwik Save	14.6	3.8
Tesco	12.1	5.1
Marks and Spencer	11.7	7.2
Argyll	10.5	4.6
J. Sainsbury	10.5	4.8
Asda	5.8	3.9
average	**10.9**	**4.9**

Continental Europe

Ahold (Holland)	5.7	1.4
Comptoirs Modernes (France)	4.9	1.7
Ava (Germany)	4.9	1.5
Delhaize-Le Lion (Belgium)	4.6	1.2
Carrefour (France)	4.2	1.7
Promodès (France)	3.9	1.3
Au Printemps (France)	3.8	2.3
Docks de France (France)	3.5	1.2
Asko (Germany)	2.4	1.5
Casino (France)	2.0	0.9
average	**4.0**	**1.5**

Source: COI

---

refused to invest in businesses which traded with South Africa because of the policy of Apartheid which formerly operated in that country. Now, however, investors have other ethical matters on their mind. The Co-operative Bank advertises that it will only invest depositors's funds with ethical businesses and not, for example, with businesses which conduct experiments on animals. Clearly the bank believes this will help attract customers.

Similarly, investment funds exist which promise not to invest in firms which damage the environment or in firms involved in the processing or sale of meat.

KEY POINTS 6.5

- **Ethics is a code of behaviour believed to be morally correct**

- **Business ethics have received a great deal of attention from the media in recent years**

- **Advertising is an area in which ethical questions are frequently asked – for example, is it ethical to advertise tobacco?**

EXAM PREPARATION

SHORT QUESTIONS

1. List three groups to whom the firm has some responsibility.
2. Name three pressure groups that might try to influence the activities of manufacturing firms.
3. State three major environmental problems caused by industrial activity.
4. Outline the major changes in the UK's population structure expected by the turn of the century.
5. Name the main pieces of legislation designed to control industrial pollution.
6. Identify two possible solutions available to a firm to help overcome the shortage of school-leavers.

DATA RESPONSE QUESTION

In February 1986, the Greater London Council introduced a policy to control the movement of heavy lorries in London.

GLC Scheme
(i) Lorries over 16-tonnes banned from 9.00pm to 7.00am every weekday.
(ii) The ban operates all day at the weekends.
(iii) Companies wishing to use heavy lorries during banned hours are required to fit 'hush kits'. Heavy lorries without such kits require a permit to enter the area.

Questions

(a) What reasons might the GLC have had for introducing these regulations?
(*6 marks*)

(b) Briefly state the arguments that firms might make publicly against the introduction of these regulations. (*12 marks*)

(c) The 'Hush Kits' have been readily available for some time. Why have very few lorries fitted them? (*2 marks*)

(AEB November 1987)

BTEC ASSIGNMENT

You are employed by the Economic Development Office of your local council. You have been asked to prepare a profile of your district which could be given to firms interested in setting up in your area.

You should therefore research the following to provide the information for your profile:

- The current and predicted population (including the structure of the population)
- A map of the region showing urban and rural areas and transport links
- The assistance offered by the council to firms moving to the area and policies on matters such as pollution
- The types of business existing in the area already
- Photographs and charts as necessary to support your profile

This list is only a guide. You may be able to think of other factors which will help to show the economic and social make-up of your area. Remember to present the information as supportively as possible so as to attract new businesses to your region.

ESSAYS

1. A large manufacturing company holds a dominant position in the economy of a town. Identify the social responsibilities the enterprise may have to the locality and its population. Discuss the ways in which the company may attempt to meet such responsibilities. (AEB June 1983)

2. In the 1990s population trends will reduce the number of young people entering the workforce. How might a firm respond to this situation? (AEB June 1991)

3. 'Advertising is unethical.' Discuss this view. (AEB November 1988)

CHAPTER 7

Business and Trading Abroad

▷ ▷ QUESTIONS FOR PREVIEW ▷ ▷

1 What are the main goods and services which the UK imports and exports?

2 In what ways can UK firms trade overseas?

3 What methods of payment exist for businesses who trade internationally?

4 In what ways can the exchange rate affect UK businesses and the country's balance of payments?

5 What are the major obstacles to international trade?

6 What are the major international economic organizations which affect overseas trade?

OVERSEAS TRADE is vital to the UK and its businesses. The UK is the world's fifth largest trading nation – after the United States, Germany, Japan and France. The UK has a population approaching 60 million and produces only a small part of the foodstuffs required by its citizens. The food produced at home therefore needs to be supplemented by that grown in other EC nations and further afield. UK businesses also import large quantities of raw materials from overseas; these materials are not available in the UK. For example, the UK imports high-grade iron ore from Sweden and tobacco from the United States of America. In spite of the decline in exports of manufactures outlined below, the UK has a tradition in trading worldwide. Many businesses and jobs depend upon the continuance of this tradition.

The UK's Changing Trading Pattern

On the first day of 1973 the UK became a member of the European Community. (In Chapter Eight we will look in detail at the causes and implications of this change.) At the same time the UK's trading pattern began to change.) Increasingly, it began to exchange goods and services with fellow members of the EC whilst at the same time ties with Commonwealth trading partners, Australia and New Zealand, for example, were weakened. The creation of the Single European Market has tied the UK further to Europe as a trading partner.

The pattern of goods and services which are traded has also changed dramatically. UK businesses have had to adapt to these changes and the rate of change is unlikely to slow. The UK's role as a major producer of manufactured goods has declined as the economy has switched to supplying services. Sales of UK manufactures have declined, both at home and abroad, mainly because of poor marketing, a reputation for poor design and quality, delays in delivery as well as uncompetitive prices.

In the late 1980s the UK became, for the first time, a net importer of manufactures. This means that for the first time the UK imported a greater value of manufactures than she exported. Among the UK's major exports currently are services such as banking and insurance.

These changes do not mean that trade is in any way less important to UK businesses. Indeed, the move to the Single European Market in 1992 meant that the UK became more reliant upon trading overseas. The Single European Market has opened up UK markets to producers from other EC members and means that UK firms will have to compete successfully at home and abroad in order to survive.

*Figure 7.1 – **The UK's Pattern of Trade***

Exports

- Total to developed countries 81%
- European Community 53%
- Rest of Western Europe 9%
- North America 14%
- Other developed countries 12%
- Eastern Europe and Soviet Union 1%
- Oil-exporting countries 5%
- Other countries 5%

Imports

- Total from developed countries 85%
- European Community 52%
- Rest of Western Europe 12%
- North America 13%
- Other developed countries 7%
- Eastern Europe and Soviet Union 1%
- Oil-exporting countries 2%
- Other countries 11%

Legend:
- Developed countries
- Eastern Europe and Soviet Union
- Oil-exporting countries
- Other countries

Differences between totals and the sums of their component parts are due to rounding

Source: HMSO, *Britain 1992 – An Official Handbook* (1992)

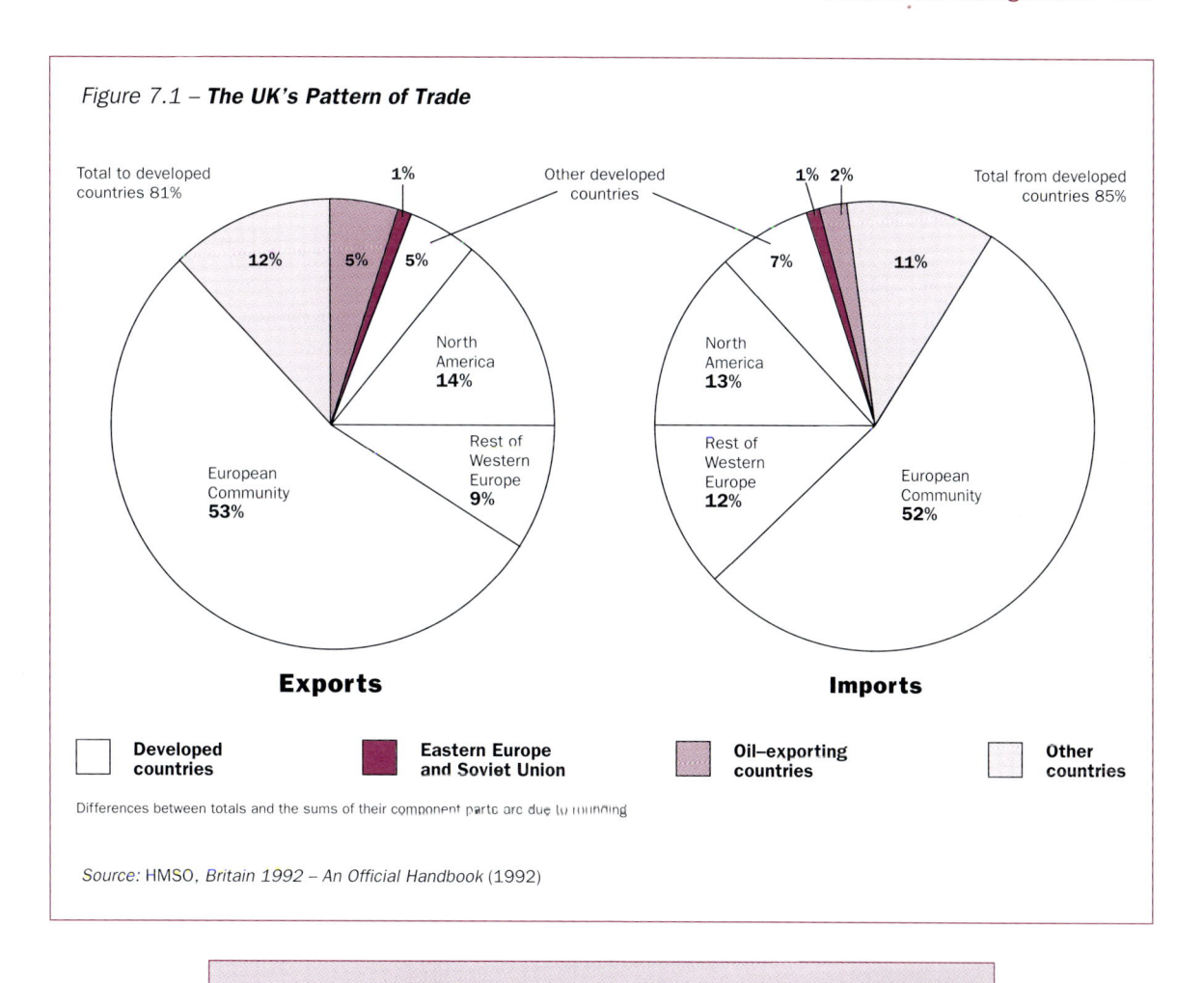

KEY POINTS 7.1

- The UK is one of the world's major trading nations
- The UK is carrying out an increasing proportion of its trade with the European Community
- The UK is exporting fewer manufactures at the same time as such imports have increased

---

Methods of Trading Abroad

There are several ways in which firms can trade abroad. Many UK firms are based in this country but sell a proportion of their output of goods and services overseas. There will be a number of firms within your locality who fall into this category. They may not be very large, but could be highly specialized and internationally successful in their field. Alternatively, they may be less specialized but are seeking to expand their market by selling abroad. Finally, you may know of some large organizations who are major sellers in international markets.

Agents or Distributors

This system was very popular with UK firms after 1945 and continues to be used, less extensively, today. It simply requires UK exporters to select foreign distributors to stock, market and sell their goods or services. In return for this service the agents retain a portion of the profit earned on each sale. This system has the advantages of cheapness and ease of establishment. It also carries a low degree of risk since the business has not committed a large amount of resources to the enterprise.

To be successful agents should be selected

carefully and trained in selling the good or service. A system of motivation is also essential if sales in this market are to grow. Financial inducements may not be sufficient to achieve this. It may be that the creation of an overseas training group to train agents is necessary. Visits by these personnel will support financial methods of motivation by creating a sense of belonging.

Activity 7.1

By consulting your local paper or *Yellow Pages*, identify garages near you that act as agents for foreign car producers. Visit one of these garages and explain to the manager that you are a business studies student. Ask the manager how their particular agency system operates. Key questions you could ask may include:

- How did the garage acquire the agency?
- Where are the nearest other agents for the same car company?
- What support does the parent company offer in terms of training, marketing, etc?
- For what length of time is the agency agreed?
- Does the parent company set sales targets which the agent must meet?

Follow this up by writing a short piece to summarize the main features of such agencies and their advantages and disadvantages to both parties.

Licensing

Through this system, a business grants permission to a third party to produce their product. This method of exporting is becoming increasingly common, particularly so in the beer and lager markets where the transport costs preclude home production in many cases. Many of the Australian lagers, for example, are produced under licence in the UK.

Licensing can take a number of forms. You will be familiar with franchises from Chapter Four. Firms such as McDonald's have used this method to expand quickly overseas and also as a means of entering centrally planned economies. Licences can also relate to the sale of trademarks or patents.

By selling a licence in whatever form the exporting firm receives a payment. Usually this will comprise an initial charge as well as payments related to each unit sold. Nowadays licensing agreements are very complex and are drawn up by international lawyers. Besides royalties, they will include conditions relating to a minimum sales quantity, renewal and termination of the contract and, in some cases, give the exporter the right to purchase equity in the licensee's business.

Licensing offers a number of benefits to the licence holder. As with agents the initial investment is very low and so, therefore, is the risk. It can be a method of establishing a business or product in a national market which has features different from those with which the exporter is familiar, or a very small market in which it is not viable to create productive capacity. Creating a successful name in other countries may assist with marketing the business's other products overseas. For example, Rolls Royce's reputation for quality and reliability in the motor car market has obviously helped its sales of aeroplane engines. It may also result in close collaboration with the other firm to the further benefit of the exporting company.

The exporter will have to ensure that – particularly in the quality conscious 1990s – all quality control standards are met by the licensee's product or service. If not, a hard-earned reputation for quality can be easily lost.

Activity 7.2

Whilst out shopping, look at labels of products which you believe to be of foreign origin. Compile a list of these products which are produced under licence in the UK. The packaging should contain this information. Note the name of the 'exporting' company and the licensee within the UK.

Establishing Joint Ventures

This involves companies reaching agreements to support one another's activities in a variety of ways. Companies may choose to undertake research and development jointly, to market one another's products in their home markets or to produce joint products or services. Such joint ventures have become common, particularly in the motor industry.

Joint ventures are a relatively cheap way of expanding into overseas markets as well as gaining technical advice and support. They are also unlikely to lead to opposition from nationalistic governments.

Joint ventures can, of course, lead to disputes between the partners. This may occur because of differing objectives in creating the partnership, differing management styles and cultures or unclear agreements. To be entirely successful such ventures have to be based upon mutual confidence. There is also a need to ensure that any differences in corporate policies and management styles do not prevent objectives from being reached. The current popularity of such

CASE STUDY

Joint Venture in the Car Market

Volvo's link up with Renault, the state-owned French vehicle giant, marks the latest in a remarkable series of deals that are reshaping the European motor industry.

For about £1.1 billion, Volvo will buy a 25 per cent stake in Renault, which – after Rover's link with Honda of Japan – had been left as the most isolated volume-car business in Europe.

Renault, in turn, will take a 25 per cent stake in the Swedish group's car operations and will buy 10 per cent of the Volvo parent company in the open market.

The deal satisfies both groups: Volvo gets a foothold in the European Community ahead of 1992 and marries its specialist car operation to a volume producer; Renault finds a strong and profitable financial partner – Volvo has about £1.6 billion in net cash.

Over the past six months the European motor industry has been in turmoil because of fears about overcapacity and competition from Japanese rivals. Quotas on Japanese cars are expected to be lifted within four years if the European Commission gets its way.

Source: adapted from the *Sunday Times*, 25 February 1990, Andrew Lorenz and Iain Jenkins.
© Times Newspapers Limited 1989.91

QUESTIONS

1 Make a list of all the benefits that you can think of that Renault will receive from its link with Volvo.

2 What is meant by the term 'overcapacity'? Why should European car producers be worried about it?

---

agreements suggests that these difficulties can be overcome.

Setting Up Overseas Companies

This is an option for larger businesses who have the confidence, capital and skills to establish a foreign business. Firms who elect to do this can either create their own business or buy an established enterprise.

A firm which chooses to export in this way will expect to sell large quantities to justify the large investment involved. This approach to exporting will be favoured by businesses who have achieved all the available economies of scale within their domestic operations and are seeking to establish a branch plant elsewhere.

This method can help firms to get around tariff or quota barriers and has been employed by a number of Japanese firms to avoid the trade barriers (known as the Common External Tariff) which surround the European Community. Prime examples are the Nissan car plant at Sunderland and the Sony television factory at Bridgend in Wales which has been operating since 1973 (see Figure 7.2 on next page). Producing overseas may also offer tax advantages to the businesses concerned.

Such a decision must be strongly influenced by the availability and cost of capital to the company concerned. It is undoubtedly an expensive option.

The risk involved in this course of action is clearly much greater than that involved in the use of agents or licensing. The more fixed assets that the company purchases, the greater the degree of risk. The failure or loss (perhaps due to political change or nationalization) of a large manufacturing plant could destabilize the entire business. As we shall see later in this chapter, fluctuations in exchange rates can alter both expected costs and revenues.

Exporters have to establish or find a business with a good track record and reputation. They have to take into account the differences in culture, personnel practice, regulations and laws which will affect the operation. They will have to consider carefully whether they have the necessary management skills within their organization to run the new enterprise successfully. Their manpower plan will have to take into account the different skills required and the training necessary to manage overseas.

In spite of these problems, multinational companies are becoming more common and important as they take an increasing share of world production and trade. Nestlé, for example, now operates more than two hundred companies in five continents.

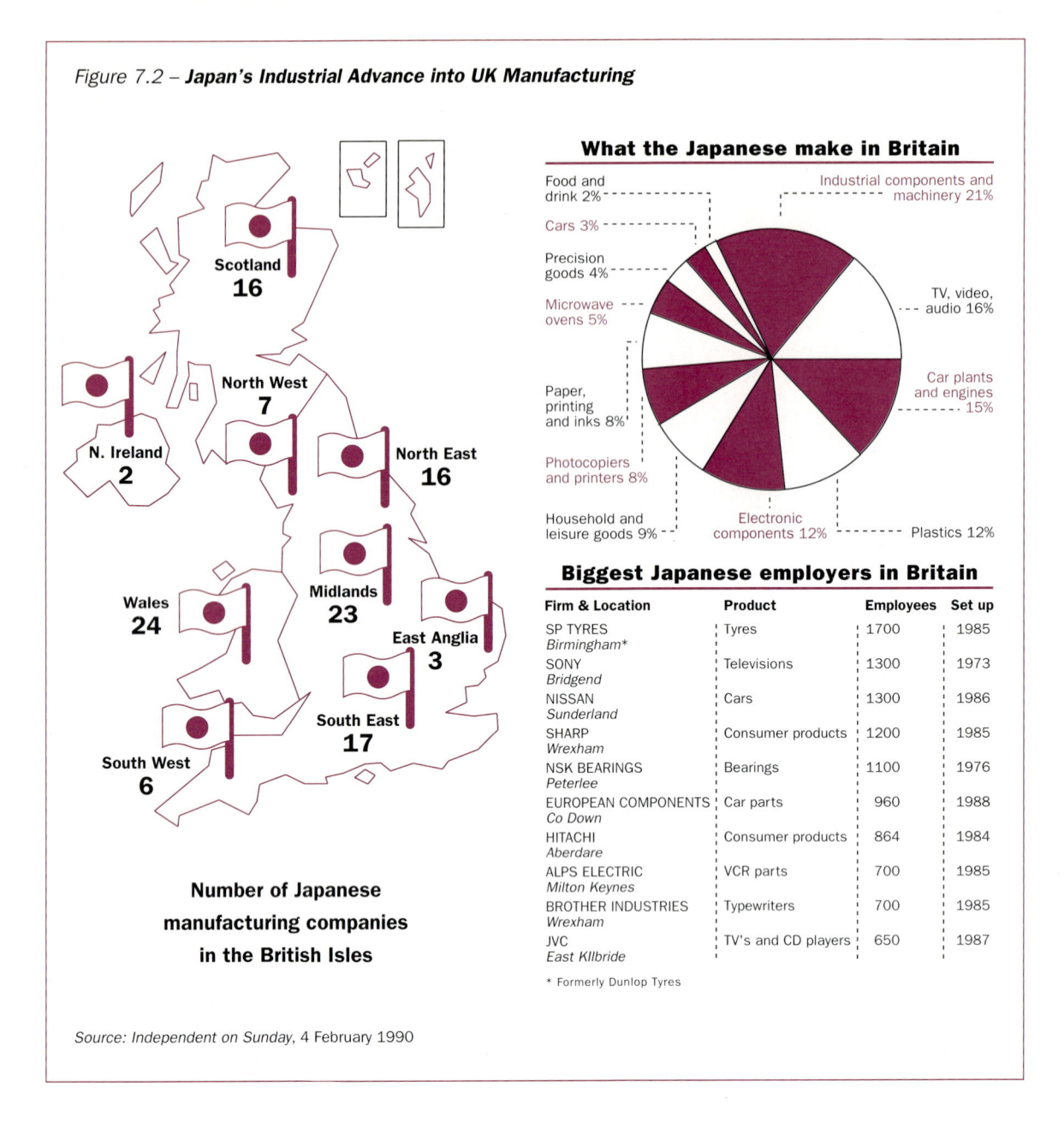

*Figure 7.2 – **Japan's Industrial Advance into UK Manufacturing***

Number of Japanese manufacturing companies in the British Isles

- Scotland 16
- N. Ireland 2
- North West 7
- North East 16
- Wales 24
- Midlands 23
- East Anglia 3
- South East 17
- South West 6

What the Japanese make in Britain

- Food and drink 2%
- Cars 3%
- Precision goods 4%
- Microwave ovens 5%
- Paper, printing and inks 8%
- Photocopiers and printers 8%
- Household and leisure goods 9%
- Electronic components 12%
- Plastics 12%
- Car plants and engines 15%
- TV, video, audio 16%
- Industrial components and machinery 21%

Biggest Japanese employers in Britain

Firm & Location	Product	Employees	Set up
SP TYRES Birmingham*	Tyres	1700	1985
SONY Bridgend	Televisions	1300	1973
NISSAN Sunderland	Cars	1300	1986
SHARP Wrexham	Consumer products	1200	1985
NSK BEARINGS Peterlee	Bearings	1100	1976
EUROPEAN COMPONENTS Co Down	Car parts	960	1988
HITACHI Aberdare	Consumer products	864	1984
ALPS ELECTRIC Milton Keynes	VCR parts	700	1985
BROTHER INDUSTRIES Wrexham	Typewriters	700	1985
JVC East Kilbride	TV's and CD players	650	1987

* Formerly Dunlop Tyres

Source: *Independent on Sunday*, 4 February 1990

Expansion into a foreign market involves many processes. The market will have to be researched to ensure that it is a viable opportunity: that demand exists, that the firm can be price competitive and that the proposed market is not affected by regulations concerning imports.

Activity 7.3

You should stop reading at this point and make a list of what you think a manufacturing company would have to do before being ready to export its product. Now contact the local office of the Department of Trade and Industry (their address and telephone number will be in your local telephone directory) and ask for a copy of a pamphlet entitled *The Export Initiative.* Compare your answers with those in the book.

BENEFITS OF SELLING OVERSEAS

Selling in overseas markets can bring many benefits (and difficulties) to firms. These include:

a Extending the life of a product

Foreign sales can provide an extension to the life of a product or service that might otherwise be in decline. The book in this series on marketing and people (*People, Marketing and Business*) highlights the point that selling a product in overseas markets can considerably extend its life and earning capacity. For example, as a reaction to declining demand in many Western nations, many tobacco companies have targeted their sales on Eastern Europe where the health lobby is less effective and consumers less sophisticated and less well informed (see Figure 7.3).

Figure 7.3 – New Markets Overseas

Firms grab chance to see East light up

WESTERN cigarette companies have moved fast to secure access to the last remaining undeveloped marketplace: Eastern Europe.

Total cigarette consumption in the old Eastern bloc, including the former Soviet Union, is estimated at around 750 billion cigarettes per year. That is nearly double the level of consumption in the US. But because the Eastern economies are weak, the revenue earned is a fraction of comparable sales in the West.

However, long-term prospects make acquisitions of Eastern manufacturers cheap at the price. Attention has been focused on the richer markets of Czechoslovakia and Hungary, whose 26 million citizens smoke well over two billion packets a year – more than 100 packets per man, woman and child.

It is a massively higher and rising rate compared with Western Europe's declining consumption.

American group, Philip Morris, won control of Czech monopoly producer Tabak, taking an initial 30 per cent stake in a deal worth $396 million. British American Tobacco (BAT) acquired Hungary's largest producer based at Pecs earlier this year. It plans to invest $34 million to increase production.

Source: *European*, 7–10 May 1992

b Achieving economies of scale

By selling in overseas markets producers can often benefit from economies of large scale production and so produce at a lower unit cost. This can increase competitiveness and enable the company to increase its market share.

c Stabilizing sales

Overseas sales can help to even out unforeseen fluctuations in sales. For example, if the UK economy is in recession and demand is reduced then some of the spare capacity may be taken up by overseas sales through an existing network.

d Difficulties for firms

Operating in foreign markets can pose difficulties for firms. There are two particular areas where the degree of risk for firms is high:

- The exchange rate
- Selling to unknown firms

The exchange rate may move against the exporter between agreeing the deal and receiving the payment. If the value of the deal is denoted in the currency of the importing country and the value of that currency falls against the exporter's currency, then the exporter's revenue will also fall.

Activity 7.4

Assume you are the manager of a small business exporting microelectronics to Austria. You have agreed a deal to supply 20 000 units at 20 schillings (the Austrian currency) for each. The exchange rate at the time of the deal is 20.5 schillings to the pound. You calculate the revenue to be earned by your company from the deal by multiplying the unit price (20 schillings) by the number of sales (20 000) to arrive at the total revenue in schillings – 400 000 schillings. To convert this into sterling it is necessary to divide this figure by the number of schillings which are exchanged for a single pound. Thus you should divide 400 000 by 20.5. The resulting figure, £19 512 (rounded to the nearest pound), is your company's earnings from the deal at the current exchange rate.

Now assume that two months have elapsed between the deal being agreed and payment being received by your company. During this period the exchange rate of the schilling fell so that 23 schillings now exchanges for one pound sterling. What is the sterling value of the deal now? What would have happened to your company's revenue had the value of the schilling risen against the pound – or indeed had the value of the pound fallen against the Austrian schilling? It should be apparent that this is the same thing.

Problems such as those illustrated in Activity 7.4 can be overcome. Companies can insist on the deal being valued in their domestic currency thus passing on the consequences of exchange rate changes to the importer. You will appreciate that this could lead to importers buying from alternative sources! An alternative approach is to use forward exchange markets which we will consider in detail later in this chapter.

A second danger is that exporting can involve selling to unknown firms and individuals, making the risk of non-payment greater. The Department of Trade and Industry operates, on behalf of the government, a scheme to protect firms against this risk. The Export Credit Guarantee Department

(ECGD), which was established in 1919, provides insurance under which exporters are protected against a number of risks, including the failure of the buyer to pay. This gives exporters certainty of payment and helps them to raise finance in advance of production. It also offers low interest loans to importers in Third World countries as an additional inducement to purchase UK goods and services. The insurance part of the ECGD is now to be split from the rest of the business and is being prepared for privatization by the government.

PROMOTING EXPORTS

Clearly the insurance scheme run by the ECGD is designed to encourage British exports. The government has other ways of promoting exports. The main government body offering such help is the British Overseas Trade Board (BOTB). The main forms of BOTB help include:

- Giving financial assistance in operating UK trade fairs
- Providing financial help in setting up UK pavilions (large stands on which all UK exporters are grouped together) at foreign trade fairs. They may also help with travel costs to fairs outside Western Europe
- Providing financial aid to groups of producers who invite foreign purchasers to visit the UK
- Carrying out overseas market research for intending exporters
- Offering monetary assistance to overseas stores who organize special displays and promotions of UK goods

You will probably be familiar with the Queen's Award for Industry. Firms who receive this Award are entitled to display a crown and the name and date of the award on their letterheads and promotional literature. The Award is made annually on the Queen's birthday (21 April). It is given to firms who have successfully entered into highly competitive overseas markets. Other categories of the award also exist (see Figure 7.4).

Figure 7.4 – Queen's Award for Exporting

Queen's Award for exporting

Winning a Queen's Award could prove to be an invaluable asset to your company, whatever its size.
Why?
Because by heightening your business standing, it gives you the edge in an increasingly competitive world.
It gives your employees greater pride in their work.
And its mark of outstanding achievement could attract the eye of new investors.
There are three Awards: Export Achievement, Technological Achievement and the newly introduced Queen's Award for Environmental Achievement.
This new UK industry award will recognise product and process developments which benefit the environment and are commercially successful.
You can enter for just one Award or all three – the choice is yours.
The Awards are granted by Her Majesty The Queen on April 21 (Her birthday) on the advice of the Prime Minister and an advisory committee drawn from industry and commerce, the Trade Unions and Government departments.
An Award is valid for 5 years, giving you the chance to make the most of all of its benefits.
Enter now and who knows? You may just have a hidden asset waiting to be declared.

Exports
To win The Queen's Award for Export Achievement your company must show a substantial and sustained increase in export earnings over three consecutive 12-monthly periods to a level which is outstanding for the products and services concerned and for the size of your unit's operations.
The final year should end as near to 31 October 1992 as your company's accounting system permits and may not be earlier than 31 December 1991.
Established exporters who cannot show dramatic export growth over three years may ask to be considered as a consistent exporter.
This is open to companies who can show outstanding achievement through a high level of exports for their industry and are able to demonstrate consistently good export growth over at least six years.

Technology
To win The Queen's Award for Technological Achievement you must show a significant advance, leading to increased efficiency, in the application of technology to a production or development process in British industry or the production for sale of goods which incorporate new and advanced technological qualities.
An Award is only made when there is evidence that an innovation has achieved commercial success.
In addition the Research and Development expenditure involved and the rate of return on this investment must be given.

Environment
To win The Queen's Award for Environmental Achievement your company must show that it has achieved significant advances in the development of products, technology or processes which offer major benefits for the environment and which are commercially successful.

Source: The Queen's Award Office, Dean Bradley House, 52 Horseferry Road, SW1P 2AG

Lastly, the Central Office of Information can also help exporters. Their role is to provide publicity overseas for UK firms who are exporters. They issue press releases overseas detailing the successes of UK businesses. Once again this body is run by the government.

Marketing Overseas

Techniques of marketing which succeed in the UK may not be appropriate in overseas markets.

The need for thorough market research is increased when selling overseas. Selling in a foreign country means that producers are facing different political and legal systems, cultures and languages. This means that intending producers have to take great care to ensure that there is a demand for their good or service. The first step in identifying possible markets is likely to be 'desk' research. Gathering information about incomes and expenditure patterns (especially on imports) for a number of markets will help to identify the most suitable markets. Firms can also use the Export Market Information Centre which provides self-help information on overseas markets. Desk research is a cost-effective way of eliminating less feasible markets.

The next step may be 'field research' where intending exporters actually communicate with potential customers. Surveys will have to overcome any language barriers and in some cultures potential consumers may be unwilling to respond to surveys or may not do so truthfully.

It is in the international marketing of a business's operation that the benefit of an agent or the system of licensing can be beneficial. Making use of their local knowledge can help avoid the many linguistic and cultural pitfalls that face an exporter. They can be particularly useful in acquiring lists for direct mailing purposes. As sales within the EC increase, it is expected the number of UK agencies who specialize in overseas markets will expand.

Promotion is important but unfamiliarity with foreign media can cause difficulties in assessing circulation figures as well as the audience at which the publications or programmes are targeted. The angle of the promotion must also take into account the culture of the country concerned. For example, Protestant European consumers do not respond well to advertisements which stress the labour-saving nature of products.

In spite of cultural differences, several large multinational companies (for example, Coca Cola) are now beginning to use essentially the

*Figure 7.5 – **Pooling Distribution Resources***

Allied signs up with Carlsberg

ALLIED-LYONS, the food and soft drinks group, and Carlsberg of Denmark shook the beer industry yesterday, announcing a plan to pool their brewing and drinks distribution operations in a 50/50 joint venture.

The new company will be marketing a portfolio of brands that includes Carlsberg, Castlemaine XXXX, Skol, Tuborg, Löwenbrau and Tetley. The deal is expected to lead to hundreds of job losses amongst sales people and depot employees.

Michael Iuul, chief executive of Carlsberg International, echoing his advertising slogan, said: 'For Carlsberg this is probably the best merger in the world.' The venture would give Carlsberg access to Allied's distribution network and its tied pubs.

Source: *Independent*, 23 October 1991

KEY POINTS 7.2

- **The use of overseas agents and distributors has been, and continues to be, important**
- **The system of licensing is being increasingly favoured by exporters**
- **In order to benefit from economies of scale joint ventures are a popular method of trading overseas in some industries**
- **Large businesses may set up overseas subsidiaries as a means of trading overseas**
- **Several government organizations help to promote UK exports**
- **Marketing overseas can differ considerably from that within the UK**

same advertisement on a global basis in order to save costs as well as to portray the same image of themselves worldwide.

Distribution patterns may differ from what businesses consider the norm. This may require greater advertising expenditure at the point of sale if distribution is – as is true in some European countries – mainly through small distributors. This is another area in which joint agreements can prove of value to both parties.

Means of International Payment

We noted earlier that trading overseas involves a high degree of risk which the government attempts to lessen. A significant problem faced by companies is how to pay for imports or, alternatively, in what form to accept payment for exports. A number of factors will determine the method employed. The main possibilities are:

a Cash
Clearly exporters would be happy to be paid in cash. However, it is not, in most cases, realistic to pay cash because the sums involved can be many millions of pounds and it is too risky to send such large sums in cash.

b Open account
This method is common where the exporter and importer are known to one another. Goods are ordered and delivered, and payment is made by cheque or money transfer within an agreed time. This is risky and would only be used when the exporter has confidence in the importer.

c Factoring
This system normally guarantees exporters up to 80 per cent of the money due at an early date after the shipment of the goods. A central role in this system is played by the 'factor' who takes on from the exporter the responsibility for collecting the debt. The difference between the full value of the debt and the price paid to the exporter is the factor's reward for the time, effort and risk involved in debt collection. Although it reduces profit margins, some exporters see it as a highly valuable service.

d Bills of Exchange
These are normally sent with the export documents to the importer. It is a document signed by the exporter and requiring the signature of the importer. By signing the bill the importer guarantees payment for the goods at a future date – usually within three months. Once signed it is returned to the exporter who can either hold it until payment is due or sell it for slightly less than its full value to their bank. If the exporter has doubts about the creditworthiness of the importer he may require the bill to be signed by a third party. This is known as 'accepting' the bill and certain banks will guarantee payment in this way in return for a fee from the importer. Thus it is, in effect, a form of insurance.

e Letters of Credit
This is the most common and surest means of payment. There are various kinds of letter of credit. The most common is a documentary letter of credit. This involves the buyer's bank issuing a letter to the seller's bank giving it authority to pay a certain sum of money to the seller. The seller will have to provide documentary proof (i.e. the shipping documents) that the goods have been exported to the buyer. Until every condition in the letter of credit has been met payment will be withheld.

Exchange Rates

An exchange rate is simply the price of one currency in terms of another. The media commonly express the price of the pound in terms of the American dollar, though increasingly the pound is being valued in terms of the premier European currency: the German deutschmark. On the financial pages of any national newspaper you will find the previous day's exchange rate for the pound usually expressed in terms of all the world's major currencies.

KEY POINTS 7.3

- Cash is rarely used in settlement of international transactions
- Open accounts are used when exporters and importers are known to one another
- The most common means of international payment are letters of credit

If the exchange rate of the pound, or sterling as it is frequently called, was set on a particular day at £1 = $1.75, for example, what would this mean? It tells us that a product or service sold for £1 in the UK would sell in the USA for $1.75, ignoring import duties or transportation costs. Similarly, a good or service sold for $1.75 in America would sell in the UK for £1, again excluding transport costs and any import duties.

The pound is not merely valued in terms of dollars, however, but in the currencies of all the countries with whom Britain has dealings. So, the pound has an exchange rate against the French franc, the Italian lira, the German deutschmark, the Swedish kronor and so on.

Why Are Currencies Exchanged?

All countries exchange their currencies for those of other nations because they wish to buy goods and services from those countries. Consider the following situation. A UK car firm is seeking to purchase tyres from a French firm whose product is renowned for its quality and durability. The French producer will prefer to be paid in francs so that domestic costs can be met. He will also avoid the consequences of exchange rate fluctuations that we discussed earlier. Thus it is likely that the UK firm will sell sterling and purchase francs in order to complete the deal.

Businesses and institutions trading abroad will require the appropriate foreign currency to finance the transactions. They will therefore sell their own currency and purchase the necessary foreign currency.

In addition, foreign currency may be demanded by individuals and businesses who wish to invest in foreign enterprises. Such enterprises will, of course, expect the investment to be made in their own currency.

The Foreign Exchange Market

This is the international market in which foreign currencies are bought and sold. The market has no simple geographical location but is made up of many dealers who communicate by telephone, telex and fax. London is one of the largest centres of the market with hundreds of institutions involved. More currency is actively traded in London than in the other major centres such as New York, Tokyo, Hong Kong, Paris, Frankfurt and Singapore. Exchange rates alter continuously according to the balance between orders for buying and selling currencies.

Most large financial institutions have some involvement in this market and all the joint-stock banks have separate departments which deal in foreign currencies on behalf of their customers.

*Figure 7.6 – **International Payments.*** This shows a typical transaction involving a French firm importing from the UK. The French firm has to exchange its own currency in the foreign exchange market for sterling in order to pay the UK exporter.

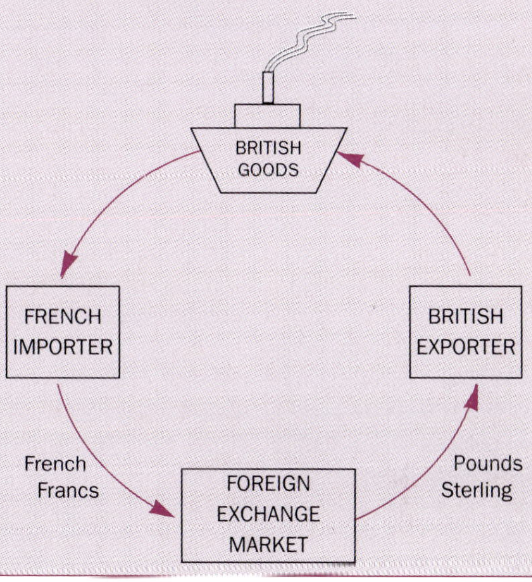

The Exchange Rate and Business

As we saw earlier, changes in the value of currencies will affect the trading position of any organization that operates internationally.

A fall in the value of sterling will have an impact both in the UK and abroad. It will mean that UK exports become cheaper and, as a result, sales are likely to rise. At the same time, imports into the UK will become more expensive and home firms will find it easier to compete.

As an example of this, suppose that the pound falls in value from four Dutch guilders to three guilders. A UK export to Holland which costs £1 will sell for three guilders rather than the four guilders it previously cost. Simultaneously, Dutch exports to the UK will rise in price. An export costing four guilders will rise in price in the UK from £1 to £1.33, assuming all other factors remain constant.

When sterling rises in value, export prices also rise, whilst imports become cheaper. You may wish to test your understanding of this by calculating the consequences for export and import prices in Anglo-American trade of a rise in the value of sterling from £1 = $1.80 to £1 = $2.00.

It may seem to you that a fall in the value of the pound is good for UK businesses and a rise disadvantageous. But, unfortunately, it is not so simple!

A fall in the price of UK exports does not automatically mean more sales. Foreign consumers

*Figure 7.7 – **The Effects of Changes in the Exchange Rates***

Sterling's value in terms of other currencies	Prices of UK exports overseas in their currency	Prices of imported goods in UK sterling
Appreciates (Rises)	Increase	Fall
Depreciates (Falls)	Fall	Increase

will obviously take into account other factors such as quality, design, after-sales service and product range. It may be that demand for British exports is price inelastic, meaning that demand is not responsive to price changes and so rises by little following a price fall.

UK exporters may be unable to respond to the increased exports sales owing to insufficient production capacity. Furthermore, enterprises may be unwilling to invest large sums in expanding capacity when a fall in the value of the pound may prove to be temporary. This would apply especially if UK interest rates were high making investment an expensive option.

Similarly, a rise in the price of imports following a fall in the value of the currency, may not be good news. In an open-trading economy like the UK's, many raw materials and components are imported and a depreciating pound is likely to push up domestic costs of production. This could ultimately result in higher export prices.

It may be that foreign firms squeeze their profit margins in an effort to hold their prices down in the UK market. If this happens then the competing UK firms will not gain a price advantage.

Finally, home consumers may prefer imported products because of their quality, design, reliability, after-sales services and other similar features.

Spot and Forward Markets

There are two types of foreign exchange transaction: spot and forward. Foreign exchange is purchased and sold for immediate delivery in the spot market. In the forward market currency is bought and sold for delivery at some future date, usually between one and four months. Forward markets help to eliminate the risk of exchange rate changes which could reduce or eliminate the profitability of any given deal.

FORWARD EXCHANGE MARKETS – AN EXAMPLE
Suppose that a deal to import American motorbikes is agreed on 1 March; the deal is to take place on 1 April. The agreed price is $4 000 dollars per motorbike. On 1 March the forward market pound/dollar price is $2.00. This means that if the importer chose to buy his currency for delivery in a month's time he would eliminate any risk and the cost of each motorbike would be £2 000 (= $4 000/2.00). On the other hand, if the importer accepts the exchange risks involved, the price in pounds of each motorbike will depend upon the spot rate between sterling and dollars when the bikes are delivered on 1 April.

For example, if the sterling/dollar spot rate were $2.15 on 1 April, the sterling price of each motorbike would be £1 860 which would save the importer £140 on each motorbike. In this case the importer would clearly benefit from the exchange movements.

Now suppose that the spot rate on 1 April were $1.86. This would result in the cost of each motorbike being £2 151. In these circumstances the importer would benefit from using the forward market.

Using the forward exchange market eliminates risk and may be attractive because of this. However, as we saw in the above example, the exchange can move in favour of the importer and increase profits. Many factors will influence companies who trade abroad as to whether they elect to use the forward exchange market. It will depend upon the proportion of the company's business which is transacted overseas, the volatility of the currencies involved, the personal judgement of the managers involved and so on. There is no 'right' answer for the firm on whether to use spot or forward markets. As with most other business decisions it depends upon the precise circumstances.

The European Community's Exchange Rate Mechanism

The pound sterling joined the Exchange Rate Mechanism (ERM) of the European Monetary System (EMS) on 8 October 1990. The then

Chancellor, John Major, announced that this would form a part of the government's monetary policy (as discussed in Chapter Three) and would help to reduce inflation.

Because of intense pressure on the pound, the UK government was forced to withdraw sterling from the ERM in September 1992. Dealers in currencies felt that the pound was overvalued in relation to the deutschmark. They doubted the commitment of the UK authorities to maintain sterling's value and, not wishing to hold a depreciating asset, sold the currency.

In spite of the intervention of fellow EC governments, the UK government was unable to continue purchasing sufficient pounds and eventually withdrew sterling from the ERM. As a consequence of this action, the value of the pound against the deutschmark fell substantially.

Since autumn 1992, the UK authorities have moved away from having a stable exchange rate as a central feature of economic strategy.

The Exchange Rate Mechanism is generally regarded as the main component of the European Monetary System. The EMS aims to promote monetary stability in Europe. Those countries that remain members of the ERM keep their currencies within agreed limits against one another with the overriding aim of creating exchange rate stability. Other features of the EMS include the European Currency Unit or Ecu (possibly an eventual EC currency), credit facilities to member nations, and arrangements for closer co-ordination of economic policies. We will discuss the Ecu fully in Chapter Eight.

Each member of the ERM gives its currency a rate against all the other currencies in the mechanism. So, for example, while the pound sterling was in the ERM it had a central rate against the deutschmark of £1 = DM2.95, against the French franc of £1 = FF9.89, against the Italian lira of £1 = L2207.25 and so on. This means that every currency has an agreed rate (also called 'central' or 'par rates') against every other currency. Changes to these central rates can only be made by agreement with all participating nations. No country can go alone and change its currency's value.

Each member of the ERM has agreed to limit the fluctuation of their currency to plus or minus 2.25 per cent against any other currency. Because they entered the mechanism at a later date, the UK and Spain were allowed wider margins for currency fluctuation of plus or minus 6 per cent.

What if one currency reaches its limit against another currency? For example, when the pound fell against the deutschmark to £1 = DM2.78, the central banks of both countries (the Bank of England and the Bundesbank) had an obligation to act to protect the weak currency – which in this example was the pound. Both banks bought sterling at a price of at least £1 = DM2.78. This prevented the rate falling below the bottom limit (to, say, £1 = DM2.72) since dealers would know that they could get this price from the central banks. However, in the case of sterling in autumn 1992, so much of the currency was sold that the central banks were unable to buy up all the surplus.

The central banks of the member states support one another in other ways to maintain all currencies within the agreed bands. Perhaps the most important is their attempt to pursue convergent and low inflationary economic policies. It is this which will, in the long term, promote exchange rate stability. Governments will have to show a real commitment to an integrated and unified European economy if a fixed exchange rate system between all the members of the EC is to operate effectively and perhaps lead to a single currency.

The ERM and Business

The principal benefit of the ERM for business is that it limits the amount by which a member nation's currency can alter during the course of an international transaction. Thus, once a deal has been agreed and priced the exporting firm can be confident that the value of the deal in its domestic currency will be pretty well unchanged. This offers certainty and security to those selling in other EC states.

It effectively removes the risk of a substantial, adverse currency movement of the kind we discussed earlier. This is intended to encourage further international trade between the member states of the EC and is an important part of the move to freeing restrictions on trade within the Single European Market.

The UK's brief membership of the ERM had another significant implication for UK exporters. Businesses must seek to control their costs in order to remain competitive. In the past, UK exporters were criticized for their willingness to allow costs (and in particular wage costs) to escalate, safe in the knowledge that a fall in the exchange value of sterling would take place if UK prices rose more rapidly than those of its competitors. The exchange rate in the past has been allowed to alter relatively freely against other currencies. Such a system was termed 'floating' exchange rates. With the exchange rate more or less fixed, firms must remain competitive or face lost orders, redundancies and possible bankruptcy. It is for this reason that politicians have said that membership of the ERM imposed an additional discipline upon the UK economy. Many politicians believe this is a powerful part of the argument in favour of the pound rejoining the ERM at some future date.

> ## CASE STUDY
> # ERM Curbs Wage Increases
>
> A survey carried out by the Confederation of British Industry has found that pay is levelling out as a result of the recession and entry into the Exchange Rate Mechanism.
>
> The CBI Pay Databank survey showed that manufacturing pay awards averaged 8.3 per cent in the first quarter of this year, which is down on the 8.9 per cent recorded for the fourth quarter of last year.
>
> In the service sector average pay is estimated to have risen 8.8 per cent in the second half of 1990, compared to average increases of 9 per cent in the first half.
>
> One in six companies has frozen pay for around two to five months.
>
> Source: *Personnel Managment*, May 1991
>
> **QUESTIONS**
>
> 1 Write a further paragraph for the above article to explain what might happen if a firm awards large pay increases to its employees when the exchange rate is fixed.
>
> 2 Under some circumstances firms might be able to award large pay rises and still remain competitive. Outline circumstances in which this might be true.

Trade and the Balance of Payments

The balance of payments is simply a nation's balance sheet of total payments to other countries and the total received from them of goods and services. As such it summarizes in value terms all transactions between one nation and the rest of the world. We need to consider briefly the structure of the balance of payments and how this affects the economic environment in which businesses have to operate.

Broadly the balance of payments falls into two categories:

a The current account
This section of the accounts records a country's sales of goods and services to other countries as well as purchases of the same from the rest of the world. This account is traditionally split into two parts: the balance of visible trade which solely refers to trade in goods; and the balance of invisible trade which records trade in services. Economists refer to that part of the balance of payments which records trade in goods (or visibles) as the balance of trade.

b The capital account
This second section of the balance of payments records investment flows in and out of the country – funds lent to, and borrowed from, overseas. This part of the balance of payments tends to receive far less attention from the media than the current account.

A deficit on the balance of payments means that funds are leaking from the nation concerned. In most circumstances this is not good news for the nation concerned or for its businesses. In terms of the economic model we developed in Chapter Two, imports represent a withdrawal from the circular flow whilst exports are an injection. Clearly, a deficit where imports exceed exports will cause the circular flow and the level of economic activity to decline. This will make the economic environment less attractive for businesses.

A deficit on the balance of payments can send a number of signals to a nation's businesses. It can mean that both overseas and domestic consumers are switching to the products or services of foreign businesses. This could be for reasons of design, after-sales service or price. A deficit on the balance of payments may mean that sales from a particular industry are declining both at home and overseas. It also means that the level of economic activity within the economy concerned may slacken leading to reduced sales, fewer orders and ultimately less output. Alternatively, it could herald a period of economic prosperity as firms import increased quantities of raw materials prior to increasing output.

The balance of payments is affected by changes in the exchange rate. If the value of the pound falls then, as we saw earlier, exports become cheaper and imports more expensive. In such circumstances we should expect export sales to rise and purchases of imports to decline. However, whether or not this happens will depend upon the extent to which export and

KEY POINTS 7.4

- A fall in the value of the pound means that UK exports will be cheaper and imports more expensive

- Other factors affect UK export sales apart from price – for example, design, quality, after-sales support, etc

- Foreign currencies can be bought on forward markets to protect against exchange rate movements

- The objective of the EC Exchange Rate Mechanism is to reduce currency fluctuations

- Membership of the ERM means exporters must be cost-conscious

- A decline in the value of the pound can result in an improvement in the balance of payments

---

import sales are price sensitive. Only if demand for these internationally traded goods and services is elastic will a decline in the value of the pound improve the current account of the balance of payments. Similarly, a rise in the exchange value of the pound may improve the balance of payments on current account.

Barriers to Trade

As we saw in Chapter Three, a major government objective in controlling the economy is to increase the level of economic activity in order to achieve economic growth and the higher standard of living associated with this growth. When a deficit on the balance of payments occurs, the government is likely to take action to prevent it from having an adverse affect on the economy.

It may decide to impose a tariff on imports. This is simply a tax on imports designed to increase their selling price and to reduce sales. This policy may not be successful if demand for these goods or services is inelastic or insensitive to price changes. Equally, tariffs will be ineffective to some extent if no substitutes exist or if foreign goods are of better quality.

An alternative is to impose quotas which place a physical limit on the quantity of a particular good which can be imported. The authorities issue licences without which the good cannot be imported. By restricting the number of licences the authorities impose the quota on imports.

In some cases governments have negotiated limits on imports with representatives of exporting nations. This was the case with the UK and Japanese car imports in the 1980s.

Such restrictions on imports can be used to protect domestic businesses and to maintain levels of employment by lessening the 'withdrawal' of funds to overseas businesses. Critics of such policies say that countries which employ them are effectively seeking to 'export' their unemployment. Countries imposing such restrictions on trade are likely to be subject to retaliation by other nations. This will make it more difficult for domestic firms to maintain export quantities.

Figure 7.8 **Duty on Photocopiers.** The European Community as well as domestic governments impose duties. It can be seen from this cutting that firms derive considerable benefits from being protected in this way. Do you think that EC consumers benefit from this tariff?

Duty to stay on cut-price copiers

THE European Commission has begun an investigation into whether it should continue to impose a 20 per cent duty on photocopiers imported from outside the EC.

The duty, introduced in 1986 to stem the flow of cheap Japanese imports, expired last week.

However, European photocopier manufacturers successfully lobbied to have the duty extended until the EC enquiry is completed, a process that is expected to take several months.

Five years ago there were ten European photocopier manufacturers. Growing competition from the Far East has reduced that number to only three. Rank Xerox, Olivetti of Italy and the Dutch company Oce van der Grinten together hold a share of the world market of about 20 per cent.

Source: European, 5–11 March 1992

The free flow of goods and services, which is a central feature of the Single European Market, limits the UK government's ability to restrict imports from other EC member states by use of such techniques.

> ## KEY POINTS 7.5
>
> - Tariffs are a tax on imports designed to reduce purchases of such imports
> - Quotas place a physical limit on imports
> - Restrictions on imports are often used to protect domestic industry

International Economic Organizations

A number of international or supranational organizations exist which have a major influence on businesses which trade overseas. In Chapter Eight we will look in detail at the structure and significance of the EC. With the creation of the Single European Market in 1992, the influence of this organization on UK exporters has increased. A number of other organizations are also worthy of consideration:

a The International Monetary Fund (IMF)
The IMF was established during the Second World War to promote international trade and to prevent a return to the protection of domestic industries which characterized the inter-war period. It assists nations with balance of payments difficulties by providing loans and advice on the management of their economies. It also attempts to maintain stable exchange rates. By promoting trade in this manner, the IMF seeks to increase the level of economic activity and thereby improve the business environment.

b The International Bank for Reconstruction and Development
The IMF's sister organization is the International Bank for Reconstruction and Development (IBRD or World Bank). This was set up at the same time as the IMF with the objectives of encouraging the international exchange of capital as well as encouraging loans to Third World nations. This assists the economic development of these less developed countries and provides larger markets for exporters. A similar function is performed by the International Finance Corporation (IFC) a United Nations Agency formed in 1957 to encourage private enterprise in member states, and particularly in less developed countries.

c GATT
The General Agreement on Trade and Tariffs (commonly known as GATT) is an international agreement, reached in Geneva in 1947, which attempts to reduce tariff barriers between the eighty-six nations who are currently signatories to the agreement.

d OECD
The Organization for Economic Co-operation and Development (OECD) was set up in Paris in 1961 to help the economic growth and the standard of living of its members. It currently has twenty-four members, mainly developed Western countries.

All of these organizations, and other less significant ones, can impact upon UK businesses. Broadly, they aim to promote greater trade between the countries of the world; this will increase the exporting opportunities for UK businesses. However, a part of this freeing of world trade is greater access to UK markets for foreign producers. Trade is not solely a one-way affair!

> ## KEY POINTS 7.6
>
> - The Single European Market ensures the free flow of goods and services between member states of the EC
> - The International Monetary Fund assists nations with balance of payments difficulties
> - The International Bank for Reconstruction and Development encourages international exchange of capital as well as loans to Third World nations
> - GATT lobbies powerfully for the reduction and elimination of barriers to trade

EXAM PREPARATION

SHORT QUESTIONS

1. The government imposes tariffs on a range of goods. Explain why demand for these imported goods may not decline.

2. Give two advantages of using agents in overseas trade.

3. Give two ways in which an exporter can ensure that he receives payment for his goods.

4. What effect might an increase in the value of the pound have on the balance of trade?

5. Name two means by which a government can restrict the volume of imports entering a country.

DATA RESPONSE QUESTION

How to unite women of the world

SELLING the same magazine title on news stands from Shanghai to New York is a wonderfully enticing idea for publishers. But there is never any guarantee that a successful domestic product will please foreign tastes. The French publishers Hachette, however, have achieved this with their flagship women's magazine, *Elle*.

In 1985 *Elle* was a French magazine with an international reputation for style. By 1990, it had followed its reputation by establishing markets in 15 other countries.

The *Elle* look would appear to be a constant: the cover of the magazine in Shanghai (an estimated 100,000 copies are sold in China) is largely similar to that on sale in Brazil (where it sells 120,000).

But the secret of the magazine's expansion lies in its reliance on partnerships with foreign publishers as much as in its ability to sell the *Elle* look abroad. Twelve of the company's 15 foreign publishing deals are joint ventures.

'When we move into a market, we generally do so in partnership with a strong local publishers,' said Louise Cardwell, international advertising director.

'This is where the strength of the partnership system lies,' said Francois Vincens, director of *Elle*'s international strategy. 'It allows us to break into a market swiftly, using local knowledge.'

Elle's joint-venture approach has not been favoured in the magazine world. Expansionist publishers like Germany's Bauer (with such mass-market titles as *Bella* and *Take-A-Break*) and Gruhner & Jahr (*Best*) favour following their own global plans rather than joining forces with local publishers.

Hachette has used the joint-venture principle to reach a sizeable pan-European audience of like-minded readers. Maggie Alderson, editor of UK *Elle*, described them as 'intelligent, affluent, outgoing, post-feminist women'.

Hachette has taken advantage of *Elle*'s pan-European positioning to establish a kind of one-stop marketing shop for advertisers called Interdeco, which the company claims is unique. Though a single agency, advertisers are now offered an *Elle* marketing package that reaches like-minded women from Brussels to Milan.

The company claims to be the world's largest publisher of consumer magazines, with 75 titles boasting a combined circulation of 650 million and a vast pooled research facility.

Source: Independent on Sunday, 24 March 1991

Questions

(a) Using Hachette as an example explain the advantages of breaking into foreign markets by forming joint ventures.

(b) In view of these advantages why do publishers like Germany's Bauer not favour this approach?

(c) Why do you think that advertisers would find the 'Interdeco' system attractive?

BTEC ASSIGNMENT

You are a civil servant employed by the government as part of the 'Export Initiative' team and have been assigned to prepare the stand for a forthcoming exhibition to promote and encourage UK exports. Your brief asks you to illustrate the main countries with which the UK trades and the goods and services which make up this trade.

Working as a group you should prepare the materials for this stand. The precise content of the materials is your decision, but it should explain the processes involved in trade, any difficulties or barriers faced by those trading internationally and, importantly, all aspects of the financing of international trade.

These materials can be in the form of graphs and charts, pamphlets, videos or audio tapes, maps or any other medium you think appropriate.

You should display your work in a suitable fashion and answer questions on trading overseas that may be asked by other groups.

ESSAY

1 In 1989 Jaguar cars blamed their poor profit performance on the fluctuating value of the US dollar. Explain why fluctuations may have had such an impact and analyse what could be done to improve the position in the

CHAPTER 8

Business and Europe

▷▷ QUESTIONS FOR PREVIEW ▷▷

1. How has the UK's relationship with Europe changed over the last twenty-five years?
2. How is the EC managed?
3. What changes will be brought about by the move to a Single Market in Europe?
4. What are the implications of these changes for European businesses?
5. What opportunities are offered to Western businesses by the recent liberalization of East European economies?

THE UK's position in relation to Western Europe has changed steadily since the end of the Second World War in 1945. This change has accelerated lately, particularly in the years following the UK's entry to the EC in January 1973. During this period of change trading links with the former Commonwealth nations have weakened and the UK economy has become more integrated with Europe and in particular the EC.

The closer ties which have developed between the UK and Europe have relevance for everyone in the country, but especially for business. Businesses have experienced significant changes in the products they produce, their markets and their competitors since the UK's entry into the EC. Businesses need to adjust their behaviour in response to these changes in Europe. Indeed, most managers would argue that there is a need to be proactive – that is, to take action to prepare for change before that change takes place.

It is important that we first look at the changes that have taken place in Europe over recent years in order to assess their impact. This will afford us a better perspective when we discuss the changes inherent in the move to the Single European Market in 1992 and the implications of the introduction of democracy in many Eastern European states.

The European Community

The origins of the EC lie in the creation of the European Coal and Steel Community (ECSC) in 1952. The original members who signed the Treaty of Paris were Belgium, Holland, France, Italy and Luxembourg. West Germany later became a member. The UK participated in the negotiation but refused to join having yet to be convinced that her economic future lay with Europe. The objective of the ECSC was to abolish restrictions on trade in coal and steel between members and to co-ordinate production.

In 1957 the six members of the ECSC met in Rome and negotiated two Treaties of Rome which established the European Economic Community and the European Atomic Energy Community (EURATOM). In 1967 these two organizations were amalgamated with the ECSC and the resulting body is correctly termed the European Community. We use this label throughout this book.

The EC has expanded on three occasions since 1957 and this is shown in Figure 8.1 (next page).

A number of other nations in and on the fringes of Europe have expressed varying degrees of interest in becoming members of the EC. In 1991, negotiations between the EC and the European Free Trade Association (EFTA) resulted in agreements to allow the EFTA members to become a

*Figure 8.1 – **The Growth of the EC.*** This figure highlights the growth of the EC since 1957. You will see at the bottom of the figure that it says 'now the next move is coming'. What do you think the 'next move' is? If you do not know, read this chapter and then consider the question again.

1957 The Six

- Belgium
- Netherlands
- Luxembourg
- Federal Republic of Germany
- France
- Italy

1973 The Nine

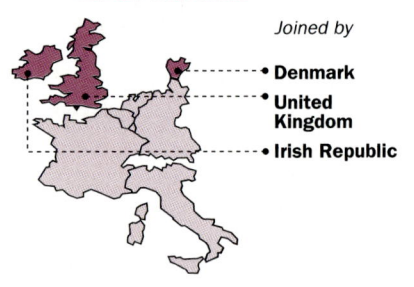

Joined by
- Denmark
- United Kingdom
- Irish Republic

1981 The Ten

Joined by
- Greece

1986 The Twelve

Joined by
- Spain
- Portugal

Now the NEXT move is coming . . .

Source: DTI, *The Single Market*

part of the EC's Single Market – something which we shall consider in detail later in this chapter. EFTA is a trading agreement between Austria, Finland, Iceland, Liechtenstein, Norway, Sweden and Switzerland with the objective of increasing trade and prosperity. Figure 8.2 illustrates those nations interested in becoming members of the EC.

Activity 8.1

Find out the following data for the members of the EC:

- Capital city
- Population
- Major industries
- Current rates of unemployment and inflation
- Indicators of living standards such as income per head or cars
- Doctors per 000 inhabitants

In what ways might businesses use this type of data? Which of the Community's members are the richest according to your figures? Do you think your figures accurately reflect relative living standards?

KEY POINTS 8.1

- The UK economy has become more integrated with Europe in the years since 1945
- The European Community was created out of the European Coal and Steel Community
- The UK declined the chance to join the EC at the outset and did not become a member until 1973
- The EC is likely to gain new members in the near future

The Institutions of the EC

The main EC institutions currently are:

a The European Commission
This is based in Brussels. It proposes EC policy and legislation which is then passed on to the Council of Ministers. The Commission executes the decisions taken by the Council. It also has the responsibility to ensure that member states comply with EC rules.

*Figure 8.2 – **Possible New EC Members***

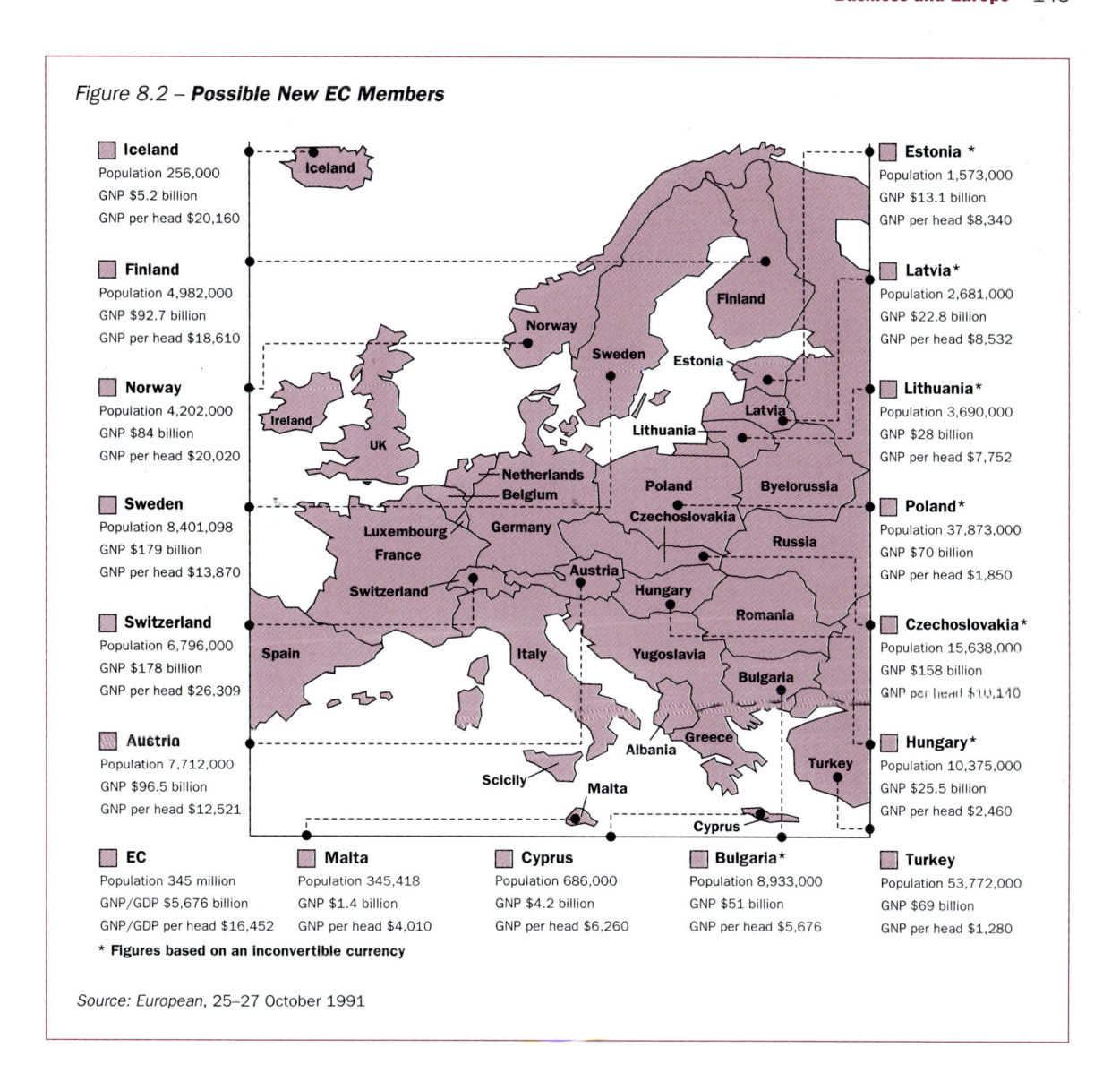

Iceland
Population 256,000
GNP $5.2 billion
GNP per head $20,160

Finland
Population 4,982,000
GNP $92.7 billion
GNP per head $18,610

Norway
Population 4,202,000
GNP $84 billion
GNP per head $20,020

Sweden
Population 8,401,098
GNP $179 billion
GNP per head $13,870

Switzerland
Population 6,796,000
GNP $178 billion
GNP per head $26,309

Austria
Population 7,712,000
GNP $96.5 billion
GNP per head $12,521

EC
Population 345 million
GNP/GDP $5,676 billion
GNP/GDP per head $16,452

Malta
Population 345,418
GNP $1.4 billion
GNP per head $4,010

Cyprus
Population 686,000
GNP $4.2 billion
GNP per head $6,260

Bulgaria*
Population 8,933,000
GNP $51 billion
GNP per head $5,676

Estonia*
Population 1,573,000
GNP $13.1 billion
GNP per head $8,340

Latvia*
Population 2,681,000
GNP $22.8 billion
GNP per head $8,532

Lithuania*
Population 3,690,000
GNP $28 billion
GNP per head $7,752

Poland*
Population 37,873,000
GNP $70 billion
GNP per head $1,850

Czechoslovakia*
Population 15,638,000
GNP $158 billion
GNP per head $10,140

Hungary*
Population 10,375,000
GNP $25.5 billion
GNP per head $2,460

Turkey
Population 53,772,000
GNP $69 billion
GNP per head $1,280

* Figures based on an inconvertible currency

Source: European, 25–27 October 1991

The Commission comprises seventeen Commissioners: two from the UK, France, Italy, Germany and Spain and one from the other members. Commissioners represent EC rather than national interest. They are supported by a staff of 10 000 – 50 per cent of whom are translators!

b The Council of Ministers
This is the Community's decision-making body. It agrees or adopts legislation on the basis of proposals from the Commission. It is, in effect, the Cabinet of the EC. It meets in Brussels and occasionally Luxembourg. Meetings are held each April, June and October. One minister from each state attends the Council; his or her office depends upon the matter being discussed. If the community budget is being discussed then finance ministers will attend; if the Common Agricultural Policy (CAP) is the main topic then agricultural ministers will attend and so on.

Twice yearly, heads of government meet in what is called the European Council.

c European Parliament
The European Parliament meets in Strasbourg in eastern France. It has 518 members of whom 81 are elected by Britain. Members of the European Parliament (MEPs) are elected by proportional representation (except in England, Scotland and Wales) for a fixed period of five years. The Parliament's opinion is needed on proposals before the Council can adopt them. In spite of this the Parliament has little authority or power.

d The European Court of Justice
This Court rules on the interpretation and application of EC laws. Its aim is to ensure that the law is observed in line with the Treaty of Rome. Thus,

144 The Business Environment

*Figure 8.3 – **The Voting Power of the EC States***

	Commission members	Council members/votes		Parliament members
Belgium	1	1	5	24
Denmark	1	1	3	16
Germany	2	1	10	81
Greece	1	1	5	24
France	2	1	10	81
Eire	1	1	3	15
Italy	2	1	10	81
Luxembourg	1	1	2	6
Holland	1	1	5	25
UK	2	1	10	81
Spain	2	1	8	60
Portugal	1	1	5	24
TOTAL	**17**	**12**	**76**	**518**

*Figure 8.4 – **The EC Institutions***

The Commission make proposals

The European Parliament gives opinions and proposes amendments

The Council decides

Source: DTI, *The Single Market – The Facts*

it is the judiciary of the EC and deals with disputes between members.

It has thirteen judges, including one from each member state. Judgements from the Court are binding in each member state and its rulings take primacy over national law.

e   The Economic and Social Committee

This is based in Brussels and is an advisory body consisting of representatives of employers, trade unions and consumers. The Commission is obliged to consult it on economic and social proposals.

f   The European Investment Bank

This has its headquarters in Luxembourg and is the EC's bank. The EIB lends money to finance capital investment projects which help all areas of the Community to enjoy economic prosperity.

Types of EC Legislation

The Council and the Commission can impose their will upon the Community by means of:

- Regulations, which have binding legal effect without confirmation by member countries' parliaments. These regulations have primacy over national law if any conflict arises
- Directives, which require member states to introduce legislation in their national parliaments to enact certain Community decisions. If the member does not introduce the directive the Commission may refer the matter to the Court of Justice as a last resort
- Recommendations and opinions, which have no binding force but state the view of the issuing institution

CASE STUDY

EC Plans for 'Green' Labels

European Community plans to label the 'greenest' brands of consumer products are heading for delay due to ministerial wrangling and problems working out what is 'green'.

Instead of having many eco-labelled items, ranging from washing machines to toys, in the shops by the end of next year, as the European Commission aims, none is likely to appear until at least the summer of 1993. There are fears that the scheme means trouble and cost for manufacturers.

Ken Collins, MEP for Strathclyde East and head of the EC environment committee, says he 'will be surprised if the Council [of Ministers] agrees' the latest eco-labelling draft regulation at its meeting in December, because each country wants its plans incorporated and the measure must be passed unanimously. The twelve cannot even agree on what the label will look like.

Source: Independent on Sunday, 8 December 1991

QUESTIONS

1 What does the article tell you about the relationship between the European Commission and the Council of Ministers?

2 Why might a scheme such as this cause 'trouble and cost for manufacturers'?

3 What advantages might result to EC businesses from the creation of a single 'green' label?

Figure 8.5 illustrates the sequence of actions involved in decision-making within the Community. It also confirms the relationship between the major institutions of the EC.

European Monetary Union (EMU)

This is a topical and controversial aspect of the EC. Monetary union – the establishment of a single currency – is a major objective of the EC. This target has come about because many people believe that different currencies are a significant barrier to increased trade and competition within the EC.

In 1979 the EC established the European Monetary System (EMS) as a means of achieving a single currency. There are two parts to the EMS.

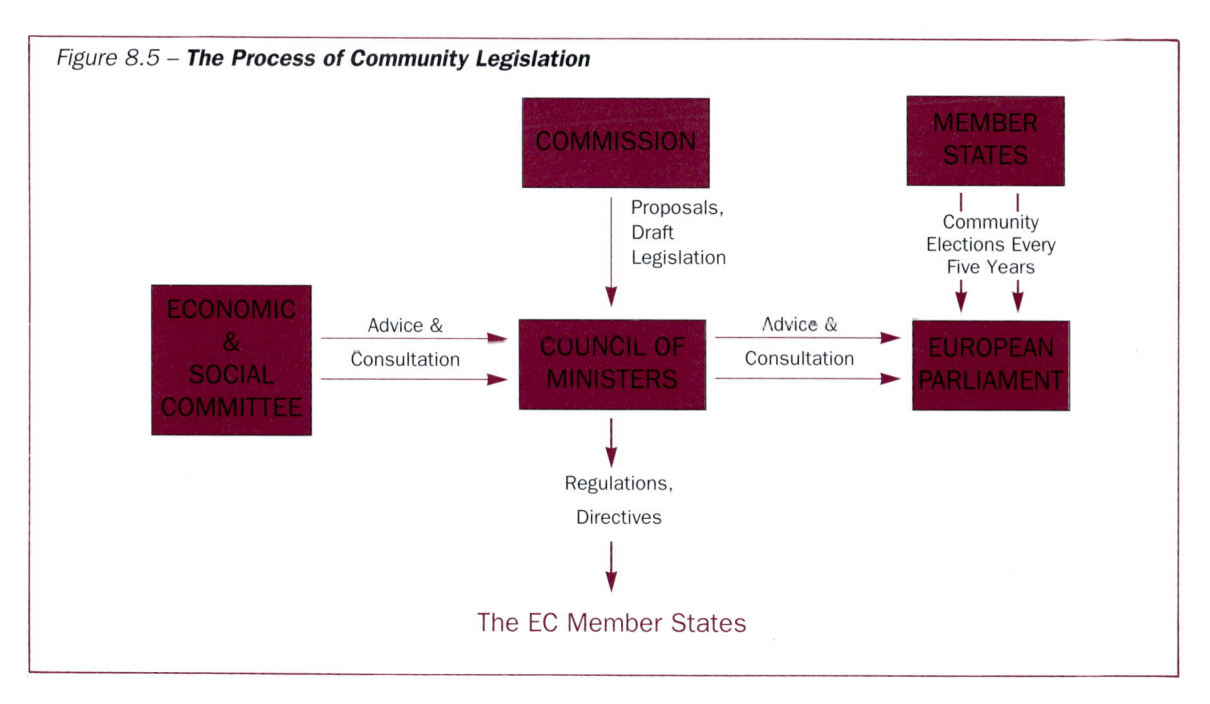

*Figure 8.5 – **The Process of Community Legislation***

The first, the Exchange Rate Mechanism (ERM), is based on what will possibly become the common European currency – the European Currency Unit or ECU. Member countries of the EC have their currency valued in terms of the ECU (i.e. in terms of each others' currencies). The governments of participating states have to maintain their country's currency within at most 2.25 per cent of the agreed value (or in exceptional cases up to 6 per cent). All EC members co-operate in maintaining exchange values. You will recall that we looked at the operation and implications of this Exchange Rate Mechanism in Chapter Seven.

The second part of the EMS is the European Monetary Co-operation Fund (EMCF) which provides funds to stabilize currency values within the agreed bands. For example, if the franc is falling in value, then this Fund can be used to purchase francs on world markets, thus increasing demand for it and of course its value. By 'currency value' we mean the currency's exchange value, as discussed in Chapter Seven.

The ECU

In the long term it is planned that the ECU will replace individual members' currencies and act as the single Community currency. The value of the ECU is determined from a basket of all the EC members' currencies. The importance of each national currency in the calculation depends upon the size and trading importance of the country's economy. The basket of currencies is revised regularly to reflect changes in underlying economic circumstances.

The current value of the ECU in pounds sterling is about 78 pence. The currency is not in general use and so far only special commemerative gold ECUs have been produced. It is, however, used as a basis for settlement of debts between governments, banks and businesses. It is possible to buy traveller's cheques denoted in ECUs, but these will be converted to the appropriate currency when encashed.

The Creation of the Single European Market

The EC is passing through a period of dramatic change. The catalyst for this change was the Single European Act of 1987. This Act is an attempt to achieve the original social and economic objectives of the 1957 Treaty of Rome. The Treaty of Rome begins by stating the signatories' determination 'to lay the foundations of an ever closer union among the peoples of Europe' their resolution 'to ensure the economic and social progress of [their] countries by common action to eliminate the barriers which divide Europe'. The 1987 Act confirmed the intention of the member states to have a Single European Market and to remove the barriers that still existed even in the mid-1980s.

These barriers took a number of forms:

- Customs barriers still existed and the paperwork required to export goods to other EC states made it difficult and expensive (in terms of administration and delays) to trade outside national boundaries
- Lack of information made many firms unaware of trading possibilities abroad. This was particularly true when governments were seeking tenders for the supply of goods and services. Most governments favoured domestic suppliers through the simple expedient of not advertising across national frontiers
- Differing technical standards made products acceptable within one country but not in others. This also involved firms producing different models with an associated rise in the cost of production

These factors led to the heads of government of the twelve EC states signing the Single European Act in February 1986. The Act came into force on 1 July 1987. It committed the EC to the creation of a Single European Market by the 31 December 1992. To create a Single Market of 332 million people required the passing of over 300 measures by the Community's institutions.

KEY POINTS 8.2

- Four major institutions govern the EC: the Commission, the Council, the Parliament and the Court of Justice
- The Council is the main decision making body in the EC
- The Commission proposes and implements policy whilst the Parliament discusses it
- Three types of European law exist of which Regulations are the most powerful
- The major aim of EMU is the creation of a common European currency

Activity 8.2

You have been asked by your boss to plan a journey for an articulated lorry carrying engine parts from Newcastle in the north east of England to Naples in the south of Italy. You have been asked to plan the quickest possible journey in terms of time so as to minimize transport costs. You have been given the following information:

- You can use any ferry crossing you like
- The lorry can travel for ten hours each day at an average speed of 80kph
- Crossing by ferry does not count as 'driving time'
- Crossing frontiers takes an average of two hours 'driving time'. This does not apply in the Benelux countries as they have no customs barriers

You will need a European road atlas which shows distances and borders. Additionally, you will have to discover the time taken on various ferry routes. Once you have calculated the time for the outward journey you should double it to allow for the return trip.

Your objective is to find the quickest possible route.

The Single European Act – The Changes

The creation of a Single – or Common – Market embodies many changes.

THE CREATION OF SINGLE STANDARDS

The governments of all the member states impose standards relating to matters such as safety and quality in the products and services available within their countries. You may be familiar with the Kite symbol in the UK which means that the product in question has met the standards required by the British Standards Institute (BSI). Germany has a similar system called DIN. These standards all aim to protect the consumer. However, such standards differ between the twelve EC states and have become technical barriers to trade. Goods which meet BSI standards may not meet DIN standards and vice-versa. Many exporters cannot send their products to other member states without adapting and altering them. This reduces the opportunity for the exporter to benefit from economies of scale.

The EC has sought to remove such technical differences since 1983 by insisting that members inform the Commission of new technical regulations. Standards imposed by a single state can be banned by the Commission if they might exclude the products of other member states and so act as a barrier to trade. At the same time, the Commission has created a new body – the Comité Européenne de Normalisation (CEN) – to create new, harmonized standards. New products which are acceptable throughout the EC will carry the Community's CE mark (see Figure 8.6 on next page).

Developments in this area have led to steps being taken to create a community patent. We discussed the workings of the UK patent system in Chapter Four. The EC proposals could create a simpler method to give protection of ideas. Currently, those wanting protection in the EC must obtain a bundle of national patents either by making a single application to the European Patent Office (EPO) or individual applications to each member state. The establishment of a patent for the entire Community subject to a single legal system and administered by the EPO is thought to be of much benefit to industry and commerce in the EC.

ELIMINATING FRONTIER CONTROLS AND DELAYS

Plans to remove all frontier controls by the end of 1992 should have been completed by now, assuming that agreement has been reached between all the EC states. The intention was that this should be attained by a policy of gradual reduction of barriers. The harmonization of VAT levels and the removal of differences in technical standards will have assisted in reducing frontier delays. Other causes of delays have resulted from the need to collect statistics, to limit the spread of animal diseases and to prevent the entry of banned products. Progress has been made in reducing the time spent by export vehicles at frontier crossings. In January 1988, a Single Administrative Document was introduced for vehicles crossing international boundaries. This single document replaced approximately 65 separate documents!

THE FREE MOVEMENT OF PEOPLE

The Single European Act provides for the removal of all restrictions on the movement of people within the EC. This simply confirms Article 3 of the Treaty of Rome, which states 'the activities of the Community shall include the abolition between member states of the obstacles to the free movement of persons'. The major forces preventing Europeans from working in other member states is the failure to recognize mutually educational and vocational qualifications. Relatively few UK citizens currently live and work in other EC countries, though the figure is rising steadily.

For many years the EC has struggled to harmonize qualifications and many courses in further and higher education are being adapted to meet this aim. Further obstacles to labour mobility have been the need to obtain work permits, difficulty in acquiring entitlement to state education for children overseas, lack of rights regarding access to the local social security system and

148   **The Business Environment**

---

*Figure 8.6 – **The New EC Standard.*** The Department of Trade and Industry has mounted a major campaign to inform UK industry and commerce of the changes inherent in the move to the Single European Market. This advertisement offers firms the opportunity to receive details on the changes that standards harmonization have brought about in various product areas.

Get up to the mark!

CE Mark

Look in the shops this Christmas and you'll see toys carrying the CE mark. For the toy industry the single market has arrived.
The toy industry is not alone; it is simply the first.
Toys will soon be followed by a wide range of other products which will also have to show they meet new EC requirements.
Whether your markets are just in the United Kingdom or elsewhere in the Community, the same rules will apply for you and your competitors. You can't opt out.
To help you prepare, a range of DTI booklets is freely available. They're just a few ticks away.

STANDARDS AND THE SINGLE MARKET

- STANDARDS ACTION PLAN
- TOY SAFETY
- SIMPLE PRESSURE VESSELS
- CONSTRUCTION PRODUCTS
- ELECTROMAGNETIC COMPATIBILITY
- MACHINERY SAFETY
- PERSONAL PROTECTIVE EQUIPMENT
- DIRECTIVES UNDER DISCUSSION
- NEW APPROACH TO TECHNICAL HARMONISATION AND STANDARDS
- AVOIDING NEW BARRIERS
- TESTING AND CERTIFICATION
- *GAS APPLIANCES
- *NON-AUTOMATIC WEIGHING INSTRUMENTS
- *ACTIVE MEDICAL DEVICES
- *ACTIVE IMPLANTABLE ELECTROMEDICAL DEVICES

*When available

SM5

PLEASE COMPLETE IN BLOCK CAPITALS
NAME _____
POSITION IN COMPANY _____
COMPANY NAME _____
ADDRESS _____
_____
POSTCODE _____ TEL NO. _____
No. of employees in Company: 1-24 ☐ 25-99 ☐ 100-199 ☐ 200-499 ☐ 500+ ☐
Nature of business: Manufacturing ☐ Service ☐ Construction ☐ Other ☐

Source: DTI

---

differences in language and culture.

The Community intends to produce a Vocational Training Card which will entitle its holder to work throughout the EC. Similarly, it has agreed a 'right of establishment' for some of the professions – notably those involved in health care. This 'right of establishment' is the outcome of lengthy negotiations and many directives to create a common basic training for all those professions to whom it applies. As a result, doctors, dentists and nurses can now practise anywhere in the EC.

The EC is now considering applying the principle, that if a person is entitled to follow a vocation or profession in one EC state then he or she should be able to operate anywhere within the EC.

CAPITAL AND FINANCIAL SERVICES

From the end of December 1992 onwards all financial transactions will have been liberalized. What does this mean? Cash, bank transfers, loans, international investments, etc will all be freely transferred within the Community. This means that individuals and firms can freely transfer capital and currency between states. Thus, French banks may lend funds for mortgages to UK citizens, or a Spanish firm may transfer its reserves to a Dutch bank without restriction.

Most of the EC members, including the UK, have already removed their exchange controls to allow the free movement of capital between states. All member countries will be required to remove their controls within a few years.

A significant part of this change is the freedom to provide financial services, such as insurance and banking, throughout the EC. Traditionally, the UK has been a major seller of insurance policies worldwide and has high hopes of substantial sales in the Single European Market (see Figure 8.7).

Already, a basic 'right of establishment' exists in the EC for providers of financial services. Firms from one member state can, in general, compete on equal terms with domestic firms in other member states so long as they establish local offices in conformity with national rules and regulations. Thus, the National Westminster Bank can open a branch in Paris if it conforms with French law and banking regulations.

However, a true Single Market will require the creation of a single authorization or passport which is valid in all member states and can be issued by any EC government. Negotiations are now in progress to achieve this aim.

GOVERNMENT PURCHASING

This is sometimes termed 'public procurement'. It simply refers to the huge amount of goods and services which are purchased each year by the EC governments.

In the past EC governments did not always award contracts for supplies and services to firms that offered the cheapest deal. Many governments tended to favour domestic firms to protect employment and prosperity. For example, the UK government may have decided to purchase military clothing from a firm in Leeds even though cheaper supplies of equal quality were available overseas. Such national favouritism was encouraged by governments employing complex tendering systems, failing to publicize fully the opportunity and requiring bids for the work to be in within a very short time.

New EC directives which formed part of the move to the Single European Market in 1992 are intended to ensure that governments buy from the cheapest and best sources within the EC and that free competition genuinely exists. Regulations concerning public procurement also covers the energy industry, water supplies, transport and communications.

OTHER HARMONIZATION POLICIES

The EC is seeking to harmonize Value Added Tax, other indirect taxes and the corporate tax systems of the twelve. These proposals have met

---

*Figure 8.7 – **Insurance Sales in Domestic and European Markets.*** This figure shows the relative domestic and European sales for a number of major European countries. Successful companies in the new European market will have to seek to gain significant sales in other European countries. However, the figures may be distorted in that some firms may have a tradition of selling in several different national markets. The Royal Insurance Case Study (next page) takes a closer look at a particular insurance company.

Proportion of premium income coming from European countries other than home country

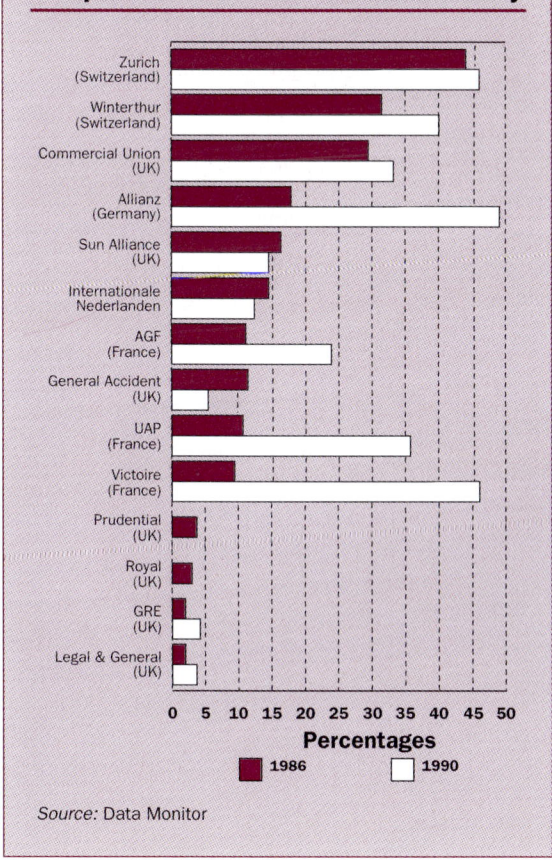

[Bar chart showing percentages for: Zurich (Switzerland), Winterthur (Switzerland), Commercial Union (UK), Allianz (Germany), Sun Alliance (UK), Internationale Nederlanden, AGF (France), General Accident (UK), UAP (France), Victoire (France), Prudential (UK), Royal (UK), GRE (UK), Legal & General (UK). X-axis: 0 to 50 Percentages. Legend: 1986, 1990]

Source: Data Monitor

CASE STUDY

Royal Insurance

The UK's leading insurance group, Royal Insurance, operates in the UK and eighty countries around the world. One of its subsidiaries, itself a holding company, is the Liverpool-based Royal Life which provides a range of financial services. The Royal Insurance company intends to establish a firm European presence in advance of 1992 as part of its growth strategy.

The company welcomes the harmonization of the EC's insurance regulations even if it will take a long time. They believe that it will be the mid-1990s before it is sorted out. David Graham, an overseas actuary, notes that 'the technical problems which have to be solved are immense. Each country has its own regime and taxation system which will affect how the final regulations take shape. Here in the UK we have a fairly liberal attitude towards insurance and investments but in Germany, for example, there is more rigid control.'

David Graham is optimistic and confident that the creation of a single authorization or licence to offer insurance services throughout the EC will create an insurance market that is more integrated and larger than even the USA.

A successful selling network is already in place in the Netherlands and Royal Life Spain has recently been launched with offices in Madrid and Barcelona with further offices planned in all major cities.

Says David Graham: 'The life insurance market is less developed in Southern Europe than in, say, France and Germany. We have chosen Spain because there is a perceived need by the Spanish to catch up and the government has a very open attitude to licensing.' The investment will be in people, too, because Royal Life aim to provide a service which is sensitive to local needs, a factor which is felt to be very important.

Source: adapted from the DTI's *Single Market News*, Spring 1990

QUESTIONS

1. Find out the meaning of the terms 'actuary' and 'holding company'.

2. What does David Graham mean when he says that the authorities in Spain 'have a very open attitude to licensing'?

3. Construct a list of the problems involved for a UK firm in setting up and operating an insurance office in Spain.

Figure 8.8 – **The Single European Market: The Main Measures**

Adopted/agreed	Under discussion	Project
Abolishing remaining exchange controls	Harmonizing rules on patents, copyright etc. including introduction of Community trademark	Further liberalization of transport
Mutual recognition of higher education diplomas	Indirect tax harmonization and fiscal frontier controls	Further measures to open up the market in telecommunications services and equipment
Removing restrictions in international road haulage	New system for collecting indirect taxes (eg VAT) when frontier controls abolished	Further opening up of public purchasing in services
Removing restrictions on non-life insurance services for large commercial risks	Further directives on manufacturing and food standards	Definitive arrangements for liberalization of road haulage cabotage*
First step towards freeing air transport from restrictions	Opening up of public purchasing in transport, energy, water and telecommunications	Setting standards for plant health
Directives on common quality standards for industry	Directive to liberalize investment services	Further measures to open up market in life and non-life insurance
More competition in public purchasing and measures to ensure compliance	Further measures on mutual recognition of higher education diplomas	
Arrangements for control of major EC mergers	Liberalization of air transport	
Directive to liberalize banking services		
Opening up market in life assurance services		
Transitional arrangements for liberalization of road haulage cabotage*		

*'Cabotage' is the name for carrying loads on stages of international round-trips.

Source: Economic Progress Report, No 206, February 1990, published by the Treasury

KEY POINTS 8.3

- A common system of technical standards is being established within the EC by CEN
- The EC is working to eliminate delays at frontiers. Eventually all customs barriers between the twelve may be removed
- Workers and capital will be able to move freely within the EC following the establishment of the Single European Market
- Complex negotiations are taking place to create a single authorization or licence to offer financial services throughout the EC
- The EC intends to harmonize indirect and corporate tax systems

---

a lot of opposition from some members, including the UK, because they can limit each country's independent control of its monetary and fiscal policies. The EC also intends to harmonize depreciation allowances for tax purposes.

The Implications of the Single European Market

The implications of this change for UK firms will be far reaching and substantial. Not all firms will be affected in the same way. The precise impact will depend upon the nature and size of the business, the structure of the market in which it operates and the reaction of its management team. It is certain, however, that all businesses will be affected in one way or another by the move to the Single European Market.

LARGER MARKET

The most dramatic and obvious change is that firms will now be selling in what is effectively a domestic market of 332 million people. Economists estimate that the spending power of the EC market will grow by between 4.5 and 7.5 per cent as a result of the integration of the twelve economies. The number of jobs throughout the EC could rise by up to two million. However, these benefits will not be equally shared around by a benevolent bureaucracy – companies and countries will have to compete for their share!

LARGER SCALE OF PRODUCTION

A larger market will encourage a larger scale of production as firms seek to gain the full benefits of economies of scale. Firms will possibly become more specialized as they concentrate on the enlarged domestic market. The increase in scale may be achieved through mergers between national companies to create European conglomerates.

Small and medium-sized companies may find the competition fierce as a result of such restructuring within their particular industry. All companies are likely to experience stronger competition in their domestic markets as the barriers which previously protected them are dismantled. This change will apply to both public and private sector markets. Firms who supply the Health Service and other public bodies will not be unaffected. Those companies who only trade within the UK will also be affected by the growth in foreign competition.

IMPLICATIONS FOR MANAGEMENT

The change in this external environment will have significant implications for the internal management of businesses. The production departments of many manufacturing firms may have to redesign their products in preparation for the Single European Market and to meet the new specifications that are emerging from CEN. Once redesigned, the new products will have to be manufactured possibly using different machinery and techniques.

The free movement of labour will clearly affect the availability and price of a vital resource to business. Employees may move overseas if higher wages are offered and this could create shortages in certain labour markets in the UK. This shortage could prove critical if the workers are highly skilled. Firms may have to work existing employees for longer hours or use more capital equipment. Another scenario might see an influx of cheaper foreign labour (possibly from the Mediterranean countries) and a resultant reduction in UK costs and improvement in competitiveness.

We should remember, however, that the UK's competitors will also have access to similar sources of cheap labour. The exact impact on the labour market is hard to predict and will vary from industry to industry and firm to firm.

Marketing and sales departments will have to prepare to sell a higher proportion of their output overseas. Different strategies and techniques will be necessary to achieve success in what may be unfamiliar territory. Advertisements that are successful in one society and one culture may be inappropriate and even positively harmful in another. Many firms may choose to either merge with competitors in different parts of the EC, and so use their local expertise, or employ local agents to act on their behalf. We considered the difficulties of marketing overseas in Chapter Seven.

TRAINING REQUIREMENTS

We should not expect firms and their employees to respond to such an immense change without a major training programme. Businesses will have to be educated to the implications of the Single European Market for their particular industry. The Department of Trade and Industry has played a leading role in fulfilling this training need.

Within firms, more specialized training will be called for. Language training for many employees will be essential: from the receptionist to the sales director. Language is one barrier to free trade that the EC cannot legislate away. Governments and firms must take responsibility for reducing this barrier. Training needs will occur in other areas, too. Workers will have to be prepared to manufacture new CEN approved goods. Managers will need training to acquaint themselves with new EC directives and regulations that relate to their industry. Marketing staff will need to be educated to sell in new areas of the EC. The move to the Single European Market has presented a great opportunity to those firms who specialize in industrial and commercial training.

This change will not happen overnight. Many firms have prepared for the Single European Market since it became a reality in 1987. Others have put their head in the sand and were not ready. Many businesses have sold to parts of the EC for a long time and are familiar with local markets and customs. Equally, many UK firms are accustomed perhaps to a relatively uncompetitive domestic market. Change will affect all firms: to different degrees and in different ways.

Is UK Business Prepared for the Single European Market?

The British Market Research Bureau has been employed by the DTI to undertake a programme of research into business attitudes to the Single European Market. Awareness of the Single

Figure 8.9 – **The Response of UK Businesses to the challenge of the Single European Market**

Measures taken or planned amongst those having taken action or intending to act

Measure	Have done	Intending to do	Total
Researching, reviewing situation	66	23	89
Monitoring progress	64	24	88
Considering implications	59	21	80
Devolping aspects of business	59	21	80
Meeting new standards, checking BS standards	59	20	79
Reviewing competition, taking steps to defend home market	54	21	75
Looking for business in Europe, exporting more	41	23	64
Input or communication with trade association	43	12	55
Diversifying	34	20	54
Consulting DTI/UK Government	32	18	50
Alternatives to the European market	38	10	48
Training, updating staff	23	22	45
Joint ventures	21	22	43
Forming a division to develop existing business with Europe	18	12	30
Lobbying	14	7	21
Seeking acquisition of a European company	11	10	21
Visiting Brussels, or discussion with "Brussels"	9	5	14

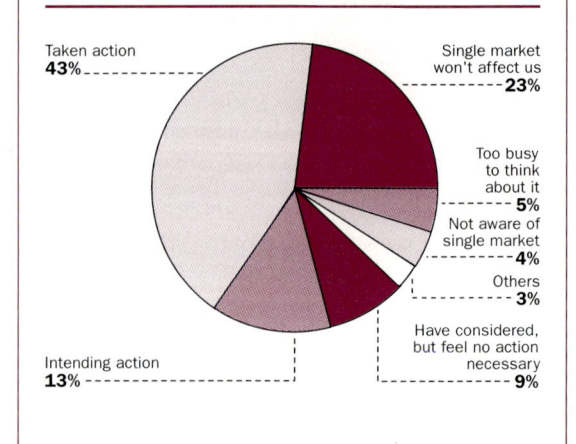

Action and Inaction

- Taken action 43%
- Intending action 13%
- Single market won't affect us 23%
- Too busy to think about it 5%
- Not aware of single market 4%
- Others 3%
- Have considered, but feel no action necessary 9%

Source: DTI, *Single Market News*, Winter 1990

European Market is at saturation point: 96 per cent of those interviewed confirmed that they had heard of plans for the Single European Market. Of the 4 per cent who hadn't, most were small, independent firms trading locally. When asked what part of their operations would actually be affected by the Single European Market, most chose to give general rather than specific answers.

The number of firms claiming to have already taken action to prepare for the Single European Market was 43 per cent of the total. Most of the firms have taken a range of actions and intend to take more.

Looking more closely at the figures, it is clear that action is closely related to the geographical extent of trade and size of the business. Thus, 75 per cent of firms with an international market have taken action compared to 20 per cent with only a local market. 83 per cent of firms with more than 1 000 employees, and 75 per cent of those employing between 500 and 999, have taken action. 55 per cent of manufacturing firms claim to have already taken action compared with 40 per cent of firms involved in other activities.

For all firms, irrespective of size, sector or location the message is clear: the Single European Market is here now. Where are you?

CASE STUDY

Flexible Manufacturing Technology Limited

Flexible Manufacturing Technology Limited (FMT) is a Brighton-based machine tool manufacturer of flexible machining cells and system tools. It already sells to the EC market including Germany. FMT's managing director, Stephen Hardy, argues that the Single European Market will, in some ways, make it easier for his company to sell in the EC. 'One of the countries into which we are selling our machines is Germany, and as they have different rules and regulations covering health and safety at work, it is more difficult for us than an indigenous manufacturer. Obviously when there is a single market, that will change. It may mean that there are certain features we shall have to add to our machines but at least it will make them all standard.' FMT believes that harmonization of standards in this area will be most strongly influenced by the Germans because they have a strong machine tool industry and other EC states will lean towards German DIN standards.

One of the biggest problems facing UK firms selling into Europe will be languages. FMT is largely over that hurdle by use of its agents appointed with the help of the local British Embassy or Consulate. FMT is not complacent, however, and does not believe that agents is the sole solution to selling abroad even if good quality agents are appointed. At every level of the company, from chairman Mike Bright downwards to the shop floor, there are bi-lingual and multi-lingual personnel. Malcolm Sheppard, FMT's sales director, argues that 'most European companies take language seriously and it is an illusion to think that you can go and sell in your own language'.

Total involvement in the marketplace is also part of FMT's strategy and the chairman sits on the committee of CECIMO, the European machine tool industry body, and is also active in Britain's Machine Tool Technology Association.

Malcolm Sheppard believes that British firms also have to overcome a reputation for poor quality and reliability. He believes the reputation to be mainly undeserved, but its existence means a greater selling effort is required from British firms compared to other EC firms.

Commercial knowledge of a particular country is seen as being of prime importance. Comments Malcolm Sheppard: 'Dealing with an Italian customer is very different from dealing with a French one and dealing with a customer in the south of France is very different from negotiating in the north of the country. In my view you will never be a good exporter if you have not travelled extensively in the countries in which you wish to sell'.

Source: adapted from DTI, Single Market News, Spring 1990

QUESTIONS

1 What evidence is there in the Case Study to suggest that FMT is well prepared for the onset of the Single European Market?

2 For what reasons might FMT find it difficult to compete in Europe once the Single European Market is fully established?

KEY POINTS 8.4

- The move to the Single European Market will affect all firms, whether they export into the EC or not
- Firms will have to adapt internally to the change in their business environment
- Training of employees in preparation for the Single European Market will be of critical importance for many firms

Developments in Eastern Europe

Eastern Europe underwent dramatic change in the late 1980s and early 1990s. The two most significant aspects of this change were:

- Many of the former communist regimes opted for economic systems along the lines of Western European countries
- One of the members of the Eastern bloc – East Germany – effectively became a member of the EC overnight when it merged with West Germany

German Unification

Having existed as separate countries since 1945, East and West Germany were reunited on 3 October 1990. On that day the population of the EC increased by 17 million as a potentially powerful new Germany was created with a population of 82 million people. This has led to a transfer of power within the EC and some apprehension in

---

CASE STUDY

Oil Giants Bid For Bulgarian Bonanza

European and US oil companies are bidding for exploration and development contracts in the Black Sea off the Bulgarian coast, but have found themselves frustrated by the slow pace of reform.

BP, Shell, Texaco and Statoil are among companies seeking a foothold in Bulgaria and other East European countries as state-owned energy monopolies are broken into smaller entities. Enterprise Oil, Shell and British Gas have recently signed substantial deals.

The oil firms and Western institutions were encouraged when last weekend's elections in Bulgaria favoured politicians who appear to be committed to large scale privatisations and the introduction of more flexible foreign investment laws.

The government has prepared draft privatization laws and opened a privatization agency in Sofia.

Foreign investors cannot invest less than $50 000. This presents difficulties for small Western firms, but for giants such as Coca-Cola and Pepsi-Cola, who have negotiated licences with local manufacturers, there are few obstacles. Foreign investment on a large scale will only come with privatisation. A team of European consultants are advising the Bulgarians, while the European Community has provided Ecu20 million to fund privatizations and restructuring.

Source: adapted from the *European*, 18–20 October 1991

QUESTIONS

1. What is the pound sterling equivalent of Ecu20 million?

2. What is meant by 'privatization' in the context of this article? (You may need to refer back to Chapter Two)

3. Draw up a 'balance sheet' to show the advantages and disadvantages to Western companies of creating production plants in Eastern Europe.

Italy, France and the UK that this enlarged state will dominate Europe economically.

The impact on the EC of this unification will be considerable. It is increased by the suddenness of the change. On previous occasions when the EC has been enlarged, several years of negotiations and preparations have preceded the entry of the new member. For example, negotiations lasted for five years before Spain and Portugal became members in 1986.

The EC will subsidize the former East German economy in a number of ways for the foreseeable future. Estimates suggest that the figure will annually be in excess of £2 billion. Subsidies will be offered to help the Germans upgrade their environmental standards. Eastern Germany will also enjoy subsidies under the Common Agricultural Policy, with its farmers receiving higher prices for their agricultural products than when under the communist regime. Finally, the Eastern Germans will receive support from the EC's Regional Policy budget to help raise living standards towards the EC average.

This means less EC funding is available for other firms, industries and regions. A benefit exists in that the Eastern German market is now open to all EC members, but exporters can expect fierce competition from Western German competitors.

The Liberalization of the Eastern European Economies

The freeing of the economies of Poland, Hungary and Czechoslovakia in Eastern Europe formerly under communist control offers opportunities to exporters from many countries. In particular, what was East Germany and Czechoslovakia offer considerable potential to multinationals. The relative poverty of these emerging economies is both an advantage and a disadvantage to potential exporters.

The economies need much development and possibilities exist for construction firms, providers of machine tools and similar products associated with the reconstruction of an economy. Eastern Europe has proved attractive to car producers and already a number of joint ventures have been established – for example, by Volkswagen and Fiat. These firms hope to produce a range of vehicles in Eastern Europe. Wage levels in Eastern Europe are well below those of the EC. This – and the closeness to major EC markets such as Germany – is a large incentive for multinational firms to set up branch plants in these countries and improve competitiveness. They also hope that Eastern Europe itself will eventually become a large potential market.

These economies are handicapped in a number of ways. Low incomes mean a lack of funds to purchase the materials and expertise they require. In particular, these economies earn relatively little Western currency with which to purchase Western goods and services. Firms seeking to establish plants in Eastern Europe will probably find it difficult to acquire materials and the necessary business information owing to underdeveloped information channels. Distribution channels are often inefficient or absent and retail outlets primitive.

However, in spite of these difficulties, opportunities do exist – even in the short term. Some firms are setting up in Eastern Europe with the help of guarantees of access to Eastern markets as a result of negotiations with the relevant governments. Loans are granted by Western firms and governments to assist the Eastern European economies to purchase the output of Western companies. Western banks and building societies are improving the quantity and quality of data available on Eastern Europe. This service encourages potential investors. In addition, many governments are providing aid to assist development in this region.

Economists predict rapid rates of growth for the Eastern European markets and this potential has not been ignored by many companies from the EC and other parts of the world. The potential of Eastern Europe is probably greater in the long term rather than the short term due to the limitations outlined above. It is likely to be exploited as a relatively low-cost base for production rather than as a market in the near future.

Now look again at your answer to the third question in the last Case Study. Can you add some more points to your answer?

KEY POINTS 8.5

- The developments in Eastern Europe provide opportunities for firms from the UK and other nations
- Such investment does, however, involve substantial risks
- It has been predicted that Eastern European nations will experience high rates of economic growth

EXAM PREPARATION

SHORT QUESTIONS

1. Which organizations make up the EC?
2. What are the four main institutions which govern the EC?
3. How do these institutions combine to produce EC legislation?
4. List four barriers which the EC has had to remove to create the Single European Market.
5. What is meant by the term 'right of establishment'?
6. What are exchange controls?
7. List four areas of training that a manufacturer might deem necessary in preparation for the Single European Market.
8. How might firms which only sell in the UK be affected by the Single European Market?
9. What is the role of CEN in the formation of the Single European Market?
10. What is meant by the term 'public procurement'?

DATA RESPONSE QUESTION

Study the information and answer the questions that follow.

The coming of the Single Market – the EC's 'big bang'

The creation of the Single European Market (SEM) involves the sweeping away of physical, technical and fiscal barriers right across the Community. What will emerge will be the world's largest market – bigger than Japan and the United States combined, totalling more than 320 million people.

Almost the first task that the present European Commission undertook was to publish a White Paper giving 300 detailed proposals requiring action and decision for a single internal market to be created by 1992. This White Paper, having first been endorsed by the heads of government when they met in Milan in June 1985, is now enshrined in the Single European Act subsequently approved by the parliaments of all member nations.

The Act defines the internal market as 'an area without internal frontiers in which the free movement of goods, persons, services and capital is ensured'.

Although the UK has so far been slow to respond to the potential opportunities offered by the Single European Market, there are now encouraging signs of awakening – following various messages of exhortation, warning and advice to companies generally. CBI President Sir David Nickson urged all chief executives in December 1989 to 'get started and set the pace'. John Raisman, chairman of the CBI Europe Committee, suggested at a recent business conference that companies should prepare for 1992 by reviewing their operational policies and programmes in Europe.

(a) Explain what is meant by the 'sweeping away of physical, technical and fiscal barriers'. *(6 marks)*

(b) What might be involved in companies 'reviewing their operational policies and programmes in Europe'? *(5 marks)*

(c) Explain **three** advantages for businesses of the Single European Market.

(*9 marks*)

(AEB November 1990)

BTEC ASSIGNMENT

You are the financial director of a Belgian subsidiary of a UK firm which has substantial export sales throughout the EC. Your board of directors is concerned with the implications of the ERM for the business and has commissioned you to write a report addressing the two issues below:

(a) Find out which members of the EC are members of the ERM. Are there any differences in the degrees to which their currencies are allowed to fluctuate? What might be the implications of these differences as well as the system of ERM for your company?

(b) How might government policy to maintain the fixed exchange rate required by the ERM affect your business? You should identify advantages and disadvantages that might result from entry to the ERM.

ESSAY

1 In 1992 all trade barriers will have been removed between member states of the European Community. Discuss the likely implications for UK firms.

Suggested Answers to Essays

Chapter One

Essay 1
The size of businesses can be measured in many ways. For example: by turnover, capital employed or number of employees.

Businesses vary in size for a number of reasons. For small businesses, it could be that their market is small – for example, a hairdresser in a village. Equally it could be that many competitiors exist which prevents firms gaining a high market share. It may be that the firm is in an industry which requires it to offer a high level of personal service, which large organizations are unable to.

Large businesses may exist because economies of scale can be achieved or because huge capital investment is required (in the steel industry, for example). The market may be worldwide and so large businesses develop to meet this extensive demand. Other factors include the management style and objectives of the owners, the amount of capital to which they have access, the extent of government support and so on.

The simple answer to the second part is, 'yes'! Those industries which produce highly technical products, which require extensive research, tend to comprise large firms. Those that produce a perishable product tend to be smaller, etc. However, there are exceptions: industries exist which have both large and small firms – for example, the retail industry.

Essay 2
The factors which shape the business environment are reflected in the make-up of this book. The government by its actions in respect of the economy or the law is a major influence. So also are supranational organizations, such as the EC and the IMF. The decisions of consumers are an important factor and these reflect their confidence in the state of the economy and the impact of social changes amongst other factors. The actions and reactions of firms – through, for example, their pricing policies and technical innovation of products – play a role.

There are a number of answers to the second part of this question. Key factors may well be the extent to which the EC centralizes, the changes in Eastern Europe, the state of the UK economy and the policies pursued by the government.

Chapter Two

Essay 1
If heavy unemployment was anticipated then firms might alter their marketing mix and place greater emphasis on price, reliability, etc. They may cut production, make employees redundant or close branch plants. They could reduce their training budgets, cut their investment programmes, merge with other firms or seek new markets. Affected firms may produce lower quality products, or a basic range to meet the lower incomes of consumers.

However, the reaction depends upon the type of firm and the style of management. Some managers will take little or no action, and hope to ride the bad period out. Those producing essentials may be little affected. Others selling income elastic goods may have to be more active. If the market is highly competitive, firms are more likely to take action.

Essay 2
The basis of this answer will be arguments for and against nationalization and privatization.

The consumer benefits from privatization in that resources should be allocated more efficiently through the market system, and so the right goods are supplied at the right time. In this sense, waste is eliminated and inefficient firms do not survive in a competitive environment. Furthermore, no public money is used in order to manage the business.

Some industries are natural monopolies and should be controlled by the state to avoid exploitation of consumers. It is possible to argue that competition would encourage wasteful duplication or that small businesses would not be capable of achieving economies of scale. Finally, the profits of the private business would go to a small section of society.

Can these two positions be reconciled? There is not just one type of privatization and some of the criticisms do not apply to certain styles of privatization. What is more, the state has attempted to remedy the worst excesses of privatized monopolies by, for example, setting up consumer watchdogs. Many shares in privatized concerns are owned by institutions and hence a substantial section of the population have an indirect interest in the well-being of the privatized businesses. Most people save with banks and building societies. Many also have endowment insurance policies which are another form of saving. The financial institutions use the savings and insurance premiums to invest in a range of stocks and shares, including companies that have been privatized. If these companies do not perform well and pay high dividends as well as maintaining their share prices, then savers and those with endowment policies will suffer from lower returns. Trade unions exist to help defend the interests of workers in these firms and the media will expose the worst excesses.

Chapter Three

Essay 1

Taxes on expenditure are known as indirect taxes and include excise duties and VAT.

A rise in indirect taxes can be expected to reduce demand for the business's output. This may be avoided by the firm absorbing the rise in tax through a reduction in its profits, thus leaving price unchanged. Clearly, this will depend upon the circumstances of the firm – notably its profitability and the competitive make-up of its market. If it is unable to absorb an effective rise in costs or simply to increase stocks, then the firm may have to accept lower sales and rationalize production accordingly. This could entail redundancies, more basic products being produced or a reduction in quality.

Firms affected may seek alternative markets or increase their marketing activities in an attempt to maintain sales.

However, a rise in indirect taxes will not affect all firms equally. It depends upon the price elasticity of demand – or sensitivity of demand to price. Essentials such as food may be little affected, but goods that have demand (for example, electrical products) will be significantly affected. Thus, firms producing goods with elastic demand can expect a tougher time.

Essay 2

a A government can restrict credit by raising interest rates to reduce the demand for credit; by shortening the repayment period and/or increasing the initial deposit on hire purchase agreements; or by imposing restrictions on lending institutions.

b (i) The motor car industry would find sales of new cars diminishing as many motor vehicle purchases are on credit. However, sales of second-hand cars may receive a boost. Sales would also decline because the credit restrictions would decrease the level of economic activity which would reduce the general level of demand (including that for cars). A rise in interest rates might lead to a rise in the external value of sterling which would make imported cars less expensive and exacerbate the effects detailed above.

(ii) Builders's merchants supplying the DIY trade would suffer two effects: demand might decline as some consumers are put off their DIY programmes by the higher cost of credit; others might choose to undertake the cheaper option of DIY rather than hiring a professional. Some may choose DIY rather than move house and incur a larger mortgage.

(iii) The overall level of economic activity would most likely decline. The impact would vary from sector to sector within the economy and from region to region. The precise impact would also depend upon the other economic policies enacted by the government and the actions of bodies, such as the EC Commission.

Essay 3

Higher interest rates will affect a firm producing consumer durables in a variety of ways. Such a policy is deflationary and will reduce the level of demand for such interest elastic goods.

Firms may react to this threat by altering their marketing mix to stress price competitiveness and durability. They may be able to reduce prices depending upon their financial and competitive position. However, this may prove difficult because suppliers's costs and prices will be rising and at the same time the consumer durable firm will face higher costs to service existing loans.

Alternative strategies may be to find new markets or to merge with competitors and/or suppliers to achieve economies of scale and reduce unit costs. Selling overseas may prove difficult as a rising pound will increase export prices.

It may be necessary to reduce production and introduce shorter working hours or negotiate redundancies or early retirements. Some increase in stock levels may be permissible if it is believed that the deflationary economic policy is likely to be short-lived.

The impact will depend upon the competitive structure of the market, the amount by which interest rates rise and the initial level of interest rates. It will also depend upon other government policies and the general level of interest rates throughout the world.

Essay 4

a Interest rates are subject to a number of

influences. A basic underlying influence is the demand for funds relative to the supply of funds. If savings are scarce this may create a shortage of short-term funds in the financial markets leading to upward pressure on interest rates.

Governments are a major influence and may manipulate interest rates as part of their economic management. Finally, other nations's rates also influence the UK's. If the UK's rates are low compared to those of other countries, then the pound is likely to fall in value. This may lead to pressure to increase interest rates

b This covers many of the areas discussed in earlier answers above. Rises in costs, declining demand and the difficulties involved in reducing output will be central factors. How this affects decisions is through the information on which decisions are based. Firms will be receiving forecasts of higher costs of raw materials and falls on demand for their goods and services. In other words, the business's environment is changing and the firm must take decisions in response to these changes.

Chapter Four

Essay 1

This is apparently about technology, but the basis of the answer lies in the theories of demand and supply – and particularly the latter.

Supply of computers has increased dramatically as technological developments have made systems easier and cheaper to produce. This has allowed economies of scale and attracted more firms into the market. Increasingly, firms have been able to employ mainly unskilled labour for assembly work with just a core of highly skilled technical workers. This process has facilitated the use of cheap labour in Africa and Asia.

Although rises in demand push prices up, it is necessary to encourage increases in supply by allowing greater returns on the capital they have invested. User friendly systems, increasing reliability, a wider range of applications and greater use for PCs in general have all fuelled rises in demand.

Chapter Five

Essay 1

In answering this, you should not lose sight of the fact that it concerns international competitiveness.

Clearly, this type of legislation imposes costs. Production will be slower and more expensive as there will be a greater number of non-productive workers. Decisions will be slower as more people have to be consulted and this may discourage managers. Costs will probably have to be passed on to consumers, resulting in a loss of efficiency and reduction of scale economies as sales slump.

Such legislation offers benefits: a protected workforce will be more content and possibly more productive. Expensive accidents may be avoided. A protected and motivated workforce should produce better quality products, enhancing the reputation of the country concerned. In any case, most advanced nations have similar legislation and are therefore competing against each other on an even basis.

However, international competitiveness depends upon other factors. Changes in the exchange rate can easily offset or emphasize rises in costs. Businesses cannot be separated from society and must reflect the values of society by not behaving irresponsibly.

Essay 2

Firstly, you need to identify the main areas of government legislation. For example, consumer and employee protection, health and safety legislation, environmental protection, monopoly and merger legislation, tax legislation, data protection and so on.

In support of the statement, it could be argued that large firms can employ lawyers and accountants to fight their cases and as such may be more willing to 'take on' the authorities. They may also feel unthreatened by the relatively small fines that some offences attract. An example of this could be the attitude of large retailers to the Sunday trading laws. Large firms are also able to lobby governments more effectively and so may persuade governments to amend legislation. Governments and local authorities may be unwilling to prosecute large firms for fear they may leave the area or nation with an adverse effect upon employment.

Alternatively, large firms are constantly in the public eye and may fear for their public image if they break the law. They may spend millions on creating a public image and will not want to damage this for what might prove to be a small saving in costs. Their workforces are likely to be unionized and so will watch over their activities and bring any infringements of the law to the attention of the authorities.

The costs imposed by such legislation can be more easily met by large firms. In fact, it is small firms that are more likely to face difficulties in this respect.

Chapter Six

Essay 1

Firms have social responsibilities in respect of maintaining employment, protecting the environment, supporting other local industries, supporting local causes and providing local amenities.

They can meet these responsibilities by investing and expanding production within the locality rather than elsewhere, by using local suppliers and by training local people. They can co-operate with local organizations, by using derelict land rather than greenfield sites, by altering production to reduce or eliminate waste and pollution and so on. They can develop playing fields and cultural centres and contribute towards transport improvements.

These policies are likely to cause conflicts within the organization. Most are expensive and may conflict with the desire of shareholders for maximum profits. It might, however, be possible to argue that meeting social responsibilities will increase productivity and reduce absenteeism and at the same time enhance local sales.

Essay 2

A firm might have many responses to the shortage of young people entering the labour force. It might offer higher wages, or make the jobs more interesting by increasing the range of tasks, or offer training and a worthwhile career structure. The firm might seek to tap the available supply of young workers by improving contacts with schools, colleges and universities. It might seek alternative supplies of labour, perhaps by ceasing early retirement schemes or employing women returners.

The firm could seek to relocate abroad in countries where there is a plentiful supply of young people. The creation of the EC's Single Market would facilitate such a move. Equally, the firm may be unaffected and do nothing or may simply replace people with technology.

The exact response will depend upon the type of business. A manufacturing firm may opt to increase its use of technology, whereas this may not be an option for some service industries. A firm with fewer competitors and a healthy profit level may elect to follow the more expensive options, such as training schemes. Another important determinant will be the management style – some managers may be proactive while others will hope that the problem will go away.

Essay 3

Advertising can take several forms: informative, telling us of a new good or service; persuasive, attempting to counter a rival's campaign or to increase market share.

Firms spend an enormous sum on advertising which wastes resources and does not add to consumer welfare. It adds to the costs of production and is sometimes used to promote harmful products such as tobacco.

On the other hand, it creates employment, maintains healthy competition and subsidizes sports and cultural activities. It can help employment by extending the product life cycle and by bringing the existence of products to the attention of the public. It can even out fluctuations in sales and improve labour relations as firms attract media attention.

Reaching a decision on this is difficult. It depends upon the moral code of the individual and how he or she assesses the factors discussed above. However, advertising does operate within a legal framework and abuses do attract penalties. Stricter control might be an alternative to banning it altogether.

Chapter Seven

Essay 1

The fluctuations may have had an impact upon Jaguar's sales because the company had a high proportion of its sales in the US and was thus vulnerable to adverse movements in the exchange rate. Changes in the value of the currency make corporate planning difficult, particularly if the product being sold is price elastic which can result in wide fluctuations in sales. This has undesirable consequences for production planning, employment and so forth.

Jaguar might have been vulnerable to movements in the exchange rate, and hence price fluctuations, because the US luxury car market is hugely competitive and other producers were queuing up to take market share.

Jaguar could seek to alleviate the impact of falling US sales by expanding in other markets such as the EC. Obviously, this entails costs and would need careful planning. It could seek to develop the home market further or, alternatively, open an American plant and thus avoid exchange rates to some degree.

Jaguar could seek to use forward markets in currency or seek mergers with other companies.

The rewards from overseas trade can be large, but as the Jaguar story illustrates, the risks are commensurately high.

Chapter Eight

Essay 1

The creation of the Single European Market will open up a huge market of about 340 million consumers for UK firms. Whilst this will create opportunities, it will also allow further competition as European firms gain further access to UK markets. Thus, UK firms will have to be highly efficient to survive. Some may seek mergers or agreements to enable them to survive in this new, tougher market.

Firms will have to transport further afield and seek new distribution outlets to ensure sales. Marketing may have to be amended to meet the cultural circumstances of the nation in question. They may have to appoint local agents and marketing agencies.

The free movement of labour will create a new cheap supply of labour, but at the same time may result in the loss of skilled workers to foreign competitors who offer better conditions or pay. Production may benefit from harmonization of standards and the economies of scale resulting from the longer production runs this allows. However, this may involve investment in new equipment and training (including language training).

Firms will be affected in different ways: the local hairdresser will be less affected than the large chemical firm. Those that do not sell overseas may face only slight increases in domestic competition. Some managers have prepared for the Single European Market and their firms have already made many of the necessary changes – others have ignored it!

Dictionary

ad valorem tax a tax which is levied as a percentage of the price or value of a unit of output.

after-sales service back-up services and facilities provided by the suppliers of goods and services to their customers, e.g. free maintenance and repairs, a telephone service for dealing with customers's queries, an express parts delivery service.

agent a person or company employed by another person or company for the purpose of arranging contracts between the principal and third parties.

authorized capital the maximum amount of share capital which a company can issue at any time.

bad debt an accounting term for money owed to a company by customers or borrowers which is highly unlikely to be paid. Such bad debts are written off against the profits of the trading period as a business cost.

balance of payments a record of a country's trade and financial transactions with the rest of the world over a particular period of time, usually one year.

balance of trade a financial record of a country's trade in goods, specifically manufactures, intermediate goods and raw materials, with the rest of the world over a particular period of time, usually one year.

bankruptcy see **insolvent**.

base rate the lowest rate of interest which is used by the commercial banks as the basis for charging interest on loans and overdrafts to their customers.

bid, 1. an offer by one company to purchase all or the majority of the shares of another company.

2. an offer to purchase an item (for example, a house or antique vase) which has been put up for sale at a specified price or is to be sold subject to receipt of 'other prices'.

bill of exchange a financial security which is used to extend business credit for a limited time period. The lender draws up a bill of exchange for a specified sum of money payable at a given future date, usually three months hence, and the borrower signifies his agreement to pay the amount involved by signing (i.e. accepting) the bill.

black economy activities which are performed in an economy which go unrecorded and hence do not appear in a country's official national income accounts.

black market an unofficial or 'under-the-counter' market trading in a product which the government has declared to be illegal (for example, narcotic drugs), or on the sale of which the government has imposed controls thus limiting its availability.

board of directors the group responsible to the share-holders for running a joint-stock company. It meets periodically under the company chairman to decide on major policy matters within the company and the appointment of key managers.

book value the money amount of an asset as stated in a company's accounts and balance sheet.

brainstorming a technique for generating ideas in which members of a group express ideas as they think of them. The object is to compile a list of ideas which can subsequently be considered and evaluated in greater depth.

brand a name, term, sign, symbol or design used to identify a supplier's good or service and to distinguish it from similar products offered by competitors.

breakeven the rate of output and sales at which a supplier generates just enough revenue to cover his fixed and variable costs, earning neither a profit nor a loss.

British Standards Institute (BSI) a body that established the UK standards of safety and quality that consumer products should reach, using its Kitemark as a recognition that the standard has been reached.

budget, 1. a firm's predetermined plan (expressed in quantitative or financial terms) for a given future period.

2. a statement of the government's financial position which is used for planning the government's economic and social welfare programmes and as part of fiscal policy in managing the level and distribution of spending in the economy.

budget deficit (government) the excess of government expenditure over taxation and other receipts.

budget surplus (government) the excess of taxation and other receipts over government expenditure.

bull market a situation in which the prices of financial securities (stocks, shares, etc) or commodities (tin, wheat, etc) tend to rise as a result of persistent buying and only limited selling.

business or **firm** a producer or distributor of goods or services.

business cycle fluctuations in the level of business activity in an economy brought about by changes in demand conditions, particularly increases and decreases in investment spending.

business objectives the goals which a firm sets for itself in respect of profit returns, sales and assets growth, etc, which in turn determine the strategic and operational policies it adopts.

capital, 1. the funds invested in a business in order to acquire the assets which the business needs to trade. Capital can consist of share capital subscribed by shareholders or loan capital provided by lenders.

2. goods such as plant, machinery and equipment which are used to produce other goods and services.

capital formation or **capital accumulation** fixed assets in a company, the process of adding (eg, by investing in new plant and equipment).

capital goods manufactured goods that are purchased by businesses to be used in the production of other goods or services.

cartel a form of collusion between a group of suppliers aimed at suppressing competition between themselves, wholly or in part.

caveat emptor 'let the buyer beware': a situation where a supplier of a good or service is under no legal obligation to inform buyers of any defects or deficiencies in the products supplied. It is thus the responsibility of buyers to determine for themselves whether or not the product is satisfactory.

census a survey carried out by a government department to obtain economic and social data which can be used in the formulation of social and industrial policies. In the UK a *population census* is carried out every ten years to obtain data on demographic trends.

central bank a country's leading bank which acts as banker to the government and the banking system and acts as the authority responsible for implementing the government's monetary policy.

Central Statistical Office (CSO) the UK government department which collects and publishes statistics concerning the economy, such as the National Income 'blue book' and the Balance of Payments 'pink book'.

cost insurance freight (c.i.f.) a method of measuring the cost of purchasing imports which includes the cost of transportation and insurance, as well as the cost of the goods itself. These represent the costs paid by the importer.

code of practice a set of guidelines used to encourage desirable patterns of behaviour but which generally lack any formal sanctions to punish inappropriate behaviour. Often codes of practice are developed as an alternative to legal regulation. For instance, companies engaged in food production might develop a code of practice between them to define hygiene standards.

collateral security an asset which a borrower is required to deposit with, or pledge to, a lender as a condition of obtaining a loan, which can be sold off if the loan is not repaid.

Common Agricultural Policy a policy agreed by all EC members which provides for the subsidization and protection of the farming industry.

common law laws based upon the outcome of previous court cases which serve as a precedent in guiding the judgement of present court cases.

competition the process of active rivalry between the sellers of a particular product as they seek to win and retain buyer demand for their offerings. Competition can take a number of forms including price cutting, advertising and sales promotion, quality variations, packaging and design, and market segmentation.

conglomerate a business that is engaged in a number of unrelated production activities.

consumer a buyer of a final good or service which is purchased to satisfy a personal consumption need.

contract a legally enforceable agreement between two or more parties. A contract involves obligations on the part of the contractors which may be expressed verbally or in writing.

contract of employment an agreement whereby a worker undertakes to work for an employer in return for a wage or salary. In the UK, employees have been entitled since 1964 to a written statement of the main elements of the contract, such as rates of pay and hours of work, known as the terms and conditions of employment.

corporation tax a direct tax levied by the government on the profits accruing to businesses.

cost of living the general level of prices of goods and services in an economy as measured by a representative price-index.

demand the amount of a product which is purchased at a particular price at a particular point in time. A *demand curve* is a line showing the relationship between the price of a product and the quantity demanded per time period over a range of possible prices.

demand forecasting see **sales forecasting**.

demand-pull inflation a general increase in prices caused by total demand exceeding current supply.

demography the analysis of human populations according to their total size, birth rates, death rates and migration; the age and sex distribution of populations and their geographical and occupational distributions; racial and religious profiles, etc.

Department of Trade and Industry (DTI) the UK government office which is primarily responsible for implementing and administering the government's industrial and trade policies.

deregulation the removal of controls over a particular economic activity which have been imposed by the government or some other regulatory body (for example, an industry trade association).

devaluation an administered reduction in the exchange rate of a currency against other currencies under a fixed exchange rate system.

developing country a country characterized by low levels of gross national product and per capita income, which is typically reliant on the production of a limited range of agricultural and mineral products to sustain its economy, but is beginning to make some progress in industry.

developing area a region of economic decline designated under UK regional policy as in need of industrial regeneration. Financial assistance from the government is available to manufacturing and service businesses prepared to undertake new investments in the area.

disposable income the amount of income which a person has available after paying income tax, national insurance contributions and pension contributions.

division of labour a process whereby each individual or firm concentrates its productive efforts on a single or limited number of activities as part of the whole manufacturing process.

DTI see **Department of Trade and Industry**.

dumping the sale of a product by a firm in an export market at a price *below* that charged in its own domestic market.

Durable consumer goods goods used by consumers that have a life-span of more than one year; that is, goods that endure and can give utility over a longer period of time.

economic efficiency the use of resources that generate the highest possible value of output as determined in the market economy by consumers.

economic growth an increase in the total real output of goods and services in an economy over time. Economic growth is usually measured in terms of an increase in gross domestic product (GDP) over time, or an increase in GDP per head of population to reflect its impact on living standards over time.

economic system, the means by which resources are allocated between alternative ends.

economics the study of the way in which countries endowed with only a *limited* availability of economic resources (natural resources, labour and capital) can best use these resources so as to gain the maximum fulfilment of society's *unlimited* demands for goods and services.

economies of scale the reduction in the unit (average) costs of producing and distributing a product as the size of the firm's operations is increased.

elastic demand demand for a product or service which changes greatly as a result of a small price change.

elastic supply supply of a product or service which changes greatly as a result of a small price change.

embargo a complete ban on all international

trade with a particular country or group of countries, or on trade in particular products such as narcotics and defence equipment.

entrepreneur a person who undertakes the risks of establishing and running a new business.

equilibrium market price the market-clearing price at which the demand for a product is just equal to the supply of it.

European Community (EC) or (formerly) European Economic Community (EEC), a regional bloc established by the Treaty of Rome in 1958 with the general objective of integrating the economies of member countries.

European Court of Justice the law court of the EC responsible for implementing the rules of the Treaty of Rome.

European Free Trade Association (EFTA) a regional free trade bloc established in 1959 with the general objective of securing the benefits to be derived from greater international trade.

European Monetary System (EMS) an institutional arrangement, established in 1979, for coordinating and stabilizing the exchange rates of member countries of the European Community (EC).

exchange rate the price of one country's currency expressed in terms of another country's currency; for example, one UK pound (£) = two US dollars ($).

Exchequer a UK government office responsible for the receipt, custody and issue of government funds.

excise duty an indirect tax imposed by the government on a product, principally those such as tobacco, petrol and alcoholic drinks, the demand for which is highly price-inelastic.

Export Credit Guarantee Department (ECGD) a UK government department which insures UK exports sold on credit against nonpayment by foreign customers.

exporting the sale in an overseas market of a product which is produced in the firm's home market.

Fair Trading Act 1973 an Act which consolidated and extended UK competition law by controlling monopolies, mergers and takeovers, restrictive trade agreements and re-sale prices.

financial year the period from 1 April to 31 March of the following year used for corporation tax purposes.

fiscal policy the regulation of government expenditure and taxation in order to control the level of spending in the economy.

fiscal year the government's accounting year which, in the UK, runs from 6 April to 5 April of the following year, and in the USA from 1 July to 30 June.

foreign currency or **foreign exchange** the currency of an overseas country, which is purchased by a particular country in exchange for its own currency, which is then used to finance trade and capital transactions between the two countries.

foreign exchange controls a means of limiting the extent to which a country's currency can be freely exchanged for foreign currencies.

foreign exchange market a market engaged in the buying and selling of foreign currencies.

foreign investment the purchase of overseas physical and financial assets.

franchise the granting by one company to another company (exclusive franchise) or a number of companies (non-exclusive franchise) of the right/s to supply its products. A franchise is a contractual arrangement which is entered into for a specified period of time, with the franchisee paying a royalty to the franchisor for the rights assigned.

free on board (f.o.b.) under a f.o.b. contract the seller pays the cost of transporting the goods to the port of shipment and loading charges, plus all insurance cover up to this point.

General Agreement on Tariffs and Trade (GATT) an international organization established in 1947 to promote the expansion of international trade through the removal of tariffs and other restrictions on cross-frontier trade.

gold a mineral that is used both as an industrial base metal and for ornamental purposes, and is held by governments as part of their stock of international reserve assets in order to finance balance of payments deficits.

good or **commodity** an economic product which is produced to meet some personal or business demand. Goods which are purchased by individuals are called *consumer goods* or *final goods*, while goods purchased by businesses are referred to variously as *producer goods, capital goods, industrial goods* or *intermediate goods*.

gross domestic product (GDP) the total money value of all final goods and services produced in an economy over a one-year period.

gross national product (GNP) the total money value of all final goods and services produced in an economy over a one-year period (gross domestic product) plus income from its investments abroad.

hard currency a foreign currency that is in strong demand, but in short supply on the foreign exchange market.

holding company a joint-stock company that controls another company or companies. Ownership may be *complete* (100%) or *partial* (ownership of 50%+ of the voting shares in the company).

horizontal integration the joining of firms that are producing or selling a similar product.

hot money money moved around quickly and/or regularly by its owners in anticipation of likely exchange rate changes (devaluations and revaluations), or in response to differences in interest rate between financial centres.

hyperinflation a very high level of inflation.

importing the sale in the home market of a product which is produced in a foreign country.

income money received by individuals, firms and other organizations in the form of wages, salaries, rent, interest, commissions, fees and profit, together with grants, unemployment benefit, old age pensions, etc.

incomes policy see **prices and incomes policy**.

inelastic demand demand for a product or service which does not change in spite of a large price change.

inelastic supply supply of a product or service offered for sale which changes very little in spite of a price change.

inflation an increase in the general level of prices in an economy that is sustained over time.

innovation see **research and development**.

insolvent a condition under which an individual or firm is unable to pay debts when they fall due.

interest the charge made for borrowing money in the form of a loan.

interest rate the particular amount of interest which a borrower is required to pay to a lender for borrowing a particular sum of money to finance spending on consumption and the purchase of capital assets.

International Monetary Fund (IMF) an international organization established in 1947 to promote, alongside the General Agreement on Tariffs and Trade, the expansion of international trade in a way consistent with the maintenance of balance of payments equilibrium by individual member countries.

investment, 1. *physical* or real investment: capital expenditure on the purchase of assets such as plant, machinery and equipment (fixed capital assets) and stocks or inventory (working capital assets).

2. *financial* investment: expenditure on the purchase of financial securities such as shares and bonds.

invisible exports/imports any services, such as banking, insurance and tourism, which cannot be seen and recorded as they cross boundaries between countries.

joint demand the sale of goods or services whose demands are interrelated, e.g. bread and butter.

joint-stock company a form of company in which a number of people contribute funds to finance a firm in return for shares in the company.

joint venture a business owned jointly by two (or more, in some cases) independent firms who continue to function separately in all other respects but pool together their resources in a particular line of activity.

labour the human input to work activity.

laissez-faire an economic doctrine which emphasizes the superiority of a 'free' market system over state regulation of individual markets and of the economy in general.

legislation the act or process of making laws; laws so made.

'lender of last resort' the role of the central bank in making money available to the commercial banks when the banks are short of funds.

limited company (Ltd) term carried by a private limited company after its name.

limited liability an arrangement that limits the maximum loss which a shareholder is liable for in the event of company failure.

luxury product/service any product or service which is above those needed for a normal standard of living, e.g. jewellery, holidays.

macroeconomics the study of how the economy as a whole works.

management the process of organizing and directing human and physical resources within an organization so as to meet defined objectives.

managing director the director of a company responsible for the day-to-day management of the company.

market an exchange mechanism which brings together the sellers and buyers of a product. Also a place in which buyers and sellers meet.

market research the collection and analysis of information about a particular market.

memorandum of association a legal document which must be filed with the registrar of companies before a company can be incorporated and which governs the external relationship between the company and third parties.

merger or **amalgamation** the combining together of two or more firms into a single business on a basis that is mutually agreed by the firms's managements and approved by their shareholders.

microeconomics, the branch of economics concerned with the study of the behaviour of consumers and firms.

mixed economy an economy in which some goods are provided by private enterprise and others supplied by the state.

monetarists individuals who believe that changes in the money supply is an important factor in controlling the economy.

monetary policy the regulation of the money supply, credit and interest rates in order to control the level of spending in the economy.

money an asset which is generally acceptable as a means of payment in the sale and purchase of products and other assets and for concluding borrowing and lending transactions.

Monopolies and Mergers Commission (MMC) a regulatory body responsible, in part, for the implementation of UK competition policy.

monopoly a market structure characterized by a single supplier and high barriers to entry.

monopsony a situation in which a single buyer confronts many small suppliers.

multilateral trade the international trade between all countries engaged in the exporting and importing of goods and services.

multinational company (MNC) a firm that *owns* production, sales and other revenue-generating assets in a number of countries.

national debt the money owed by the government to domestic and overseas lenders.

national income accounts a financial statement of the total income (or output) generated in an economy over a particular period of time, usually one year.

nationalized industry an industry which is owned and run by the government.

non-profit-making organization an organization whose major objective is not to achieve a profit for distribution to its owners or investors.

obsolescence the tendency for products to become outmoded and to reach the end of their effective life.

Office of Fair Trading an authority established by the Fair Trading Act 1973, to administer all aspects of UK competition policy.

oligopoly a market structure characterized by a few large firms supplying the bulk of industry output.

opportunity cost when a decision is made in favour of one choice, the opportunity cost of that decision is the benefit that would have been gained from the next best alternative.

ordinary shares or **equity** a financial security issued to those individuals and institutions who provide long-term finance for companies.

organization a social grouping (eg, a business, company) arranged to achieve certain goals.

organization chart a diagrammatic representation of the job titles and the formal patterns of authority and responsibility in an organization.

Organization for Economic Cooperation and Development (OECD) an international organization whose membership comprises mainly the economically advanced countries of the world.

overhead or **indirect cost** any cost that is not directly associated with a product, that is, all costs other than direct materials cost and direct labour cost.

oversubscription a situation in which the number of shares applied for in a new share issue exceeds the numbers to be issued.

overtrading a situation in which a firm expands its production and sales without making sufficient provision for additional funds to finance the extra working capital needed.

parallel importing the practice whereby independent importers buy a particular manufacturer's product from a low-priced market source and sell it in direct competition with the manufacturer's appointed distributors in the local market, usually at a lower price.

partnership a business owned and controlled by two or more persons who subscribe capital and share decision-taking as specified by a partnership agreement.

par value the face or nominal value of a share in the UK.

patent a grant of ownership rights by the government to a person or business in respect of the invention of an entirely new product or manufacturing process or a significant development of an existing product or process.

Patent Office a UK body which is responsible for the administration of various aspects of 'intellectual property rights' legislation.

per capita income or **income per head** the *average* income per head of population if it were all shared out equally.

perfect competition a market structure characterized by a multitude of small suppliers and buyers, standardized products and no barriers to entry or exit.

personnel management the branch of management concerned with administering the employment relationship and with achieving effective use of the human resources available to the organization.

planned economy a type of economic organization where the factors of production are owned by the state, and where decisions about what to produce and how to produce are also made by a central agency.

population the total number of people resident in a country at a particular point in time.

pound sterling (£) the standard monetary unit of the UK.

preference share or **preferred stock** a financial security issued to those individuals and institutions who provide long-term finance for companies. Preference shares pay a fixed rate of dividend and are generally given priority over ordinary shares in receiving dividend.

price the money value of a unit of a good, service, financial security or asset which a buyer is required to pay a seller to purchase the item.

price controls the regulation by a government agency of the prices permitted to be charged for a product.

price discrimination the ability of a supplier to sell the *same* good or service in a number of *separate* markets at *different* prices.

price index a weighted average of the prices of a general 'basket' of goods and services produced in an economy over time, which is used in particular to indicate the rate of inflation.

price leadership a situation where a particular supplier is generally accepted by other suppliers as the 'lead' firm in changing market prices.

prices and incomes policy the application of controls on prices and incomes (particularly wages) in order to stop or slow down inflation in an economy.

price war a situation of aggressive price cutting by a group of rival suppliers as a means of gaining sales at each other's expense.

private limited company (Ltd) a limited company that does not issue shares for public subscription.

privatization the transference of ownership of an industry or firm from the state to private interests. See also **deregulation**.

producer or **manufacturer** a business which is engaged in making consumer goods and capital goods using factor inputs such as raw materials, labour and capital.

production the conversion process for transforming inputs such as materials, labour and capital into goods and services.

profit the difference that arises when a firm's sales revenue is greater than its total costs.

promotion the means of bringing products to the attention of consumers and persuading them to buy those products.

prospectus a document prepared by a company as an invitation to the public to subscribe for shares in the company.

protectionism the measures taken by a country to protect certain of its domestic industries from foreign competition and, on occasion, to assist the country's balance of payments.

public limited company (plc) a form of limited company where the public are invited to buy shares through the Stock Exchange, and so become owners of the business.

public sector that part of a mixed economy where decisions about what to produce and where to produce are made by a central authority.

public utility an undertaking which provides a certain basic good or service such as gas, electricity or telecommunications.

purchasing power the amount of goods and services which can be purchased by a specified sum of money, *given* the prices of those goods and services.

quota an administration limitation on the production of, or trade in, a particular product imposed by suppliers or by the government.

raw materials basic materials such as iron ore, bauxite, wheat and coffee, which are converted into finished goods or components in the production process.

recession a fall in demand which leads to falling output and unemployment.

redundancy the termination of an individual's employment when the employer ceases trading or the job ceases to be required.

regional enterprise grants cash grants given to small manufacturing and service businesses (with under 25 employees) which are prepared to undertake new investment in areas designated as 'development areas' under UK regional policy.

regional policy a policy concerned with promoting a balanced distribution of industrial activity, employment and wealth as between the various geographical areas of a country.

research and development (R&D) the commitment of resources by a firm to scientific research (both 'pure' and 'applied') and the refinement and modification of research ideas and prototypes aimed at the ultimate development of commercially viable processes and products.

restrictive trade agreement an agreement entered into by two or more suppliers of a product which contains restrictions relating to such matters as prices, terms and conditions of supply, restrictions on the type of persons or businesses supplied, etc.

retail price index a measure commonly used to indicate the rate of inflation.

revaluation an administered increase in the exchange rate of a currency against other currencies under a fixed exchange rate system.

rights issue the issue by a company of additional shares to existing shareholders at a price which is generally a little below the current market price.

salary a payment made to employees for the use of their labour. Salaries are expressed in an annual sum, a portion of which is paid to the employee each month.

sale the purchase of a good or service by a buyer from a seller at a stated price.

sales forecasting the process of predicting future product demand to help in making decisions about marketing expenditure, investment in production capacity and the scheduling of factory output.

sales revenue the income generated from the sale of goods and services.

savings the proportion of income of a person (personal saving), company or institution (retained profits) that is not spent on current consumption.

seasonal demand when the purchase of a product by consumers varies according to the time of year.

seller's market a market situation in which the demand for a product or financial security is greater than the supply of it at existing prices, which leads to the bidding-up of prices to the advantage of sellers.

share a financial security issued by a company as a means of raising long-term capital.

share capital the money employed in a company that has been subscribed by the shareholders of the company in the form of ordinary shares (equity) and preference shares, and which will remain as a permanent source of finance as long as the company remains in existence.

shell company a company whose shares are currently listed on the stock market but which is not actively trading.

social responsibility a business philosophy which stresses the need for firms to behave as good corporate citizens, not merely obeying the law but conducting their production and marketing activities in a manner which avoids causing environmental pollution or exhausting finite world resources.

soft currency a foreign currency that is in weak demand, but in abundant supply on the foreign exchange market.

sole trader a business or firm which is owned and controlled by a single person.

speculation the buying and selling of commodities (tea, tin, etc), financial securities (shares, etc) and foreign currencies whose market prices are characterized by substantial fluctuations over time, by individuals and firms (speculators) in the hope of making windfall profits.

spot market a market which provides for the buying and selling of financial securities (shares, stocks), foreign currencies and commodities (rubber, tin, etc) for immediate delivery.

standard of living the general level of economic prosperity in an economy as measured by, for example, the level of per capita income (gross national product divided by the size of the population).

statute law the law laid down by government legislation (in the UK, an Act of Parliament).

stock the part of a firm's assets that are held in the form of raw materials, work in progress and finished goods.

stock exchange a market which deals in the buying and selling of company stocks and shares and government bonds.

subsidy the provision of finance and other resources by the government or a firm to support a business activity or person.

suggestion scheme a facility for employees to submit suggestions for revision of production equipment and working methods which will lead to improvements in efficiency or product quality.

supply the amount of a good or service at a given price that producers are willing to bring on to a market.

tax a levy imposed by the government on goods and services (indirect tax) and the income and wealth of persons and businesses (direct tax).

taxation the government receipts from taxes on personal and business income, expenditure and wealth.

technology the application of scientific principles and know-how in the development and operation of industrial processes, systems and products.

terms of trade the ratio of a country's export prices relative to its import prices. If a country's export prices rise at a faster rate than its import prices, this is an improvement in the country's terms of trade since a given amount of foreign exchange earnings from exports will now buy more imports.

trade cycle see **business cycle**.

trade fair an organized gathering of firms from different industries for the display and promotion of their goods and services to prospective customers.

trade gap when a country's payments for imports exceed receipts from the export of goods.

trade mark a symbol (a word or pictorial representation) which is used by a business as a means of identifying a particular good or service so that it may be readily distinguished by purchasers from similar goods and services supplied by other businesses.

trade union an organization of employees whose primary objective is to protect and advance the economic interests of its members by negotiating wage rates and conditions of employment with employers or managers.

transactions the activities of buying and selling in a market system.

transfer price the internal price at which raw materials, components and final products are transacted between the divisions or subsidiaries of a firm.

Treasury the UK government department responsible for managing the government's finances, authorizing the expenditure plans of government departments and overseeing the tax-gathering work of the inland revenue and customs and excise.

turnover the speed at which a business can sell its product (the word is also sometimes used to mean sales revenue).

underwriting the acceptance by a financial institution of the financial risks involved in a particular transaction, for an agreed fee.

unemployment the non-utilization of part of the economy's available labour (and capital) resources.

unlimited liability a form of liability in which the owners of the business are responsible for all the losses of the business.

unlisted securities market (USM) a market for corporate stocks and shares that have not obtained a full stock market listing.

value the money worth of a product or asset.

value-added tax (VAT) an indirect tax imposed by the government at every point when goods and services are exchanged, from primary production to the final consumer.

vertical integration when companies from different levels of production join together to become one company.

wage the money payment made to a worker, usually on a weekly basis, for the use of his or her labour.

wage differential the difference between the wage rates of different groups of workers.

yield the return on a financial security, expressed in money terms, related to the current market price of that security, to show the percentage return on the investment.

Index

References to Dictionary bear the suffix D.

Abbey National Building Society 1
accountants 6
acid rain 113
Acts of Parliament 87, 88
ad valorem tax D
advertising 4
   elasticity 81
   and ethics 119
Advertising Standards Authority 90
after-sales service D
agents 125-6 D
aims and objectives 7
Airtours 70
Allied Lyons 131
American Cyanamid 72
analysis viii
assisted areas 42
authorized capital D

bad debts 11
balance of payments 22, 34-6, 51, 136-7 D
balance of trade D
Bank of England 43, 44, 45, 46, 119
bank reserves 45
base rate D
BAT 120, 129
BCCI 119
Beeston & Co, Dennis 3
Benetton 75, 90
bid D
bills of exchange 132, D
birth rate 101
black economy 19, D
black market D
board of directors 10, D
Body Shop organization 108
book value D
Boots 9
brainstorming 59-60, 61, D
brand D
breakeven D
British Airways 114, 117
British Coal 10
British Franchise Association 63
British Gas 20, 34, 70-1, 110, 154
British Institute of Management 58
British Market Research Bureau 152
British Overseas Trade Board (BOTB) 130
British Petroleum (BP) 154
British Rail 10, 66
British Standards Institute 147, D
British Steel 4
British Sugar Corporation 121
British Telecom 20, 34
budget D
Bulgaria 154
bull market D
Bundesbank 45
Burton Group 51
business 1, D

and economy 16-54
objectives D
opportunities 55
plans 6-7
and size 3
and society 3-4, 13-14, 101-23
and technology 13

Cadbury-Schweppes 61
capital D
   account 22, 136
   and currency flows 149
   goods D
Carlsberg 131
cartel D
caveat emptor D
CE mark 148
census D
central bank D
Central Office of Information 131
Central Statistical Office 18, D
CFCs 112
Chamber of Industry and Commerce 58
Chancellor of the Exchequer 39
Ciba-Geigy 72
circular flow of income 20
civil law 87
Coca-Cola 154
collateral security D
Comité Européenne de Normalisation (CEN) 147, 151, 152
command economies 12
Commercial Union Insurance 1
Common Agricultural Policy (CAP) 143, 155, D
common external tariff 127
common law 88, D
Commonwealth 124
communication 1-2
companies 6
   private 8-9
   public 9-10
competition D
   Act, 1980 92
   law 89
   policy 91-2
concentration ratios 69
Confederation of British Industry 14, 102-3, 136, 156
conglomerate D
consideration 93
consumer D
consumer durables 45, D
contract 92, D
contract of employment 93, D
contract law 92
Cook, William 92
Co-operative Bank 121
copyright 64-6
Copyright Act 1988 66
corporation tax 41, D
cost, insurance, freight D
cost of living D
Council of Ministers 142, 143

Court of European Justice 88
credit restrictions 45
credit sales 47
criminal law 87
Cuba 13
current account 22, 136

Data Protection Act 94-5
delegated legislation 88
demand 73, D
   conditions of 74
   curves 74, 77-9
   and supply model 73
   and supply model, assessment of 78
demographic time bomb 101-4
demography D
Department of Health 121
Department of Trade and Industry (DTI) 96, 115, 129, 148, 152, D
depreciation 21
deregulation 32, D
design registration 64
designs, protection of 64
devaluation D
developing area D
developing country D
developing ideas 62
disposable income D
Domino Amjet Limited 94
dumping D

East Anglia, University of 108
Eastern Europe 129, 154-5
Eastgate Furnishings Limited 52
EC legislation, types of 144
EC merger control 89
economics 1-2, D
   efficiency D
   environment 16
   growth 31-2, D
   models 20
   objectives 24, 37
   policy 37-54
   and Social Committee 144, 145
   statistics 18
   systems 12
economy 11, 16-17
   black 19, D
   and business 16-54
   market 12
   mixed 13
   of scale 129, D
   planned 12
ECU 135, 146
effective demand 73
Elan Corporation 72
elasticity 79-81
   advertising 81
   calculations 80
   of demand 79-80
   income 81
   price and total revenue 80
   of supply 81
embargo D

employers liability insurance 94
employment 27-31
   and business 31
   Department of 96
   and income patterns 30
Enterprise Allowance Scheme 97
enterprise initiative 96
Enterprise Oil 154
entrepreneur D
environment, measures for protection of 113-15
environment and business 109-18
environment and marketing 118
environmental control 115-18
Environmental Protection Act 1991 115
equilibrium 20
equilibrium market price D
essays viii
ethics 5, 118-21
Europe 141-56
   European Atomic Energy Community (EURATOM) 141
   European Coal and Steel Community (ECSC) 141
   European Commission 11, 127, 137, 142-3, 144
   European Community 1, 115, 124, 127, 137, 141-53, D
   European Community, voting power 144
   European Community and patents 65
   European Community law 88-9
   European Council 143-4
   European Court of Justice 143-4, D
   European Currency Unit 135, 146
   European Economic Community 141
   European Free Trade Association (EFTA) 141, 142, D
   European Investment Bank (EIB) 144
   European Monetary Co-operation Fund (EMCF) 146
   European Monetary System 134-5, 145, D
   European Monetary Union (EMU) 145
   European Parliament 143, 144, 145
   European Patent Convention 65
   European Patent Office (EPO) 147
   Eurotunnel 87
evaluation viii
Exchange Rate Mechanism (ERM) 48, 134-5, 146, 157
exchange rates 47, 129, 132-5, 136, D
   effects of changes in 133-4
   policy 48
Exchequer D
excise duty D
expectations 21
expenditure, average weekly household 49
Export Credit Guarantee Department (ECGD) 129-30, D
export initiative 96, 140
Export Market Information Centre 131
exports 21-2, D

factoring 132
Fair Trading, Director General of 91, 92
Fair Trading, Office of 92
Fair Trading Act, 1973 92, D

Fiat 155
financial year D
fiscal policy 37-43, D
fiscal year 38, D
Flexible Manufacturing Technology Limited 153
Ford Motor Company 3, 6
foreign currencies 133, D
foreign investment D
foreign exchange controls D
foreign exchange market 133, D
format franchising 63
forward exchange markets 134
franchise 62-3, D
franchising 62-3
free on board (FOB) D
Friedman, Milton 44, 107
Friends of the Earth 14, 114

General Agreement on Trade and Tariffs (GATT) 138, D
General Motors 62
Germany 44, 154-5
Glaxo 59, 60
global warming 111
gold D
good D
Goodheart, Charles 46
government expenditure 21, 39, 41-3
government purchasing 149
green audits 114
Green Movement 14
Greenpeace 14, 95, 114
gross domestic product (GDP) D
gross national product (GNP) 18, D

Hachette 139
Hanson Group 60
hard currency D
Harrods 67
Hatton Garden 73
Health and Safety at Work Act, 1974 86, 88, 95
holding company D
Honda 127
Hong Kong 12, 13
horizontal integration D
hot money D
hours worked weekly 105
household expenditure 106
hyperinflation 25, D

ICI 1, 60, 75, 115, 117
ideas 56
   developing of 62
   protection of 64-6
   sources of 57
imports 22, D
income D
   average weekly disposable 30
   circular flow of 20
   elasticity 81
   tax 40
inelastic demand D
inelastic goods 79
inelastic supply D
inflation 24-7, 51, D
   cost-push 25

demand-pull 25, D
information gathering 57-60
injections 21
Inland Revenue 19
insolvent D
Institute of Manpower Studies 102
insurance, employers's liability 94
insurance, public liability 94
intellectual property 66
interest D
interest rate policy 46
interest rates 18, 21, D
interest rates, real 48
International Bank for Reconstruction and Development 138
International Economic Organizations 138
International Leisure Group 69, 70
International Monetary Fund 1, 44, 138, D
International payment, means of 132
investment 21, D
investment, gross 21
investment, net 21
investment, replacement 21
invisible exports/imports D
invisible trade 136

Jaguar 34
job enrichment 104
joint demand D
joint stock company 9-10, D
joint ventures 126, D
judicial precedent 88

Keynes, John Maynard 37-8
Korea 4

labour D
laissez-faire D
law 2, 1
   Acts of Parliament 87, 88
   Competition Act, 1980 92
   Copyright Act, 1988 66
   Data Protection Act 94-5
   delegated legislation 88
   Environmental Protection Act, 1991 115
   Fair Trading Act, 1973 92, D
   Health and Safety at Work Act, 1974 86, 88, 95
   Monopolies and Restrictive Practices Act, 1948 91
   Road Traffic Acts 86
   Single European Act, 1987 146
   sources of 87-90
legal environment 11
legislation D
lender of last resort D
letters of credit 132
Lewin 3, 4, 6
licensing 126
limited company D
limited liability 9, D
Loan Guarantee Scheme 96
Local Enterprise Companies 97
London Business School 20
luxury product/service D
Lynx 114

macroeconomics D

Index

Major, John 135
management D
managing director D
Marion Merrill Dow 72
market 73, D
   economies 12
   research D
marketing overseas 131-2
Marks & Spencer vii, 1, 17, 66
mathematics 1-2
Maxwell, Robert 11
McDonalds 126
Medium Term Financial Strategy 44
Memorandum of Association D
MEPs 143
merger D
Mexico 4
microeconomics D
mint 45
mixed economies 13, D
monetarists 43, D
monetary policy 43-8, D
money 1, 43, D
money supply 45, 46
money wages 25
monopoly 33, 70, D
   Monopolies and Mergers Commission 91, D
   Monopolies and Restrictive Practices Act 91
   monopolistic competition 68
monopsony D
Montreal Protocol 115
multinational trade D
multinationals 35, 131, D

National Council for Vocational Qualifications 97
national curriculum 6
national debt D
National Economic Development Office (NEDO) 101, 102
National Federation of Self-Employed & Small Businesses 47
National Health Service 10, 37
national income 31
national income accounts D
national insurance 50
National Westminster Bank 11, 149
Nationalized industries 33, D
New Product Development Agency 61
needs 4
Nestlé 127
News International 13
Nissan 127
non-profit-making organization D
Norsk Hydro 114

obsolescence D
Oce Vander Grinten 137
Office of Fair Trading 92, D
oligopoly 68, D
Olivetti 137
ordinary shares or equity D
open account 132
opportunity cost D
organization D
organization chart D

Organization for Economic Co-operation and Development (OECD) 138, D
overhead or indirect cost D
oversubscription D
overtrading D
owners abroad 70
ozone layer 113

par value D
parallel importing D
Paris, Treaty of 141
partnerships 8, D
Patent Office 62-3, D
patents 62-3, D
Pepsi-Cola 154
per capita income D
perfect competition 68, D
personnel management D
planned economies 12, D
Poland 4
pollution, causes of 111-13
population D
population statistics 102
Post Office 70
pound sterling D
poverty trap 25
preference share D
pressure groups 14, 114-15
price 77, D
   controls 77
   discrimination D
   elasticity of demand 79-81
   elasticity of demand, calculations 80
   elasticity of demand, factors affecting 79-80
   elasticity of supply 81
   index D
   leadership D
   setting of 77
   system 74-81
   war D
prices and incomes policies 50, D
private limited company 8-9, D
private provision 32
privatization 32-4, 97, D
   debate 32-4
   sales 3
producer D
production D
profits 41, D
promotion D
prospectus D
protectionism D
public liability insurance 94
public limited company 9-10, D
public procurement 149
public sector 10, D
public utility D
purchasing power D

Queen's Award for Exporting 130
quotas 137, D

Rank Xerox 137
raw materials D
recession 11, 29, 51, D
redundancy D

Regional Enterprise Grants D
regional policy 48, 97, 155, D
regional unemployment and expenditure 49
Renault 13, 127
research and development (R&D) 60, D
research and development expenditure for UK 60
restrictive practices court 92
Restrictive Trade Agreement D
retail price index D
revaluation D
revised data 18
Reward Group 26
right of establishment 148, 149
rights issue D
Road Traffic Acts 86
Roddick, Anita and Gordon 108
Rolls Royce 3, 126
Rome, Treaty of 88-9, 143, 146-7
Rover Group 10, 127
Rowntree 82-3
Royal Insurance 150
Rubik Cube 56

Sainsbury's 108
salary D
sale D
sales forecasting D
sales revenue D
savings 22, D
seasonal demand D
secondary activities 2
seller's market D
share capital D
shareholders 9-10
shares 9, D
Shell 117, 154
shell company D
Sinclair, Sir Clive 56, 58
Sinclair C5 56
Singapore 12
single administrative document 147
Single European Act, 1987 146
Single European Market, 34, 43, 69, 95, 96, 104, 124, 135, 138, 141, 146-53
   implications of 151-2
Small Firms Service 96
Smith, W H vii, 9
social costs 113
social responsibility 107-9
soft currency D
sole traders 8, D
Sony 127
spot markets 134, D
standard of living D
statistical seasonability 18
statistics 1-2
Statoil 154
statute law D
stock D
Stock Exchange 10, 73, D
Stockton, Lord 34
study vii
subsidy D
suggestion boxes 57
suggestion scheme 56-7, D
supply 76, D
   conditions of 76

curve 76
   and demand model, assessment of 78
   joint 77
   side policy 50
Taiwan 4
tariffs 35, 137
Tate & Lyle 121
tax D
   direct 23, 37, 39, 43
   harmonization 149
   indirect 23, 37, 39
   reliefs 41
taxation 23, D
   policy 23
technology 13, 71-3, D
terms of trade D
tertiary activities 2
Texaco 154
Thatcher, Margaret 4, 13
Thompson Holidays 70
Tobacco Advisory Group 120
toll roads 98
trade, pattern of 124-5
Trade and Industry, Secretary of State of 92

trade barriers 137
trade fairs 130, D
trade gap D
trade marks 66, D
Trade Marks Registry 66
trade unions 1, 14, D
trading abroad, methods of 125-8
training 152
Training and Enterprise Councils (TECs) 50, 96
transactions D
transfer payments 41
transfer price D
Treasury D
turnover D

underwriting D
unemployment 51, D
   social cost of 28
   statistics for UK 28
   types of 29-31
Unilever 6
unlimited liability D
Unlisted Securities Market (USM) D
value D

VAT 40-1, 43, 97, 147, 149, D
vertical integration D
visible trade 136
vocational training card 148
Volkswagen 13, 155
Voluntary Codes of Practice 90, D
Volvo 127

wage D
wage differential D
Wages Councils 50
waste 113
waste disposal 112
withdrawals 22
'women returners' 103
work of art 65
working week, length of 105
World Bank 138
writing answers viii

yield D